Money Mania

MONEY MANIA

BOOMS, PANICS, AND BUSTS FROM
ANCIENT ROME TO THE GREAT
MELTDOWN

Bob Swarup

BLOOMSBURY PRESS

NEW YORK · LONDON · NEW DELHI · SYDNEY

Published by Bloomsbury Press, New York

All papers used by Bloomsbury Press are natural, recyclable products made
from wood grown in well-managed forests. The manufacturing processes
conform to the environmental regulations of the country of origin.

LIBRARY OF CONGRESS CATALOGING-IN-PUBLICATION DATA

Swarup, Bob.
Money mania : booms, panics, and busts from Ancient Rome to
the Great Meltdown / Bob Swarup.—First U.S. edition.
pages cm
Includes bibliographical references and index.
ISBN 978-1-60819-841-2 (alk. paper)
1. Speculation—History. 2. Finance—History. 3. Investments—History. I. Title.
HG6005.S93 2013
332.64'509—dc23
2013041928

First U.S. edition 2014

1 3 5 7 9 10 8 6 4 2

Typeset by Hewer Text UK Ltd, Edinburgh
Printed and bound in the U.S.A. by Thomson-Shore, Inc. Dexter, Michigan

To Radhika for her love, for her endurance, and for her refusal to deliver our first until I had delivered the kernel of this book.

Contents

Part I
Déjà Vu All Over Again

CHAPTER 1

Of Men, Money, and Mania

When experience is not retained, as among savages, infancy is perpetual. Those who cannot remember the past are condemned to repeat it.

—GEORGE SANTAYANA (1863–1952)

Recurrent speculative insanity and the associated financial deprivation and large devastation are, I am persuaded, inherent in the system.

—J. K. GALBRAITH (1908–2006)

TAKE a deep breath.

Feel the air hit the back of your throat and disappear down the trachea. As your lungs inflate, your diaphragm pushes downward and your stomach swells. Inside, trillions of oxygen molecules within the air pass into your bloodstream, hitching a ride on the nearest passing blood cell and rushing throughout your body. Millions of cells now ignite millions of molecular furnaces, burning the raw fodder from your last meal to release energy and fuel the constant little processes that allow them to grow, multiply, and thrive, maintaining in aggregate the necessity we term life. If you close your eyes and focus, it really is the most euphoric feeling.

But there is a catch.

The sensation is always momentary, repeating a dozen times a minute as you exhale and inhale again. Try as you might, you cannot hang on to it. Nor should you.

Now try holding your breath.

As oxygen dissipates into your body, it is initially replaced by carbon dioxide—the waste by-product of all the above millions of chemical reactions. But if you don't breathe out, the trapped air soon becomes saturated, and the carbon dioxide now begins to build up in your bloodstream. Meanwhile, the oxygen levels in your blood continue to drop as your body uses up its precious stores.

A minute in, your circulation becomes inefficient, and your pulse starts to race. Your skin becomes flushed and your blood pressure begins to climb. That earlier feeling of exhilaration soon wears off, to be replaced by palpitations in your chest. Your muscles and limbs begin to twitch as your oxygen debt soars to dangerous levels and the first pangs of air hunger hit you.

Override your body's demands, and soon you feel a mild headache forming. You're tired now, and you can feel your reactions and judgment becoming impaired. But then suddenly, the confusion is soon replaced by euphoria—not a moment of Zen but the narcotic effects of excessive carbon dioxide and the growing lack of oxygen to your brain. Your body is now screaming for air, making rapid movements and fighting more viciously than ever against your conscious control.

Suppress its natural urges and your euphoria begins to transmute. Is that dizziness you're feeling now? It's hard to tell—your hearing seems to have become muffled and your eyes are finding the outside world increasingly dim. If you're still in charge, your body is now beginning to tremble.

And then, thankfully, some three to four minutes in, you pass out and your body begins to breathe again—your conscious intent short-circuited before it caused any lasting damage.

Now that you're conscious again, congratulations—you have just lived through a microcosm of a financial crisis.

The core is the same. It's not about air or money. Those are only different stage settings for the same primeval drama played out at different levels. Rather, it's all about the very human choices we make to control our environment and their consequences. Rises and falls are as natural and vital to the economic condition as breathing is to the human condition. Try to remove these ebbs and flows, and both conditions will begin to rebel against their unnatural state of being. Try too hard out of hubris to control your world and the outcome is inevitably the same, as amply demonstrated throughout recorded history.

THE MYTH OF NORMALITY

The subprime crisis and the ensuing credit crunch that began in July 2007 were the most recent reminder of how damaging financial crises can be.

It began innocuously enough, with the collapse of two overleveraged hedge funds owned by the U.S. investment bank Bear Stearns. The funds had a simple premise: borrow money cheaply, buy so-called asset-backed securities that paid attractive yields higher than the cost of funding (thanks to their specialization in a fast-growing sector of the mortgage market known as sub-prime), and keep borrowing more and more until the returns looked attractive enough to persuade investors to part with their capital. It seemed a good idea until someone realized that the mortgages weren't actually worth the digital paper they were written on and the funds even less so, thanks to the leverage hidden within their opaque financial wizardry.

I have no wish to go through the timeline and ponder details—others have spent enough hours poring over the entrails—but I remember some things well. Bear Stearns's original letter announcing this inconvenient truth ended with a chest-beating bravado that soon became a constant plaintive refrain: "Our highest priority is to continue to earn your trust and confidence each and every day, consistent with the Firm's proud history of achievement. As always, please contact us if we can be of service."

By the end of July 2007, both funds had filed for bankruptcy and a third, the $850 million Bear Stearns Asset-Backed Securities Fund, seemed to be teetering on the edge, despite the bank's shrill protestations to the contrary. Its acronym, BS ABS, would soon become an in-joke.

Three months later, the fallout had gathered pace. Vaunted buying opportunities seemed less certain now. A friend bought a financial instrument from an investment bank that I will not name—the kind of instrument that through the miracle of rapid mathematical juggling and financial sleight of hand promised the earth in terms of returns with none of the risk. All he had to do was bet that twenty-five of the world's largest banks would not default on their bonds over the next five years and he stood to make twice the current coupon.[1] With rapidly approaching hindsight, that seemed less secure and the promised paltry return of an additional 0.62

percent seemed poor compensation for agreeing to sandbag the rapidly escalating deluge.[2]

Over the next two years, many lost good money as they stooped to pick up these pennies on the highway and forgot to check on the speeding traffic.

In the meanwhile, we all clustered around our Bloomberg screens daily, waiting to see if someone had called time on happy hour. People began to obsess about the dreaded *R*: recession.

On December 1, 2007, the United States officially went into recession. It was not a surprise in hindsight, given the events of the previous few months, though few of us at the time had any inkling of how much more painful life was about to become.

Six months later, in May 2008, an innocuous conference entitled "Reporting Liquidity Risk and Liquidity Risk Frame Works" took place in Hatton Gardens in London. The keynote speaker was the head of treasury at Lehman Brothers in the United Kingdom, who outlined in a clear, articulate talk how Lehman was never going to make the same mistakes as Bear Stearns and go under. They had learned their lesson from the Russian default crisis of 1998 and knew full well the perils of illiquidity. This was the moment he and his team lived for, and at a flick of a keystroke, billions of dollars were ready and primed to be drawn down and deployed.

That September, Lehman collapsed. The money clearly hadn't been enough.

Within days, a new joke went viral around the financial community. A rich kid falls in love with the Wild West and for his eighth birthday asks his billionaire father for a horse. So his father goes out and buys him a whole stableful of beautiful stallions. The next year, he asks his father for a cowboy film and his father goes out and buys him every Wild West movie ever made. The following year, he asks his father for a cowboy outfit, so his dad goes out and buys him Lehman.

Lehman wasn't the only firm to fall afoul of its arrogance. Chuck Prince, the former chairman of Citigroup, found himself rapidly elevated to the pantheon of immortal idiocy as his moment of Zen-like honesty came back to haunt him: "When the music stops, in terms of liquidity, things will be complicated. But as long as the music is playing, you've got to get up and dance. We're still dancing."[3]

We all were. As 2008 drew to a close, I was having lunch with the former chief economist of a large bank. We were at the nadir—the banking system seemed close to collapse and the money had begun to flow from the spigots at the central banks in an effort to stem the bleeding in the global economy.

Two years earlier, he told me, worried by the growing strains in the world economy, he had gone to his boss and expressed his conviction that this was all going to end badly. His boss called in the head of trading, who said confidently that he could handle any trouble. All he had to know was when to pull the plug and he would stop all activities. "I'm an economist," replied my friend. "I can't tell you when it's going to happen, only that it's going to be painful when it does."[*]

The head of trading was flabbergasted. As he noted, he could not stop trading just because one person was worried. Who was going to make the money in that scenario? But he had an idea. All the teams would be instructed to run their positions on a very tight leash and be ready to liquidate at a moment's notice. When things went wrong, they would all be able to exit with minimal losses. My friend agreed and went away relieved.

A few months later, he was at a dinner in Switzerland—an annual event organized behind closed doors for the chief economists of all the banks. As they sat around and dwelled on the worsening economic situation, my friend suddenly had a horrifying revelation. Every person in the room had given his or her bank the same advice. Every bank sat with its finger on the trigger, ready to rush for the door at the first sign of trouble. A couple of tentative steps toward the exit by any one party would soon escalate into a stampede by all. And since no door is infinitely wide, especially in the financial markets, a bloody outcome was a foregone conclusion. It was at that point that he realized we were never going to somehow just muddle through.

As defaults soared and subprime contagion gave way to sovereign panic, the finger-pointing began. It was the fault of bankers for lending

---

[*] As Galbraith once noted, the only point of economic forecasting was to make astrology look respectable.

irresponsibly. It was the fault of central bankers for keeping interest rates so low. It was the fault of the politicians for turning a blind eye to the weapons of financial mass destruction massing outside suburbia and Capitol Hill.

Everybody else was to blame, and everyone wanted just to return to happier days when *bust* was a term confined to late-night television and poker games, growth and ever-rising financial markets were a given, and money was something we could all make or access. In short, they wanted to get back to normal.

There's only one problem. That is not normal. Easy money is not normal.

What *is* normal: a fragile financial system defined by booms and busts, where money is just another expansive synonym for the constant dance of human emotions—optimism, arrogance, greed, fear, and capitulation—around a maypole of trust.

What *is* normal: a complex world where emotion and money leverage off each other, binding us into vast instinctive herds that charge into uncertainty, striving only for forward movement with little regard for the terrain beneath our feet, running headlong into the myopic horizon and stumbling, only to pick ourselves up, shake our heads, and resume the pursuit of our peers once again.

A multitude of arguments were put forward in the aftermath to explain what happened, ranging from inadequate corporate governance to a lack of transparency to poor regulatory supervision. But among the shock, the scrutiny, and the blame merry-go-round, the biggest surprise is precisely why this crisis was such a surprise to everyone.

AS THE WHEEL TURNS

There is a popular children's story in England called "The Gruffalo." It charts a mouse's walk through a dark wood, where he protects himself from various predators by inventing a monster that he is on his way to meet. Successive fantastical details—terrible claws, huge tusks, poisonous warts, penetrating eyes, and so on—layer on to create this mythical terrible creature, the Gruffalo. Then, to his horror, the mouse actually meets a Gruffalo.

Crises are not new phenomena. They have been around for centuries and have occurred with alarming frequency—about once a decade on average for the last four hundred years in western Europe alone, by some estimations. Coincidentally, changes in banking regulations have maintained an impressive correlation in their shorter life span, occurring about once a decade as well for the last two centuries—a Sisyphean tragicomedy where the solution to the last crisis inevitably seems to blinker them to the next.

The genealogy is relentless and impressive. Before the current credit crunch, we had the dot-com crash in 2000 as hypergrowth turned out to be little more than hyperfantasy; the Russian near default and the infamous Long-Term Capital Management fiasco of 1998, which proved that two Nobel Prize–winning economists don't necessarily equal a moneymaking fund; the Asian currency crisis in 1997, which ended in the complete financial and political restructuring of the Asian tigers; the implosion of the Japanese economy in 1990, which contributed the phrase "lost decade" to the financial lexicon and is now approaching its silver jubilee without an end in sight; and at the edge of today's memory, the legendary Wall Street crash of 1987 that etched Black Monday into cultural memory.

Between the two world wars, the developed world seemed to spend the best part of two decades in perpetual crisis, the notable low points being the lengthy Great Depression and the hyperinflation in the German Weimar Republic. Go further back and there was the Panic of 1907, which led an exasperated French banker to describe the United States as "a great financial nuisance" and birthed the Federal Reserve; the recurrent stock market crises of the late nineteenth century that seemed to occur almost like leap years; the Barings crisis of 1890 and the great Latin American meltdown that accompanied it; the international panic of 1873, which gave rise to the first Great Depression[4]; the recurrent banking and railroad panics of the 1830s, 1840s, and 1850s that were birthed by the first great emerging market boom—the United States; the Latin American debt crisis of 1825, where speculative loans were even made to Poyais, a completely fictitious country; the British credit crunch of 1772, which contributed to the American Revolution; the Mississippi and South Sea bubbles of 1719–20, when the French acquired a distaste for paper money and the Bank of England nearly went bankrupt; and the legendary tulip-mania of 1637.

This is just a quick head count of some of the near and dear family. The extended family of crises has many more members. There was the disastrous Chinese experiment with paper money in the Middle Ages, the Dark Ages were punctuated by a century-long depression, and texts from long ago tell us that banking bailouts were not unknown to the ancient Greeks and Romans.

Despite this rich genealogy, our knowledge of crises is woefully limited. On the surface, they revel in diversity. Every country has a crisis to share and every story is different. For every hypothesized commonality, there is an exception. They have occurred in different eras—ancient, medieval, and modern; under democracies, dictatorships, and monarchies; before we had central banks and after we had them; when the world clung to a gold standard and when it sought out paper money instead; in complex international systems and in small isolated communities; in eras of both laissez-faire capitalism and didactic state commerce; and in diverse asset classes from stocks to property to tulips to red mullets.

All it seems you need are people and a medium—money by any other name.

The other common feature is that the wise men of the day—astrologers, shamans, viziers, courtiers, and economists—miss the signs that are all too obvious in hindsight. In the aftermath, explanations and solutions abound, but again diversity reasserts itself. No two are ever the same, though all claim to have a lasting answer.

In time, the cycle repeats—the words, symbols, and resolve spent on modeling and solving the last crisis to theoretical perfection typically impotent once again. Even today, for all our knowledge, we struggle. The copious economic data accumulated only tell us that we do not know enough to answer the question of why, let alone the thornier issue of when again. That we soldier on regardless is testament to our optimism and stubborn ego.

Financial crises are for us what natural disasters were to our ancient ancestors. Their unpredictability and their punishing aftermath—capable of rending societies in extremis—make them objects of mystery and morbid fascination. Thousands of years ago, the causes took the form of whimsical gods in an ever-growing pantheon while the solutions lay in an ever-growing religious litany to carefully placate each and every one. Today, our new gods come from the theories of economics and finance, while the litany is replaced by a growing body of bureaucracy and regulation. In common, the answer still evades us.

But like tales often repeated, gods are transient. They change their names; they change their ways. New ones arise to challenge the old, and just when we think we know the answers, the pantheons disperse and reassemble anew. This failure to learn only emphasizes the fact that we cannot take too narrow a view and focus on the fine details of any given crisis. Rather, the roots to all our crises past, present, and future are to be found in the clash between our simple human nature and the complex societies and economies we create. The psychological mechanisms that drive us have not changed in thousands of years and naturally give rise to speculative booms, thanks to our propensity toward herd behavior. Their punishing aftermath is also born of human psychology as trust evaporates and self-preservation becomes paramount.

Galbraith noted in his erudite tome *A Short History of Financial Euphoria* that the "circumstances that induce the recurrent lapses into financial dementia have not changed in any truly operative fashion since the tulipmania of 1636–37." He was right: we all love making money and accruing status. By looking at the long history of endlessly repeated cycles—optimism, arrogance, greed, fear, and capitulation—this fascination entails, we perhaps might come to an understanding of our human foibles and even glean some lessons to guide us through the next inevitable *Ring of the Nibelung.*

Galbraith's only error of assertion is on dates. Modern accounts began in 1636, but the behavior they so carefully noted began far earlier.

This book had its genesis in a casual mention of the first documented sovereign default in a 1933 book entitled *Foreign Bonds: An Autopsy.* The author was one Max Winkler, an overachieving Jewish immigrant from Romania who became a professor of economics at the College of the City of New York, ran the foreign department at Moody's, and founded a brokerage firm on the eleventh floor of the New York Stock Exchange in

1929. Four years later, in January 1933, Winkler stood in front of the U.S. Senate Committee on Banking and Currency and found himself picking through the rubble of the Great Depression, trying to make sense of what had just occurred. As president of the American Council of Foreign Bondholders—a sorely aggrieved lot if ever there was one—he had a ringside seat to the whole debacle as country after country reneged on its obligations.

The primeval default Winkler chronicled itself took place some millennia earlier, in 377 B.C. in ancient Greece. The culprits were ten city-states that borrowed heavily and then defaulted on their debt to the Temple of Apollo at Delos. But as Winkler discovered, this was no isolated incident. Subsequent accounts tell us that economic recessions were not uncommon and the orators of the day found time enough between the speeches that have made their way down to us to also vent their spleen at a nascent banking community for its periodic and contagious paroxysms. While the recessions were triggered by the changing fortunes of wars between the different city-states such as Athens and Sparta, these were only catalysts. What was common was credit, euphoria, and a financial banking system reliant on confidence. Nearly twenty-five hundred years later, the spectacle of a Greek default plays out once again.

Plus ça change . . .

THE UNCHANGING ID AND THE PLIANT EGO

As a species, we believe that everything that happens to us is unique and unprecedented, making it all the more important to put current events in some historical perspective. The many financial crises that have occurred over the last three millennia can be used as lenses to understand why crises seem to occur with such regularity and why we never seem to learn.

Poring over the follies of the past is not an exercise in schadenfreude. Financial crises and the speculative booms that birth them have important and lasting effects on economies. At the same time, economies are not closed cocoons but have social, political, and, increasingly, international dimensions. Therefore, crises also have important and long-lasting effects on governments, hegemonies, and societies. They accentuate tensions, expose structural frailties, and, through repeated application, usher in dramatic shifts in existing paradigms. The Roman Empire's history is in part a reflection of how it dealt with its financial fragilities, while the French Revolution was in part a society's dismay at the dystopia wrought by a century of financial folly. No other recurrent event encapsulates the intellectual onanism at the heart of human nature better than financial crises do.

For all their notional diversity, financial crises are bound by the common factor of human nature. We humans are intendedly rational, but in practice, what we term rationality is actually bounded on all sides by experience, emotion, and environment. These give us shortcuts that allow us to make quick decisions but also leave us with a host of unconscious behavioral biases that find their collective expression in a crisis. A simple example may be found in the customary stroll to dinner. Two restaurants present themselves, one empty and the other with some people already within. Our automatic response is to infer that the second is in some way better and go there. We do not check menus, study layouts, ask to sample the wares, weigh ambiences, and so on. That may be the rational way to make the best decision, but it would be a waste of time and the evening would soon pass the truly rational man by. Instead, we trust our peers and follow the herd.

Like geese flying in formation, each of us moves individually through the world but never in isolation. If one changes course, his or her actions impede on neighbors, affecting their behavior. Our bounded rationalities overlap and cascade through the flock until suddenly the whole formation changes course, the new order emerging unbidden from the initial random movements of a few.

Other biases abound. For example, we care more about today than about the distant future. The young couple will always prioritize paying for home and school today over saving for a secure retirement tomorrow. The drug addict will care more about the hit in a few seconds than the far worse comedown in a few hours. The money to be made today is more real and alluring than what lies ahead next year, even if the latter may be much greater. Our long shared history is a monument to this common temporal myopia in which the urgent usually trumps the potentially more important.

Life is simply too short for us to be truly rational. But there are benefits to our shortsightedness as well. If entrepreneurs were truly rational,
they would never set up businesses. Any genuine assessment of the risks
tells you that there are just too many uncertainties. The majority of new
businesses will always fail, but we still continually plow on. The blinkered
taking on of risks, the relentless focus on the here and now, the ability to
persuade your peers into your vision, and so on—these are also all qualities
that led to the creation of successful empires, fed innovation, built economies, and allowed us to progress from lone hunters in caves to the
sophistication we have today. As George Bernard Shaw noted, all progress
depends on the unreasonable man.

All these episodes we discuss have something in common: they
involve people. A financial market is not a static entity. It is a collective
noun for the actions born of the hope, greed, and fear of countless human
participants. Like the refrain from John Gay's *The Beggar's Opera*, man
truly is the most sociable of predators. Though we may prey on each other,
we still herd together. Our collective emotions and the actions born of
them ebb and flow over time, euphemistically creating the booms and
busts we term cycles.

The psychological factors are invariant in every recurrent episode of
financial euphoria, panic, and denial, whether it be Greece in the fourth
century B.C. or Greece in the twenty-first century A.D. That we greet each
episode with surprise is telling of how often we fail to see beyond the
outside ornamentation and how quickly we choose to forget. Can we
prevent them? Not if we choose to study the minutiae of each crisis—the
wealth of data accumulated has filled countless books but shown us
remarkably little about the causes, prediction, and prevention of crises.
There is no simple early warning system. Rather, the answers lie in understanding the human element and how it relates to money.

Money is only a medium, a transient store of value. It provides a way
of keeping score, an abstract means of exchange and payment. Our tragedy is that we are always looking to stay in the present, not realizing that
it is always doomed to become the past. And money is a physical reflection of this fact. We hoard it believing that it will keep its value while the
world conspires to prove us wrong, be it through devaluation, inflation,

repossession, usurpment, destruction, or confiscation. Money is another dogma like religion. In the shifting sands of time, it provides a seeming certainty, and therein lies its chief attraction. Whether it be a medieval merchant counting his precious reserve of gold coins or a modern trader eyeballing the digital decimals of his worth, we have changed little in thousands of years.

This construct of money both unites and divides us. By giving us all a common reference point, it brings us together irrespective of affluence, geography, or language. The coin or note becomes a constant thread, weaving together a disparate and growing society every time it changes hands. But that same medium emphasizes inequalities between us and eventually widens them by giving our innately competitive natures a simple means of keeping score. Social harmony and stability come to be inextricably linked to our perception of money and its value.

FROM BOOM TO BUST

Our psychology lends itself naturally to boom and bust. What raises it to the architecture of crisis is the addition of money to the mix. The two feed off each other, leveraging our innate biases till an entire economy and society resonate in sympathy. Self-belief is buttressed by the enhanced status that money imparts. Initial speculation leads to over-confidence and a growing illusion of skill. What is for now a virtuous circle—a boom, in everyday parlance—soon buoys up the egos of those involved, though this becomes increasingly suspect as asset prices become ever more inflated.

Alongside, money booms. Speculation needs money. As investors bid up the prices of commodities, property, food, gold, stocks, bonds, and so on, it becomes easy for us to imagine ourselves rich. This nebulous creation of wealth means we can borrow more and funnel it into our investments, leading to an explosion of debt. There is now a race on to ensure that we are all making money, whether it be by lending or investing. Where there is insufficient money, people find ways of creating more—the history of finance is replete with innovations such as bills of exchange, bonds, paper money, and derivatives.

The phenomenon is understandable. Speculation conquers sense. Ego denies the hand of luck and instead thanks skill, knowledge, and pre-science. In an economic boom, there is also no shortage of oracles and cheerleaders, whether it is John Law in the eighteenth century, Irving Fisher prior to the Great Depression, or Michael Milken in the junk bond boom of the 1980s. Each increase in value rubber-stamps and diffuses the innate superiority of our chosen gurus until by the end we are all self-affirming experts and inevitably oblivious to the increasingly shaky ground underneath.

Intelligence and idiocy are often two sides of the same coin, sepa-rated only by a sliver of time. When the bubble bursts, it causes surprise every time. Inevitably, the triggers are innocuous, though all too obvious in retrospect. It is the failure of some small link in a complex financial chain, misdirected imperial or sovereign edicts that accentuate rather than amel-iorate crises in confidence, new opportunities elsewhere that promise more and steal our limited attention span, the flooding of the system with money through debasement or printing only to learn Gresham's law yet again, and so on.[5]

Irrespective of this diversity, at its core a crisis is always a question of trust. That same knife-edge of trust that allows every bank to take liquid deposits from us and return illiquid loans back to purchase whatever takes our fancy is sharpened by euphoria till it glides through our illusions and fancies to reveal our base human motivations and fears.

In the wake of a crisis, those baser elements take center stage. The extreme brevity of financial memory ensures that people do not learn from the last crisis, preferring instead to find external scapegoats in the after-math, whether individuals or groups. As the tide departs and shipwrecks surface, allegations of fraud and deceit abound. There is the self-righteous belief—but always excusing oneself—that excesses need to be purged and speculation punished. There is hope that policy makers will provide answers and create a utopian world where economies are no longer subject to the vagaries of boom and bust.

But hope is not a strategy. The introspection needed is sorely lacking, and myopic postcrash mutterings only contribute to the brevity of financial memory. The tools of the boom—stocks, tulips, derivatives, mortgages, and so on—are scrutinized, demonized, and finally rehabilitated through regulation. But the all-too-human wielders of those tools and the societal incentives that drove them are never mentioned.

It is hardly surprising, then, that there is such a strong correlation between regulation and crises. Sheathing the sword does not make it any less dangerous—it only presents the illusion of doing so. If we do not address the underlying causes, crisis and regulation are forever condemned to follow each other like night and day.

Crises are endemic, and efficient markets—the core commandment of modern finance—are a lie. The regularity of crises and our persistent failure to avoid them hint that markets are inherently unstable and fragile. To ignore the human actors within them is to ignore the lifeblood that drives our history. Like the drunken man zigzagging back home after a night out, we lurch from crisis to our notion of normality to crisis again.

The same pattern repeats in financial crises from the Greek and Roman bailouts of the ancient era to the follies of tulipmania in the seventeenth century to our modern experiences in the twenty-first century, even as the human race steadily marches on through history, progressing to new heights of achievement.

THE MARCH OF COMPLEXITY

We live in a world that is more interconnected and complex than ever. You don't have to look far to see how rapidly it has evolved, particularly over the recent past (see Figure 1 in the photo insert, graph of estimated global GDP).

Till about 1700, the world grew on a Malthusian dynamic—that is, its growth was linked to the growth in population, increasing steadily. Communities ran into each other more often, explored new lands, and traded more widely. Productivity increased steadily and there were periodic technological breakthroughs (e.g., gunpowder), but the pace of these was slow. The world was divided into those who had a lot of money and those who had very little. The middle class, as such, was thin on the ground and largely composed of the merchant class and occasional urban gentry. Agriculture was the dominant profession and contributor to global growth, its upward trend ensured by a steady increase in the mouths that needed to be fed.

The crises we see during this period are often fiscal crises of empires and nations. They borrowed too much money or spent too heavily in pursuit of their interests. As money ran short, they resorted to watering down the metal content of their coins—debasement or inflation the old-fashioned way—and found themselves losing all credibility. Insurrections, invaders, and assassinations purged the system and collapsed its nascent complexity before it could encompass too large a population. Bankers were few and debt was limited.

There were exceptions to the above. Rome was one, where the system evolved a rare complexity of economy. The influences of that complexity still echo in our language and laws today. But it also came with costs in the form of repeated battles between debtors and creditors, numerous financial crises, and a state that grew so large and dominant within the Roman hegemony in its pursuit of certainty that it became a financial black hole, causing the system to implode.

Post-1700, however, we see a distinct change. The Industrial Revolution unleashed a surge in productivity thanks to technological innovation, and growth suddenly took off. Thereafter, economic growth appeared to decouple from population growth and was driven by the ever-increasing pace of technological progress.

With this sustained exponential surge in growth, society became increasingly complex at an accelerated rate. As interactions between people as well as demand grew apace, money flowed into the system in response. Innovation was fueled and productivity increased dramatically. A virtuous circle of leverage was created. The promise of enhanced status, driven by a slice of future growth, enticed more people to commit ever more capital. Where they did not have any, intermediaries sprang up to manufacture this for them by mortgaging the future, increasing the stock of money in the system. An arbitrage of location between supply and demand became one of time. By pulling the future earnings of many people into today, you financed growth in the present, so when tomorrow arrived, you were already far richer.

A secondary industry based around money arose. By taking resources and lending them out repeatedly to others, it deepened the links across the network. Trust became commoditized and an efficiency of allocation emerged. The result was the distribution of money across a far wider swath of people, all of whom now acted to further grow their individual influence (and, thereby, their status) within this complex network by moving their money to where growth might emerge.

The nature of financial crises changed as well. Losses of trust grew more pervasive. Debt and leverage increasingly became a structural part of the link. Thus, the failure of a link affected more people and for longer. The phenomenon of contagion was born. As herds moved around this new ecosystem, rotating through different opportunities, a more distinct boom-and-bust cycle was created.

Recessions and crises have become more common over recent centuries. Their impact has also grown. Both are in proportion to the growth in complexity and the more efficient transmission mechanisms created by this. The debasing and defaults of sovereigns have been joined by the defaults and restructurings of smaller collectives and individuals as they seek to alter the promises made in headier times.

One may see the transition as akin to the transition from an oxcart to a car. The latter will get you to where you want to go much faster, but it also has far more moving parts that can break down unexpectedly. However, that is a compromise we make willingly every time because we value the added benefits.

THE GOOD, THE BAD, AND THE UGLY

Given their roots in the excesses of human nature, it is easy to typify all crises as bad. But this is too simplistic a view. Throughout history, progress and growth have always been linked to the capacity for error. Speculation and overlending may cause bubbles if unchecked, but at the same time, it is the taking on of imprudent risks that has often led to many of the advances throughout history.

It was likely a speculator who left his milk out too long one day and discovered cheese, and possibly a greater fool who came to the party even later to discover blue cheese. The rise of the Internet spawned an infamous dot-com bubble. However, that same bubble also financed a paradigm shift in the global exchange of information and social interaction that is now increasingly defining our modern world.

Conversely, attempting to dampen down too far is stifling. The Dark Ages may possibly be construed as a greater depression, as the Christian ban on usury and the lack of a financial framework to support speculation slowed economic growth to a crawl. Legend has it that when the great Mongol warlord Tamerlane reached the borders of eastern Europe in the fourteenth century, after scything his way through Asia, he looked across and deemed the continent too insignificant and poor to pillage. A third of global GDP during those times resided in China, which was experimenting with the concept of fiat money—money based only on trust, as we have today. Along the way, the Chinese created a legendary empire and discovered gunpowder and paper as well as new financial phenomena such as hyperinflation. It was only when greedy banking families such as the Medicis began to fraudulently lend money without holding sufficient reserves—a necessary if criminal speculation—that the Renaissance and the ascendancy of European culture actually began. Other examples abound. The South Sea bubble in the eighteenth century was intrinsically tied both to governments' need to develop a functioning bond market to help finance them and to the growing popularity of the stock company, financing the dreams—for better or worse—of countless entrepreneurs (and a few criminals) through to the present day.

But though birthed from the same socioeconomic DNA, crises can evolve down very different paths. Some crises, such as the Wall Street crash of 1987 and tulipmania, only lead to brief lulls in economic activity and little lasting damage. Others are more scarring. Almost all of the 1400s were beset by inflationary forces, while 1929 and its aftermath have been seared into cultural memory as the Great Depression.

Depressions have deep roots. The amount of debt is critical. When the borrowing has been far too excessive such that the deleveraging required is monumental, then that may necessitate years and perhaps even decades of liquidation to return to some semblance of normality.

The long-term planning and management of a society's different aspects also necessitate a long-term perspective. But in practice, the actions of those charged with this task always have a horizon far shorter than the complexity of the system they manage. Little decisions today play out in big ways tomorrow as the actors in the economy respond individually to them and the incentives they procreate. New permutations of group behavior and, thereby, complexity are born. Some will inevitably reinforce existing bubbles or create new ones. However, these bubbles also have a critical point they will reach at some time in the future when emotions tip over and confidence turns to growing concern.

At these turning points, when the disequilibrium beneath the surface comes to the fore, failing to appreciate the complexity of what you are dealing with can cause great harm despite all the best intentions. The small decisions can accumulate, allowing the herd to grow far larger than it might do otherwise, yet always too little to right the structural weaknesses when the cycle turns. In time, they crescendo over successive crises, and what would otherwise be a recession becomes something far more scarring that can threaten the sustainability of an economy and way of living.

A depression then becomes fundamentally a tragedy of small decisions. Bubbles are born in the minds of individuals, nurtured by the incentives of their environment, and grow to adulthood in the complexity of economies. Their aftermath is dictated by these same forces as well.

Because we are human and seem to have a preference for capitalism, we may not be able to prevent the contagion. But knowing how to manage crises and minimize their wider impact—both economic and sociopolitical—is still an important goal. As I noted at the start of the chapter, rises and falls are as natural to the economic condition as breathing is to the human condition. Removing these ebbs and flows would be to stifle progress, as has been amply demonstrated throughout history. But a clear perception of the characteristics common to these episodes can also help in warning of and curbing our enthusiasm so that we minimize the risk of our speculations becoming systemic. While this may be less mechanical than many hope for, the signs of delusionary euphoria are still unmistakable. When the world is increasingly convinced that something can only go up, it is time to gently bring it back down to earth.

The importance of that cannot be overstated. Beyond the systemic risks, an economic crisis left to go on for too long always becomes a political and social one. The Europeans' impotent obsession with reparations and war debts led to the rise of Nazism. The Spaniards' love of gold in the sixteenth and seventeenth centuries eventually bankrupted their nation. China's dalliance with floating exchange rates in the late 1930s led to hyperinflation and the advent of Chairman Mao. The lessons of history and the human imperative underlying them are clear; we simply have to recognize them.

In our language, we talk constantly of flows: the flow of water, the flow of money, the flow of ideas, the flow of our thoughts, the flow of the words on these pages. It is an unconsciousness acceptance of the fact that we live in a dynamic world and that all life is movement.

You hold in your hand a history of financial speculation and its consequences. It tracks and analyzes the persistent seduction of our senses by new investment opportunities; the subsuming of individuals into the euphoria of the crowd as the illusion of insight takes hold; the never-ending, ever-enriching boom, fueled by a surfeit of money; the complexities we never understand till it's too late; the unexpected catalysts that expose the emperor's new clothes; the inevitable crash as investors scramble to realize their monies and salvage their egos; and, finally, the brevity of financial memory that allows us to repeat the cycle endlessly without ever critically evaluating our own failings.

In short, it is the story of what makes us human.

CHAPTER 2

Deconstructing the Gruffalo:
A Roman Parable

Past things shed light on future ones; the world was always of a
kind; what is and will be was at some other time; the same things
come back, but under different names and colors; not everybody
recognizes them, but only he who is wise and considers them
diligently.

—FRANCESCO GUICCIARDINI (1483–1540)

All the perplexities, confusions, and distresses in America arise,
not from defects in their constitution or confederation, nor from
want of honour or virtue, as much from downright ignorance of
the nature of coin, credit, and circulation.

—JOHN ADAMS (1735–1826)

IN A.D. 33, a certain Jesus of Nazareth, also known as the Christ, was
crucified by Pontius Pilate, the fifth prefect of a distant province of the
Roman Empire called Judaea.

A few paragraphs may have been devoted to the abovementioned
unfortunate in Pilate's regular report to Emperor Tiberius on tax collec-
tions and the general mood of the local populace. It certainly earned a
passing mention in the Roman historian Tacitus's diatribe against the
"Chrestians" in his *Annals* some eighty-three years later.

Otherwise, this distant death was of little consequence to the
ancient world. Tiberius was busy throwing his friend Sextus Marius to his
death off the Tarpeian Rock in Rome, some 1,434 miles away. He and
the rest of Rome had their hands full dealing with their deepest financial
crisis to date.

AN EMPIRE OF COMMERCE

The year began as any other for a Roman Empire seemingly in its ascendancy. Roman legions had conquered much of Europe, and the empire's borders now stretched from Spain in the west to Syria in the east, from the length of the Danube in the north to Egypt and Libya in the south. A constant stream of people from the outlying provinces flooded Rome in search of prosperity and status. Despite periodic skirmishes with those unenlightened enough to resent Rome's rule, peace was the order of the day, and the Pax Romana was rapidly becoming the cultural myth that future generations would aspire to.

Long before our own modern globalization, a dense web of interconnected economies and trade—all supported by a complex morass of banking and credit—already existed. Rome was the economic and cultural capital of the Mediterranean world, the city where all roads led. Nowhere was this more evident than on the Via Sacra, the main street of ancient Rome, which meandered from the great temples at the top of the Capitoline Hill through the Forum with its bankers and traders before finishing up at the Colosseum, where ordinary Romans went to enjoy an afternoon of gladiatorial combat or highbrow drama.

This was the most expensive retail street in the ancient world, the Fifth Avenue or Champs-Elysées of its day. Here you could pick up a slave for a lifetime, or a whore for the afternoon, if the price of the former—often more than a year's wages for the typical Roman legionnaire—was too steep. Find a backstreet gambler to chance your precious monies with or instead trust them to one of the many bankers or companies dotted around the fora. Traders vied with one another to sell you exotic spices from India or holy scarabs from Egypt. Little eateries set up shop next to each other, tempting you with fine wines from Spain, hams from Germany, and olive oil from northern Italy. If nothing else, one could saunter down the paved street and admire the many architectural delights left by generations past, from triumphal arches to sycophantic statues to the pagan magnificence of the Pantheon.

Smaller tendrils reached out, catering to the wants and whims of those unable or unwilling to afford the wares of the Via Sacra. These economic contours radiated outward, delineating the strata of Roman society, until finally, on the Tiber, one reached budding Monte Testaccio, the future eighth hill of Rome and a testament to how much Roman commerce had come to dominate the world. A dumping ground for disused amphorae, Monte Testaccio would eventually become the resting place for some fifty-three million amphorae, rising in a mound nearly 160 feet high and with a circumference of more than half a mile.[1] Today it forms the grassy hub of a bustling working-class neighborhood of Rome, many of whose visitors are oblivious to the ancient clay beneath their feet as they stock up for weekend picnics at its famous market by day and at night venture into the many nightclubs carved into the hill.

The Via Sacra was a true melting pot for the whole empire. Around this artery of commerce, a burgeoning financial district had taken shape to cater to Roman denizens of all strata. Hidden in the markets were the moneychangers, each hard at work at his *bancu*—a long bench that would in time give us the words *bank* and *banker*. Foreign coins were weighed, checked for quality and purity, and then converted into the gold denarii, silver sestertii, and other lesser coins issued by the imperial mint.

A step above were the *argentarii*, professional bankers who received deposits and made loans. They advanced credit to buyers at auctions and also collected money on behalf of the sellers. Over time, other types of bankers would spring up who combined varying aspects of the moneylenders and *argentarii*.

Finally, at the other end of the scale were the financiers. Akin perhaps to the merchant bankers of the nineteenth century or the private-equity powerhouses of today, these were entrepreneurs who took part in financial enterprises and speculations on a grander scale. They lent money to cities and kings, created large companies to bid for public contracts and collect taxes on behalf of Rome, and dominated ancient mining and shipping.

Between all these echelons, a complex financial network extended throughout the empire. It bound society as well as provided the fuel for economic growth. Most important, it instilled a sense of trust that was vital to the success of the Roman economy.

A FOUNDATION OF DEBT

Modern banking is typified by fractional reserving, a notion under which money deposited is loaned out repeatedly, with only a small amount held back in reserve. Through this provision of credit, the money supply is boosted and the economy receives a huge influx of capital to help it grow. Behind this lie two calculated risks: first, that the profits on loans made will exceed any losses suffered and provide the banker with a return over and above the deposits entrusted to him; and second, that depositors will not ask for their money back all at once. All banks always have only a small amount of liquid cash on hand to manage their daily outgoings. The rest is all tied up in longer-term loans that are not so easy to call in at short notice and unlikely to retain more than a fraction of their value in any disorderly liquidation. Therefore, trust is all-important to this façade: people are unlikely to make a run on the bank as long as they have confidence that they will be paid back their money whenever they need it.

However, this concept of a leveraged economy sustained by trust is not a modern invention. The word *credit* comes to us from the Latin verb *credere*, "to trust or believe," and ancient civilizations were well versed in the use and abuse of credit.

Many temples across the ancient world from Greece to Egypt to Asia took full advantage of their privileged position in society and had a profitable sideline in taking deposits, extending loans, and changing currencies. Credit was a vital part of facilitating trade and arguably predated the medium termed money. Ancient legal codes such as Hammurabi's Code from the eighteenth century B.C. prescribe the treatment of debt and debtors in extensive detail. The cultural pervasiveness of credit may be judged by the repeated mention—rarely flattering—of bankers by ancient orators such as Isocrates and Demosthenes, while other records demonstrate that the ancient Greeks at least were able to add default to their list of accomplishments alongside democracy.[2]

Nevertheless, it took the Romans to elevate credit to the architecture of an economy. Roman law made distinctions between money handed over to a banker for a period of time or to be available on demand (*mutuus*), typically with interest, and money that was given explicitly for safekeeping (*depositum*), often in a sealed bag. The former could be lent out at will by the bank, while the latter was strictly off-limits. These concepts have lasted through to modern times and even as late as the nineteenth century were being cited in U.S. court cases. Today we still unconsciously distinguish between them by choosing to put money in our bank accounts or valuables in a safe-deposit box.[3]

Credit was fundamental to both the growth and sustenance of the Roman hegemony. Rome was one of the earliest mercantile powers, where trade and empire went hand in hand. As Cicero noted in one of his speeches, "All Gaul is full of traders—Roman citizens. No Gaul does any business without a Roman's aid."

The size of the Roman Empire demanded both extensive infrastructure and finance to facilitate trade across this growing commercial reality. The evidence lies strewn across Europe and Africa in the remains of countless aqueducts, Roman roads, and Mediterranean shipwrecks. This commerce allowed Rome to spread its influence, laws, and culture across much of their known world, binding people into a common society that stretched across thousands of miles. As long as everyone was making money, few had reasons to disturb the Pax Romana.

At its zenith, the city of Rome had a population of over a million people—a number thereafter unmatched until London in the early nineteenth century laid claim to being the largest city in the world. Meanwhile, the growing number of cities across Italy and the empire added their own demands for wheat, oil, and luxuries.

Loans were advanced to traders, with wheat and dried fruits as security. Contracts for future delivery—a rudimentary form of what we term today financial derivatives—provided insurance against crop loss and the risks of long-distance commerce.[4] As ships set sail for distant lands, bankers provided the guarantees that allowed merchants to chance the uncertain journey.

Famous Romans over the years such as the orator Cicero, the philosopher Seneca, and Julius Caesar's assassin, Brutus, competed to provide the grease to lubricate the growing Roman economy and made handsome profits as a result. Senators, knights, and rich plebeians all congregated around the Forum to trade in debt claims and the shares of *publicani* and shipping companies, deposit their monies with the financiers of the day, or take loans for that other perennial Roman speculation, land.[5]

Financial speculation was the quickest way to climb or sustain your position on the greasy pole of Roman society. Like many ancient societies, Rome had a hierarchical structure. At the top were the privileged senators, originally the old landed gentry who had founded and ruled the republic for many years. Beneath them were the equestrians or knights, ambitious junior members of the aristocracy who took advantage of a burgeoning Roman Empire to accumulate vast estates and fortunes. Then there were lesser elites—typically the aristocracies of other cities—and the poorer strata of Roman society, culminating in the freedmen (ex-slaves) and slaves at the very bottom.

However, this hierarchy was remarkably fluid and one could move in either direction by virtue of fortunes made or lost. The role of money in determining status in society was eventually codified by the first Roman emperor, Augustus (63 B.C.–A.D. 14). Senators required a minimum property threshold of 250,000 denarii (about 1,100 times the annual wage of a legionary), while knights required 100,000 denarii.

The role of trade and finance in aiding this social mobility is best illustrated with two examples. The Latin poet Horace's father was first a slave, then a freedman, and eventually, a professional banker. The fortune he made enabled him to build up a significant real estate portfolio and provide his son with the best education money could buy. Horace in turn became eventually a knight and one of the most famous Latin poets, immortalizing his father's contribution in verse.

> And yet if my disposition be culpable for a few faults, and those small ones, otherwise perfect (as if you should condemn moles scattered over a beautiful skin), if no one can justly lay to my charge avarice, nor sordidness, nor impure haunts; if, in fine (to speak in my own praise), I live undefiled, and innocent, and dear to my friends; my father was the cause of all this. . . . As long as I am in my senses, I can never be ashamed of such a father as this, and therefore shall not apologize [for my birth], in the manner that numbers do, by affirming it to be no fault of theirs. (Satires 1.6.65–92)

Still more remarkable was the story of the family of Vespasian, one of the preeminent Roman emperors in the late first century A.D. His grandfather Titus Flavius Petro was one of the earliest recorded professional bankers, offering the full gamut of services from receiving monies at auctions to deposits to exchanging money, in the time of Julius Caesar during the early first century B.C. His father, Titus Flavius Sabinus, built on this foundation to establish a significant fortune. He began his career as a private tax collector in Asia and then moved on to advancing loans to various tribes across the Roman Empire. The Swiss, in particular, were among his best clients, giving him the distinction of being history's first recorded Swiss private banker. Thanks to his father's enterprise, Vespasian himself ascended to the ranks of knight, senator, and eventually emperor, though he lost little of his family's taste for making money.[6]

THE ARCHITECTURE OF CRISIS

By A.D. 33, many senators and knights were not averse to making money through commercial and financial ventures, such as lending, banking, and tax farming. It was a way of growing their patrimony and ensuring their preeminence at the political dinner table. It was also their share of the spoils of a growing empire. These few thousand men and their families dominated the Roman economy and were to play a vital role in the future history of the empire.

Much of this growing optimism and attendant mobility was thanks to one man: Augustus, the first Roman emperor. Born Octavian, he was a short, quiet man who lacked the charisma of his great-uncle Julius Caesar but was blessed with superior political acumen. As Octavian, he ruthlessly maneuvered his way through a bloody civil war in the aftermath of the assassination of Julius Caesar to emerge the unchallenged victor. Then, as Augustus, he adopted a more benevolent façade as the kindly emperor and father of the nation. His chameleon-like ability to play the political game was evident in his dying words: "Since well I've played my part, all clap your hands and from the stage dismiss me with applause."

But it was not an easy path. In 30 B.C., surrounded by Octavian's troops in Alexandria, Mark Antony—once Caesar's confidante and Octavian's co-ruler—fell on his sword and killed himself, pausing only to have a final glass of wine. As he died, the Egyptian queen-pharaoh Cleopatra clasped an asp to her breast, according to the legends, and chose death over the humiliation of being paraded in the inevitable triumphal march in Rome.

The civil war now over, Octavian's challenge was immense. Rome was decimated and impoverished after the latest episode in over a century of civil wars. High taxation, the dearth of commerce, punishing inflation in the prices of basic necessities, and numerous debt and liquidity crises had reduced economic growth to a theoretical term.

Rome and its businessmen needed stability to recover. Octavian provided this by hunting down and killing the eldest of Caesar's, Antony's, and Cleopatra's children. With that accomplished and a vast army at his call, all political threats were removed. By itself, that would have led to a recovery in time as Roman commerce recolonized Europe and reopened trade routes. Octavian, however, was impatient. He was also mindful that social tensions between debtors and creditors had been at the root of Rome's troubles for the last century.

This was the flip side of the complex economy built over successive generations. Money permeated throughout Roman society. The growth of Roman power and wealth had led also to a growing inequality in society, as rich landowners accumulated vast estates and a large number of commoners found themselves increasingly impoverished and unable to compete with the influxes of cheap labor flooding in from distant conquests in the form of slaves. The rise of the knights as a new breed of entrepreneurs only exacerbated this disenfranchisement and led to growing tensions within society in the absence of political reforms. Tax farming—the use of private *publicani* to collect taxes from the provinces—was particularly lucrative and open to abuse. The method employed was unique. The state wanted the stability of revenues, so contracts were auctioned for different territories. Companies bid for these and paid the expected revenue up front. They would then go out and extract the taxes from the local populace, taking on the risk of any shortfalls. Naturally, the desire to maximize profits soon meant that the focus was on extracting as much as possible in excess of the bid paid to the Roman state. For the populace, the need to pay taxes soon meant that moneylenders had a captive clientele, and many cities found themselves perilously and perpetually in debt. Brutus infamously lent money to the city of Salamis in the first century B.C. at the generous rate of 48 percent and then tried to coerce the local governor into using his troops to collect on his debt when they began to default.

The Romans soon found themselves learning the now familiar cycle of boom and bust as the market economy grew more complex and credit percolated throughout Roman society. Financial crises driven by debt or liquidity began to be recorded in the historical annals with increasing frequency from the early second century B.C. onward, both in Rome and in its provinces.[7]

By the end of the second century B.C., land reform and debt relief were major political issues and led to the splitting of the Roman elite into two rival factions supporting debtors and creditors, respectively. The class struggles that Karl Marx would write about two millennia later were being played out in all their brutal glory in the streets of Rome. Echoes of this cultural memory may be found in the name Marx gave his working-class heroes: the proletariat. The word derives from the Latin word *proletarii*, for the lowest rung of Roman society, who had little to no property and whose only contribution to Roman dominance were the *proli* or offspring they produced to fill the ranks of the army and colonize new provinces.

Given the intractability of both sides, war and crisis were inevitable and chronic. The Social War of 91–88 B.C. between Rome and its vassal Italian city-states was a bitter struggle over the thorny issue of land redistribution and a growing inequality divide. It led to a financial crisis, as a fall in real estate values was compounded by the hoarding of money by cautious Romans and troubles in the province of Asia Minor, where considerable Roman money was invested. The interconnecting threads linking the new Roman economy became a noose for many as investments went sour and debts fell due. As deflation took hold, debt burdens grew harder to shoulder, forcing yet more people into selling their lands and possessions at any price to settle their books, and creating a vicious cycle that we now know today as the debt-deflation spiral. Resolution was reached only when one side emerged victorious and the new consuls Valerius Flaccus and Marcus Cinna pushed through a debt relief bill that cut all debts by three-quarters.

But the pattern was now set, and debt was rapidly becoming a structural part of the economy. Roman demands for reparations from the cities of Asia Minor for their impudent rebellion soon created another financial crisis, resulting in the first-ever documented banking bailout: a ten-year moratorium on the return of deposits for the troubled banks of Ephesus in 85 B.C. Two decades later, in 64 B.C., another looming financial crisis led to the infamous Catiline conspiracy. Debts had again grown across Roman society. Rome strained under an influx of dispossessed farmers and ex-soldiers looking for jobs and money. Many senators found themselves unable to repay their debts without sacrificing the patrimony that gave them their privileged place and political clout. The senator Catiline demanded the abolition of debts and attempted a coup to overthrow the Republic, only to be foiled by the great orator Cicero, who summarily executed the conspirators to remove any potential threat to the state.[8] Possibly Cicero was also influenced by his own partisan pursuits, as he lent large sums of money often and traded in debt claims. In later years, as his own debts piled up, Cicero ruefully remarked to a friend that he would gladly join in some conspiracy but that none would have him after his punishment of Catiline.

Barely fifteen years later, the latest round of civil war—now between Julius Caesar and Pompey—triggered another crisis in 49 B.C. Worries about political instability led to the hoarding of coins and a drying up of the money supply. Creditors began to call in their loans, but debtors found themselves unable or unwilling to sell. The economy once again ground to a halt.

A functioning and growing economy depends on how fast money moves through the system. In Rome, as for us today, the velocity of money is determined by the entities that buy and borrow and lend, that is, banks, businesses, and ordinary consumers, as an economy is fundamentally nothing more than the sum total of their interactions. In order to have an effect on the economy, money needs to move through the system, and that can only be determined by these participants' willingness to borrow and lend rather than hoard and save. When banks refuse to lend, businesses begin to conserve cash and consumers stop buying and borrowing, choosing instead to save and hoard money. Monetary velocity crashes, transactions dry up, and the economy begins to shrink in recession—the bogeyman of kings and politicians through the ages. Deflation becomes the order of the day as asset prices fall in an attempt to become attractive enough to entice those hoards out of hiding and kick-start a stalled economy.

Then, much as in the following passages of human history, the resulting panic and hardship led Caesar to negotiate settlements between debtors and creditors as well as bring in new laws that limited the amount of interest that could be charged on loans. Senators such as Brutus were unlikely to have been supporters of such measures, given their lucrative dealings. There are suggestions that Caesar even tried to fix the maximum proportion of a patrimony that could be loaned out by the upper class going forward. If true, it would have represented the earliest equivalent of asking banks to limit their leverage and hold more regulatory capital. Caesar's reforms were soon ignored, making him among the first to learn that one cannot legislate away market forces of supply and demand.

THE CUSP OF MANIA

All this history was fresh in Octavian's mind. Political stability had already been ensured for now through the sword. Dragging Rome out of its deflationary spiral and reigniting growth were critical if Rome was to manage its social tensions and create an empire that could withstand the test of time.

We often debate today what the right policies are to engineer growth and maintain it. Schools of thought inspired by economists such as Keynes, Hayek, and Friedman dominate the exchanges between policy makers and central bankers on key issues such as taxes, interest rates, and the supply of money in the economy. Recent events such as the credit crunch of 2007–9 can add urgency to some of these discussions as each school trumpets its favored solution to end an ongoing crisis and restore growth.

John Maynard Keynes would advocate during the Great Depression of the 1930s that in times of severe stress, the government should step in and alleviate the burden through cutting interest rates and increasing its own spending on areas such as infrastructure to keep the economy going and minimize the downturn.[9]

A few decades later, the chairman of the U.S. Federal Reserve, Ben Bernanke, earned himself the moniker "Helicopter Ben" when in a speech at the National Economists Club in Washington, D.C., in November 2002 he argued that a government that owned the physical means of making money could always outfox deflation by simply issuing more money.

> U.S. dollars have value only to the extent that they are strictly limited in supply. But the U.S. government has a technology, called a printing press . . . that allows it to produce as many U.S. dollars as it wishes at essentially no cost . . . [and] reduce the value of a dollar in terms of goods and services. . . . [Sufficient] injections of money will ultimately always reverse a deflation.

It was a new recasting of Milton Friedman's famous "helicopter drop" of money, but the speech could have been written by Octavian. The brevity of our memory coupled with misplaced pride makes it hard to imagine that anyone could have appreciated the tools of monetary and fiscal policy in the distant past. But nearly two millennia before either Bernanke or Friedman spoke or wrote a word, Octavian was grasping toward the same techniques that others advocate today for repairing a broken economy. The military power he wielded, coupled with his vast inheritance from Julius Caesar and the legendary riches of the conquered kingdom of Egypt (designated now as his personal property), gave him the ability to retool an economy in a way that today's politicians and central bankers can only envy.

The unpopular practice of tax farming was abolished and replaced with a simple system of flat wealth and sales taxes.[10] The Roman Empire became a free-trade area comparable in size to the European Union today, with only a few port duties and some agricultural subsidies for local Roman farmers. Commerce flourished under this system as people began to retain more of the money they made.

Octavian also significantly increased both spending by the state and the money supply—powerful antidotes to the economic malaise afflicting Rome. Over the next two decades, Octavian—now known as the benevolent Augustus—spent lavishly. His personal fortune was not just vast. It was a significant proportion of all the wealth in the known world and his spending was a public stimulus likely unmatched till recent decades. Roads across Italy were upgraded or rebuilt anew, with many being financed by Augustus directly. Eighty-two temples in Rome alone were restored, and some of the city's most famous monuments, such as the Pantheon, the Temple of Caesar, and the Baths of Agrippa, sprang up in these golden years. Other cities across the burgeoning empire found themselves receiving gifts of aqueducts, temples, baths, and statues. Augustus triumphantly proclaimed toward the end of his life, "Behold, I found Rome made of clay, and leave her to you made of marble."

The money supply was also dramatically increased. Augustus owned gold and silver mines, which were all turned over to producing coinage. Mints were opened in Spain and Gaul. Gifts of cash were made from Augustus's personal fortune to the populace on a regular basis. In one year, 29 B.C., he paid 400 sestertii—just under half a legionnaire's annual wage—each to at least 250,000 citizens, and 1,000 sestertii each to 120,000 army veterans in the colonies. It was not an isolated act of generosity and would be repeated several times over the coming years. He spent some 700 million sestertii over the years purchasing land for his soldiers to settle upon and gave another 400 million as cash gifts to these same soldiers when they retired. Even the public purse was not left out, as Augustus donated 150 million sestertii to the public treasury and another 170 million sestertii to the military treasury.

We do not know the full quantum of Augustus's largesse over these years, but the gifts that were recorded in his memoirs totaled over 2.5 billion sestertii. It is hard to draw direct comparisons between the value of the sestertius and, say, the U.S. dollar today. However, we can make some estimates based on a purchasing power parity basis—how far your money went in each age—thanks to the detailed records of prices for basic goods such as bread and wine. A loaf of bread cost half a sestertius and a flagon of wine a sestertius, while a typical daily wage for the average Roman might be 3–4 sestertii. Meticulous records kept by Roman brothels over the years have also been very helpful. A higher-end prostitute charged about 6 sestertii for a good time, while the ubiquitous streetwalker commanded about a sestertius. These give us estimates that one sestertius equaled anywhere between $10 and $100 in today's terms. Assuming a conservative valuation of $30 for the sestertius, Augustus's cash gifts were the equivalent of $75 billion today. This was stimulus in its most naked and direct form.

These policies not only revitalized the economy but also fueled an explosive credit expansion and business boom. Archaeologists have found a sharp increase in the number of known shipwrecks dating from the late first century B.C. and first century A.D. This is hardly surprising, as maritime commerce was a key part of the Roman economy and its success reflected the thriving business in trade and maritime loans. Roman merchants began to travel further than ever and established a lively trade with far-off places such as India. Roman coins appear with increasing regularity in Indian archaeology from the first century A.D. onward and the obligatory wrecks began to appear off its coast as well. Ancient texts talk of enormous trading ports such as Nelcynda and Barbaricum, where Roman merchants sold "figured linens, topaz, coral, frankincense, vessels of glass, silver and gold plate, and a little wine" in exchange for "turquoise, lapis lazuli, Seric skins, cotton cloth, silk yarn, and indigo," not to mention rice, sesame oil, cotton, ebony, ivory, and exotic animals. The output of commodities such as copper, lead, and iron reached levels that would not be seen again till after the Industrial Revolution took place more than seventeen hundred years later.

Aided by Augustus's extensive public works program as well as by the rapid growth of Rome and other cities, many new fortunes were made. At times, the flood of new money meant that speculation tipped into idiocy and perfunctory mania. The craze over red mullets in these early decades was a case in point. These were not epicurean fish, but they became a morbid centerpiece at the finest dinner parties. The philosopher Seneca in the mid-first century A.D. described the fascination with these in detail:

> A red mullet, even if it is perfectly fresh, is little esteemed until it is allowed to die before the eye of your guest. They are carried about enclosed in glass vessels, and their coloration is watched as they die, shifting as they struggle in the throes of death in varied shades and hues. . . . There is nothing, you say, more beautiful than the colors

of a dying red mullet; as it struggles and breathes forth its life, it is first red, and then gradually turns pale; and then as it hovers between life and death, it assumes an uncertain hue.

Large red mullets became particularly prized because of their relative rarity, and the wealth of Rome found in them an outlet. In the absence of Ferraris and Lamborghinis, competitive bidding for red mullets soon sent prices soaring to stratospheric levels. Augustus's successor Tiberius complained bitterly that three mullets had been sold for 30,000 sestertii—enough to pay the annual wages for thirty-three soldiers. On the Via Sacra, enterprising fishmongers installed stone tables with water-filled bowls carved into them, where their clientele could observe the live fish swimming within. Meanwhile, some speculators tried unsuccessfully to farm and breed mullets into ever larger specimens. We have little information as to how long the craze lasted, but some twenty years later Seneca talked of a sizable red mullet going for 5,000 sestertii—a bargain at half the price—and in the late years of the first century A.D., the poet Martial mentions a far lower price of 1,200 sestertii. By the second century A.D., the red mullet was an expensive but eminently affordable fish for any pescatarian.

Much of the new money, however, was plowed into land. Petronius's Trimalchio, a humble freedman of literary satire, spoke for much of Rome when he gloated in the *Satyricon* as to how he had made his fortune:

> For on just one voyage I scooped in 10,000,000 sesterces and immediately started to redeem all the lands that used to be my master's. I built a house, bought some cattle to sell again—whatever I laid my hand to grew like a honeycomb. When I found myself richer than all the country round about was worth, in less than no time I gave up trading, and commenced lending money at interest to the freedmen.

Land conferred prestige and, as noted earlier, allowed the nouveau riche to acquire a sizable patrimony and aspire to aristocracy. Real estate prices in Rome and elsewhere boomed as the new money sought out new homes.

This isn't just conjecture. Suetonius noted in his biography of the emperor that "when Augustus brought the royal treasures of Egypt to Rome, money became so abundant that the rate of interest fell and the value of real estate rose greatly." These are familiar words to any who recall the various real estate bubbles from the 1980s through to the early part of this century. The historian Dio confirms this, recording that interest rates fell from 12 percent to 4 percent—their lowest levels in Roman history—and "the price of goods rose."

However, there is also a side effect to having such low interest rates. Though they may stoke growth and reduce the cost of servicing debts today, they also accentuate the boom-and-bust cycle of an economy. It is a truism of banking systems that an excess of money will always be lent out at any cost. The availability of cheap credit leads to higher and higher levels of debt, fueling asset price bubbles that soar to unsustainable levels. Human myopia cannot conceive of a time when money might not be so freely available. The previous crisis recedes in memory and, like Trimalchio, we can do no wrong.

Augustus was the greatest beneficiary of this boom: Romans and generations of classical scholars would henceforth look at this period as the beginning of the golden age of Rome, ushered in by the greatest of its emperors. But the aftereffects of his policies would be felt keenly a few decades later in the financial panic of A.D. 33.

There was an additional complication with Augustus's prescription. Financial crises are rarely just financial. They often have social, political, and fiscal dimensions. A state that spends money so freely and places such an emphasis on financial stability must necessarily grow in size to reflect its role in the economy. However, that added burden of expense is not so easy to roll back afterward—bureaucracies, like turkeys, rarely vote for Christmas. Under Keynes's future musings, increased government spending in a downturn would be counterbalanced by increased taxes or cost cutting by the selfsame government and a reduction in size once the boom years came. History tells us governments rarely follow this prescription of their own volition. The mantra often is to spend in the bad times to ignite growth, and to spend in the good times to achieve political and social agendas. The result is an ever-growing state apparatus until external circumstances—be they financial shocks or social turmoil—enforce a rollback.

Under Augustus, the Roman state exploded in size to match the stimulus and growing empire. The tax reforms instituted by Augustus necessitated regular censuses. The large infusions of public money and extensive infrastructure projects required a competent and deep bureaucracy to administer. Rome and other cities acquired the trappings of modern civil society with police forces, firefighters, and planning authorities. The army grew as the mercantile Roman Republic with its vassal states transformed into an empire of direct rule. A standing army of 170,000 soldiers maintained the Pax Romana, aided by additional legions recruited from local populations and supported by a comprehensive communications and supply infrastructure. The costs of the state rapidly spiraled upward as what we term today the public sector took shape and grew rapidly.

Alongside, a proto–welfare state came into being. The need to address the social tensions that caused the civil war led Augustus to institute a mammoth program of benefits. A thousand sestertii was given to every Roman family to encourage them to produce more offspring. It became accepted practice to give every soldier a lump sum equivalent to thirteen years' salary upon retirement—the beginnings of a pension.

Since the first stirrings of social tension a century earlier, generations of Roman politicians had instituted the distribution of subsidized grain to the sprawling Roman underclass, who typically spent more than half their income on food. Over time, this became a free distribution as subsequent consuls found it an expedient way of cushioning the high levels of structural unemployment in Rome and avoiding the thornier issue of social reform.[11] By the time of Julius Caesar, nearly a third of the population of Rome received free grain—an enormous drain on the exchequer. Caesar more than halved this number by limiting eligibility and introducing means testing. Under Augustus, the number began to climb again, rising back to over 320,000 Romans, and proved stubbornly hard to stabilize despite his repeated efforts.

Lavish circuses and mock battles were now laid on regularly to entertain the crowds. Augustus meticulously recorded many of these in his memoirs:

Three times in my own name I gave a show of gladiators, and five times in the name of my sons or grandsons; in these shows there fought about ten thousand men. . . . In my own name, or that of my sons or grandsons, on twenty-six occasions I gave to the people . . . hunts of African wild beasts, in which about three thousand five hundred beasts were slain. . . . I gave the people the spectacle of a naval battle beyond the Tiber . . . [where] thirty beaked ships . . . and a large number of smaller vessels met in conflict. In these fleets, there fought about three thousand men exclusive of the rowers.

Panem et circenses—bread and circuses—became the basic political strategy for Augustus and his successors. Later Romans such as the poet Juvenal lamented what had become of the Roman populace: "Now that no one buys our votes, the public has long since cast off its cares; the people that once bestowed commands, consulships, legions and all else, now meddles no more and longs eagerly for just two things—Bread and Circuses!"

It was a cynical ploy to stupefy growing anger at the structural inequity within the Roman system with empty largesse. In the short term it was effective, but in the long run it was an additional fiscal burden that only exacerbated the impact of any financial turmoil. Today the phrase has entered our lexicon, referring to the purchase of political goodwill through extravagant but ultimately empty gestures.

THE WAVE CRASHES

By definition, stimulus is transient. After the early decades of free money, Augustus sought to impose some fiscal discipline as the costs to the state grew unsustainable. There were external pressures also as the early mines began to run empty. The deluge of new money became a trickle.

Rome had seen enormous asset price inflation, particularly in property, thanks to the Augustan boom. Occasionally, inflation encroached into wider society. Riots over rising grain prices were a regular occurrence, and the army had been called on to put down revolts caused by high grain prices in A.D. 5, A.D. 6, and A.D. 19. However, the booming economy and regular grain handouts had glossed over these little bumps in the road.

But the warning signs were mounting. As money poured into Rome from Augustus and new conquests, it left almost as quickly to search out new luxuries for Romans to enjoy. Rome had grown into a negative trade balance with the rest of the ancient world, with some 100 million sestertii worth of gold flowing out annually to India, China, and the Arabian peninsula in return for exotic animals, spices, and silks. "So dearly do we pay for our luxury and our women," complained the polymath Pliny the Elder about the imbalance in his *Natural History*, uncharitably blaming only the fairer sex. As the flow of money inward decreased, this outbound drain soon had a further pauperizing effect on the system.

Augustus passed away in A.D. 14, oblivious to these growing pressures on the Roman economy. His successor Tiberius—altogether a more prudent man by all accounts—continued the fiscal discipline of recent years. Perhaps because he was traumatized to find that his uncle had left him only 100 million sestertii, austerity became the new watchword. Tiberius was also keen to avoid further taxation. When some of his governors wrote recommending increased taxes for the provinces, the emperor wrote in return that "it was the part of a good shepherd to shear his flock, not skin it." Building projects dried up and lavish entertainments grew rare. Budding construction tycoons found themselves with vast numbers of idle slaves on their hands and a blushing balance sheet. Only grain distribution continued to increase as Tiberius sought to contain increasingly regular food riots.

Money is a commodity. Therefore, it is subject to the same law of supply and demand as any other commodity. As money becomes scarce, the demand grows and what we are willing to pay for it—its value, in other words—goes up. The most common metric is that interest rates begin to rise. As they rise, loans that made sense previously—and were within the power of borrowers to sustain—become strained. Debtors become distressed and creditors grow nervous. The same myopia that fueled the boom ensures that we worry more about tomorrow than next year, and our survival instinct tells us to hoard in times such as this. A virtuous intention soon becomes a vicious circle and, if it is left long enough, a common crisis.

THE GREAT DEPRESSION OF A.D. 33

A financial crisis does not send a town crier in advance to announce its arrival. Disbelief is a more common greeting. Few—be they soothsayers or economists—see it coming, even though stresses and fragilities are endemic to every financial system. The event that kicks off the crisis is typically innocuous. The problem is that as the system becomes more complex and leveraged, its capacity to deal with shocks, even minor ones, rapidly declines. Like a spinning top, its equilibrium soon rests on a fine point. Social, political, and fiscal pressures all serve to restrict the freedom of movement further till finally the economy runs out of steam and topples over inelegantly.

The fateful year A.D. 33 began with little inkling of the credit crunch that would be so carefully chronicled by numerous Roman historians later. The catalyst in this case was a series of accusations that bankers and financiers were charging more than the legal interest on loans.

Debt had become a structural part of every Roman's balance sheet. Mortgages to purchase properties and land were common. Many a Roman also mortgaged existing holdings to acquire the liquidity to chase greater fortune. Senators and aspiring politicians took loans to throw banquets and give gifts as means of gaining and maintaining their popular support. Merchants borrowed to build ships, finance lucrative trade routes, and further the expansion of the Roman hegemony.

Under Tiberius, as the money supply shrank and the debt burden grew, an increasing proportion of borrowers found themselves struggling to service debts. The situation was complicated by one of Tiberius's regular purges, born of paranoia in his old age. Two years earlier, the seventy-two-year-old Tiberius had grown suspicious of the ambitions of his loyal lieutenant Sejanus, the commander of the Praetorian Guard—the emperor's personal elite army of bodyguards. Sejanus was the archetypal ambitious Roman knight. Over the previous decade, he had ruthlessly parlayed his friendship with the aging Tiberius to make the Praetorian Guard into a powerful political force and himself the most powerful man in Rome after the emperor. Seeing Sejanus as a threat, Tiberius moved to reassert his authority. In the space of a single day, Sejanus found himself suddenly denounced before the Senate and thrown to his death down the Gemonian Stairs. His family followed soon after, and over the next two years his supporters across Roman society were purged and their estates confiscated. As their belongings were auctioned off, much of the liquid cash in Rome ran to find new bargains among the spoils.

The praetor Gracchus suddenly found large numbers of debtors swarming his court on the Forum in A.D. 33, complaining loudly that they had been deceived.[12] The chief accusation was that the creditors had broken Caesar's original laws on moneylending, which had set the maximum rate of interest at 12 percent. The laws had long been discarded. Every now and then, some populist would seek to reaffirm them, but regulatory arbitrage and the demand for money soon carried the day. "At length, usufruct was unconditionally banned," Tacitus noted, "while a series of plebiscites strove to meet the frauds which were perpetually repressed, only, by extraordinary evasions, to make their appearance once more."

Overwhelmed by the numbers, Gracchus passed the buck up the chain of command. Faced with a wave of popular unrest, Tiberius upheld Caesar's 12 percent rate of interest. The senators—"for not one member was clear from such a charge"—faced a growing pool of loans that were now uneconomic in the current climate. A deputation immediately went to the emperor and pleaded for amnesty. Tiberius with imperious magnanimity granted them a year and a half to adjust their private finances to conform to the letter of the law.

It was a disaster. The senators, knights, and other creditors went straight out and began to call in all their loans at once. Debtors, in turn, sought to sell their lands and goods to raise the cash, only to find that the purges following Sejanus's downfall had drained liquidity from the system. As ready money today became the new imperative, prices began to fall and rapidly escalated into a real estate crash.

Desperate to stabilize prices and buttress the property market, Tiberius now ordered that every creditor had to invest two-thirds of his capital back into Italian property. At the same time, all debtors were required to immediately repay two-thirds of their outstanding loans.

The situation only worsened. Creditors now began to pursue their debts all the more furiously so that they could comply with the emperor's latest edict. Many also began to realize that as prices fell, it made more sense to wait, as land would only get cheaper. The debt-deflation cycle was reborn. Negotiations between creditor and debtor became pleas for mercy, and the hapless Gracchus found himself overrun with yet more litigants.

Prices fell all the more as the deleveraging of the Roman economy gathered momentum. The crisis grew systemic as the complex web of the Via Sacra and Roman commerce unraveled. Merchants who were waiting for their trade ships to arrive, deposit bankers who had lent out the monies entrusted for safekeeping, politicians attempting to largesse their way into power—all suddenly found creditors knocking on their doors and asking for their money back. Many of these lenders had taken out loans themselves for other purposes. Creditors became debtors overnight as the cash on hand proved insufficient to meet all these demands. The property market began a precipitous decline as money fled and the financial system hollowed out. With every fall in values, defaults grew.

This was a credit crunch par excellence. Ruin struck rich and poor alike. Fortunes were lost and reputations rendered naught. The knight Vibullius Agrippa swallowed poison and died in the Senate house itself. The senator Nerva starved himself to death, dismayed at the "great loss of confidence and financial confusion." Not even Tiberius's entreaties could urge him to reconsider. The fragility of fractional reserving—for so long the engine of Roman growth—now threatened the collapse of the whole system.

The parsimonious Tiberius was forced to take radical steps. A public "bad bank" was set up and funded with 100 million sestertii. A senatorial commission was charged to use this to make interest-free loans to the chronically indebted for up to three years. In return, every borrower had to give to the state securities that were backed by landed property and double the value of the money borrowed.[13] Credit—belief in the system— was restored gradually, and slowly private lenders began to come back out of their burrows. This is a familiar solution for even the short memories of today: a government forced to become the lender of last resort and recapitalize the system, taking mortgages as securities.

In the meanwhile, Tiberius busied himself with replenishing the imperial treasury and building up a buffer against future crises. The socialization of debt was easier in those autocratic days, and he soon hit on an ingenious solution. A vast program of nationalization and confiscation began across the Roman Empire.

The unfortunate Sextus Marius was one of the best known of Tiberius's victims. Marius was the richest man in Spain and Tiberius's close friend. He owned significant gold and copper mines in the region, and his wealth and power were legendary. The historian Cassius Dio relates a story about a dispute Marius had with a neighbor. Marius invited the man over to his estate for two days. On the first day, he had his unsuspecting neighbor's villa razed to the ground before rebuilding an even more magnificent one the next day. When the neighbor returned home and wondered who could have done this, Marius revealed it was him and noted, "This shows you that I have both the knowledge and the power to repel attacks and also to requite kindness."

But in these strained times, friendship was a luxury. Marius found himself accused of incest with his daughter. After a speedy trial, both were flung from the Tarpeian Rock—a steep cliff on the Capitoline Hill over-looking the Forum and reserved for the most heinous criminals.

Tiberius now took personal ownership of Marius's mines and wealth. Other senators and provincial aristocrats also found their property confiscated, often thanks to another ancient law of Caesar that limited the amount of ready money to be held by any Roman to 60,000 sestertii, lest anyone foment rebellion. Tributes from vassal states were replaced with a more formal system of tax revenues and an encroaching bureaucracy.

On his death, Tiberius left somewhere between 2 and 3 billion sestertii to his successor, Caligula. The first rumors of his passing were greeted with joy by Rome, which had tired of his financial repression, and many welcomed his death as his having paid "the debt of nature." When word spread that "Tiberius was recovering his speech and sight . . . [a] general panic followed." The new commander of the Praetorian Guard, Macro, immediately suffocated his charge under a pile of bedclothes. The populace now ran about shouting "Tiberius to the Tiber"—being thrown in that river was the punishment for notorious criminals—and many called for his body to be burned in the amphitheater.

Memories faded as Caligula soon loosened the public purse and lending followed suit—"a vigorous beginning lapsing as usual into a careless end," as Tacitus noted. The credit crunch of A.D. 33 passed into obscurity and became a footnote to the death of the aforementioned Jesus of Nazareth.

A SENSE OF PERSPECTIVE

It is a sign of our brevity of memory that each financial crisis is often viewed and analyzed in isolation. Its cause determined and its immediate resolution identified, we move on contented. But given that all crises spring from a common economic and human foundation, this seems simplistic.

As our brief canter through Roman economic history shows, crises have deep roots, sometimes far back in antiquity. Their genesis lies not just in the boom-and-bust cycle, which is a natural extension of human psychology and the use of credit to grow. They are also born of underlying fragility in the economic system. Combined together, people, credit, and structural fragility provide the perfect auditorium for the echoes of the past to reverberate loudly.

Some fads, such as the red mullet craze, are fascinating speculative manias—often with humorous tinges—but do little lasting harm to the wider economy. They represent optimism, exuberance, and an excess of money that finds new avenues to explore, like a river overflowing its banks and flooding the surrounding terrain. The waters eventually recede, and they often also prepare the soil for future progress.

The Roman merchant always went before the imperial army in search of speculative fortune. Thanks to their efforts, there were countless little asset bubbles that sprang up, such as the trade in exotic animals for circuses, and many others that we will never know. A few businesses would be inevitably ruined in their aftermath and the odd financier or speculator burned. But none of these threatened to infect the entire economy and become systemic. Consequently, they sidestepped the veil of memory.

It is this systemic dimension that separates the speculative mania from the financial crisis. The latter is the confluence of the gambler in us all with the fiscal, social, and political imperatives of current and past generations, which accentuate the cycle of boom and bust and spread it far and wide, leaving us with a lingering hangover.

Despite our best intentions, this is not necessarily avoidable. We are always a product of our proclivities and times. The social status associated with the ownership of property meant that in the run-up to the Roman crisis of A.D. 33, loans to purchase property rapidly became common in Roman society. In time, it was inevitable that any financial prudence found itself sacrificed at the altar of social ambition.

It is impossible to separate the financial from the other sociopolitical facets of the world. For Rome also, these different strata were all part of the complex environment that unconsciously influenced choices and made it ever harder to maintain a fine equilibrium.

Augustus's loose monetary policy and growing bureaucracy were the natural result of wanting to turn around an ailing economy and provide stability after a century of strife. They also served the political ambitions of a greater Roman hegemony. In this, they succeeded. Even today, a Latin tinge lingers in our political and legal structures.

The expensive attempts to maintain social peace were understandable in the light of Roman history and the growing inequality that rapid economic growth brings in its wake. The government's resulting paucity of money was another natural outcome. Each of these had a cumulative impact on human behavior, adjusting rewards and sanctions till people found themselves focused in the same direction. As one moved to arbitrage the new rule book, others followed in their wake until systemic risk was born. It was like the childhood game of Buckaroo, where children load ever-increasing burdens on a mechanical mule until, suddenly, it can take no more and throws everything off violently.

In hindsight, it is easy to identify the structural weaknesses of Rome born of their choices. The proliferation of slave labor drove real wages to near nothing. The ordinary Roman could not compete and found himself sustained only by the state, ever resentful at the growing inequity. That same slave labor held back innovation and the development of technology that might have accelerated growth and allowed the system to sustain itself. The state failed to balance its growth against the need for adequate revenue to maintain its expanding size. The laissez-faire attitude toward commerce made sense, but it should never have extended to the same degree to the provision of credit. The nature of money and its supply were continually misunderstood.

There will be others I have not noted above. But they are all manifestations of an overriding human weakness: in life, there are urgent matters and then there are important matters. The two are not always the same. When problems expose themselves, our myopic response is to deal with the urgent, and the important is often left unattended. In a crisis, stanching the wound takes precedence. Its healing is a matter to be considered tomorrow, though usually by then another urgency has intervened.

A financial crisis is not an isolated incident. It exposes structural frailties in the system. These rarely vanish and indeed become more pronounced as the economy and society increase in complexity over time. More crises follow, escalating and compounding with each iteration. Financial crises are, therefore, interlinked—peaks and troughs in a greater wave of history that can stretch for centuries before it finally crashes in a crisis of social gravity.

The aftermath of A.D. 33 was just as prolonged and painful.

THE AFTERMATH

Following Tiberius's death, financial crisis became a perennial. His successor Caligula—often portrayed in later history as a debauched and sadistic tyrant—restarted the Augustan tap with new vigor. Palaces were built; the circuses made a welcome and extravagant return; ambitious new aqueducts and engineering projects were commissioned. Gifts of cash were made to the army and Roman citizens, while taxes were reduced or abolished. Philo of Alexandria, a contemporary Jewish philosopher, chronicled this golden age:

> On this occasion the rich were not better off than the poor, nor the men of high rank than the lowly, nor the creditors than the debtors, nor the masters than the slaves, since the occasion gave equal

privileges and communities to all men, so that the age of Saturn, which is so celebrated by the poets, was no longer looked upon as a fiction and a fable.

Within two years, the billions carefully saved by Tiberius had been squandered and a new financial crisis beckoned again. Political unrest rose as grain grew scarce. The reversal of imperial generosity was just as swift. Confiscations returned with a vengeance. Those with money found themselves impelled to donate or purchase from the state. One poor senator, Aponius Saturninus, fell asleep at an auction only to find upon waking that he had purchased thirteen gladiators for 9 million sestertii. New taxes appeared, ranging from a sales tax on food and a levy on litigation and marriages to the first beginnings of income taxation, initially on porters and prostitutes.

Within another two years, Caligula was dead at the hands of his Praetorian Guard. His uncle Claudius found himself thrust into the limelight as the new emperor and set about reforming the system. The *panem et circenses* remained along with gifts of money to the army to ensure loyalty. These were now an accepted part of the structural fabric of Rome. Building projects continued and a particular effort was made to strengthen the food supply network. Ambitious projects, such as the construction of a new harbor at Ostia near Rome and the draining of local marshland by the Fucine Lake, provided fiscal stimulus and sought to consign the regular crises in the grain market to the past. Claudius was familiarizing himself with the common obsession of many a politician: to never let the system break down. Alongside this began an ambitious process of expansion. Rome needed growth, and only the acquisition of new lands and tributes could provide this. Roman citizenship was granted to a wider number of people, particularly in new colonies—an extension of the tax base, as only Roman citizens paid taxes to the state. The bureaucracy grew apace as more power was centralized to ensure that much-needed revenues flowed to the treasury.

But the demand for revenue continued to grow, driven by the costs of a large standing army and the subsidies of cash, grain, and entertainment to the masses. Additionally, the negative balance of trade with the rest of the ancient world persisted. As gold came in, it rapidly left again. The availability of plentiful slaves and cheap labor in the frontier provinces meant that much of the manufacturing moved out of Italy as well. Areas such as Gaul and North Africa became the new centers of production for earthenware, weapons, and other goods. Rome became a center for government, services such as banking, and trade in luxuries. Behind the imperial façade, the economy wilted in the face of this exodus.

Under the emperor Nero, the growing deflationary forces were soon catalyzed into an economic malaise by the Great Fire of Rome in A.D. 64. The ambitious rebuilding of the city placed yet another burden on a strained treasury. Facing a limit to how many new taxes could be imposed, Nero took another modernist approach—the introduction of inflation through a debasement of the currency.

Roman currency consisted of the copper sestertius, the silver denarius (equivalent to 4 sestertii), and the gold aureus (denoted as 25 denarii). Nero now proceeded to reduce the weight of the gold and silver coins as well as the purity of the more commonly circulated silver denarius from Augustus's original prescription. Inflation became a facet of Roman life. Nero committed suicide in A.D. 68, another Caesar sacrificed on the altar of public opinion as the army and populace rebelled at his economic policies.[14]

A brief civil war later, Vespasian was emperor. He was a practical and pragmatic man who understood how to balance the books and immediately set about stabilizing the empire and its finances. The public reconstruction of Rome continued, with the magnificent Colosseum his most lasting legacy, but modesty in public life now began to be stressed. The relentless expansion halted for a while, to be replaced by a focus on consolidation and the maximizing of revenues. Ever the capitalist, Vespasian began to auction imperial posts to the rich and even found a way of turning the chronic public corruption of Rome to his advantage. Corrupt officials were encouraged to rise up through the ranks and accumulate money. Vespasian called them his sponges, as he let them soak up the wealth, only to squeeze it out of them later as they were arrested for corruption and their estates confiscated.

The coinage was debased further. New taxes were introduced, most notably a tax on public urinals. When his son Titus complained that this was unbecoming of an emperor, Vespasian is alleged to have picked up a coin and held it under his son's nose. "Does that smell bad to you?" he asked. Today, Italians pay homage to this zeal in their language—the word for "urinal" in Italian is *vespasiano*.

His sons Titus and Domitian continued this program of careful stewardship. Expansion was rejected, corruption checked further, and taxes meticulously assessed and collected. Domitian was even able to increase the proportion of silver in the denarius, reversing the earlier inflation. The economy seemed on a firmer footing, and even capable of sustaining the public works and *panem et circenses* that continued.

But fiscal discipline is transitory and perhaps too dull to hold our attention. Their successors restarted the expansion of the Roman Empire. In the absence of deeper internal economic reforms, Rome could not stay static, as there was insufficient growth for the revenues needed. However, this fast became a pyrrhic undertaking. The new gold and tribute flowing in were rapidly offset by a growing military budget and subsidies. Compounding this, taxes were rolled back, particularly for the poorest Romans. In light of the mistaken perception of prosperity, new welfare programs were added that sought to provide food and education for poor children as well as land for the poorest Romans. These were often funded through the interest generated by lending money from the state to rich landowners at reduced rates. However, this means of funding the social welfare program often defeated the purpose of the program, as the loans simply allowed the rich to utilize the state's resources to accumulate greater fortunes and increase the divide between rich and poor. The devaluation of the denarius was the common prescription for solving all of the empire's economic problems and its periodic financial crises.

As expansion came to an end in the second century A.D., inflationary pressures soon came to the fore as the prices of commodities began a century of rises. The value of the denarius fell so much that the Romans also found themselves increasingly acquainted with Gresham's law, which holds that bad money will always drive out good money. The money-changers in the Forum found their *bancu* in much demand as people sought to differentiate the older, higher-value coins from the newer, debased versions. The former began to be hoarded and disappeared from circulation, resulting in further loss to the imperial treasury.

By the end of the second century A.D., the emperor Commodus was resorting to increasingly punitive taxes and enforced labor as the denarius dropped to just a third of its original value. The high inflation and resulting crisis of confidence resulted in a debilitating financial crisis that led to widespread defaults.

The slave and future pope Callistus found himself one of these unfortunates. Given a sum of money by his master, the freedman Christian Carpophorus, the enterprising Callistus set up a bank and began to take in deposits from widows and Christians. The bank soon ran into trouble, however, and was unable to pay back its depositors. Callistus blamed a liquidity crunch caused by problem loans, but others accused him of fraud. His master denied knowledge of these difficulties. Callistus attempted an escape by sea, only to be captured and sentenced to hard labor. The favors of the emperor's concubine Marcia saved him and secured his release. Nearly three decades later, the rehabilitated freedman Callistus became the seventeenth pope of the Roman Catholic Church, dying a saint five years later when he was flung into a well by pagan rioters in A.D. 222. It is not recorded whether any of his former clients were among the mob or whether his experience had anything to do with the Church's later distaste for usury.

Following Commodus's inevitable assassination in A.D. 192, Cassius Dio remarked, "[Our] history now descends from a kingdom of gold to one of iron and rust, as affairs did for the Romans of that day." The next century was one of constant crisis—a period now known as the Crisis of the Third Century. What had been a financial crisis evolved into a crisis of empire.

Civil wars and thirty emperors followed in quick succession, with only one of those rulers managing to die a natural death. Successive emperors debased the currency ever faster to raise revenue as the demands of the military and state remained stubbornly high. No would-be emperor could afford to ignore the army, the arbiter of power. The donative—a cash gift to the Praetorian Guard and army by the incoming emperor—became de rigueur, and Rome even suffered the ignominy of the Praetorian Guard auctioning the title of emperor to the highest bidder in the closing years of the second century.

By the beginning of the reign of Claudius II Gothicus in A.D. 268, the silver content of the denarius was at just 0.02 percent, down from its purity of 99.5 percent under Augustus. Hyperinflation now became a reality, and the few reference points we have for basics such as grain imply a change in inflation of 1,500,000 percent over the third century.[15]

The economy collapsed in response. Any coin of value disappeared into private pockets, only to reappear in recent centuries in the hoards of Roman coins regularly found by archaeologists. Merchants found it hard to obtain credit, and barter became increasingly common. Alongside, commerce suffered another blow as barbarians grew emboldened by the constant civil wars and the empire began to lose ground under their assault. Internal trade began to shrink as a result, and the records of our aforementioned shipwrecks and mining output show a steep decline.

The banking *argentarii* had begun to decline toward the end of the second century, and now they disappear entirely from the record. Presumably, with the hoarding of coin and the precipitous drop in trade, there were few calls for their services. A half century later, the word would be resurrected, but now to denote a silversmith. The professional banker had retreated into his shell for the next millennium.

The state—still as large and complex as ever—grew ever more desperate for revenue. Confiscations rose and the aristocracy were now compelled to use their own monies to help the emperor of the day placate the crowds. One emperor, Caracalla, issued an edict in A.D. 212 granting Roman citizenship to every free man in the empire in a vain attempt to widen the tax base. Where coin failed to be found, direct requisitions of grain, cattle, and other goods took its place. Unable to move forward, Rome was retreating back to its earliest days at a breakneck speed.

The emergence of a dominant victor in the form of Diocletian at the end of the century restored some stability. But the changes that had begun in the third century were irreversible. Diocletian's attempts to introduce fixed prices and capital controls were a miserable failure. Goods disappeared from sale, only to reappear in black markets, and inflation proved too capable an opponent.

Diocletian eventually accepted the new status quo. New laws were introduced that collected taxes in kind rather than money. The market economy transformed into a state-controlled one that could ensure a steady and dependable supply of goods and services. People were now tied to their land, while employment became hereditary to ensure continuity.

Under these financial and fiscal pressures, society began to transform. Urbanization gave way to depopulation as increasing numbers went back to the land and subsistence farming became common. Large landowners began to break free of the oppressive tax regime through tax evasion and bribery, and by forming small closed economies centered around their estates. As these exited the larger economy, it shrank further, and pressure grew on the lower strata, particularly the middle classes, comprising merchants, smaller landowners, and other professionals. They found not only their livelihoods fast vanishing but also their money as the state's attention increasingly turned toward them as the primary source of tax revenue. To escape their tax burden, many Romans began to attach themselves to larger estates as semi-servile tenant farmers or even slaves. In exasperation, the emperor Valens passed an impotent law in A.D. 368 that made it illegal for any man to become a slave for the purpose of acquiring protection from taxation. But these *coloni*—later the serfs of medieval Europe—were here to stay.[16] The feudalization of society was beginning.

Higher taxes had little impact, for there was an increasingly smaller number of people to pay them. Emperors such as Constantine realized where the wealth now truly resided—in the East. The capital moved eastward to Constantinople, where there was a plentiful supply of trade routes with Asia and the Middle East to cultivate and tax. The focus and power increasingly shifted there, and the Western Roman Empire found itself in terminal decline. Italy and Rome moved from the center to the periphery.

Finally, in A.D. 476, the barbarian general Odoacer invaded Rome and deposed the last emperor, Romulus Augustus. It was not a great victory, more a gentle assent to the new reality. The last Caesar found himself not fighting to the death in glorious battle but rather being pensioned off to spend the rest of his days in ignominy.

Money died, feudalism was born, and the embers of a once great empire finally burned out. Its passing was greeted not with sadness but with relief by many Romans, for whom it had come to represent nothing more than an overlong financial repression.

CHAPTER 3

All Things Being Unequal:
Redefining Economics

Logic: The art of thinking and reasoning in strict accordance with
the limitations and incapacities of the human misunderstanding.
—*THE DEVIL'S DICTIONARY*, AMBROSE BIERCE
(1842–1913)

We build the best possible story from the information available . . .
and if it is a good story, we believe it.
—DANIEL KAHNEMAN (1934–)

WORDS seduce. They nuance human expression and add subtle emotional overtones when we communicate ideas. They dominate religious texts, historical tracts, and scientific commentaries. The works that thrive and achieve the status of dogma are often the ones whose words are best crafted to appeal to the psyche of the time.

But words also obfuscate. Wars have been fought over them. The Great Schism between the Roman Catholic and Eastern Orthodox churches in A.D. 1054 can be traced to the addition of a single word, *filioque* (and from the Son), by the former into the Nicene Creed, the universal profession of faith espoused by Christians.

Language naturally conveys hidden biases. The *filioque* may have been a technicality once, but it soon became symbolic of the battle between the two churches over the future direction of the growing and powerful Christian community. Accusations of heresy, excommunications, and eventually the sacking of Constantinople by Western Crusaders in A.D. 1254 followed, as the word exposed divisions along political, doctrinal, geographic, and ethnic lines.

Words are open to interpretation. A simple term or elegant turn of phrase can hide a wealth of assumptions within. All too often, if an argument is well constructed and written, we are seduced by the verbal skill on display. An illusory train of logic drives us toward an inescapable and compelling conclusion.

Economics is no exception to this rule. Theories and verbosity abound in splendid isolation from the real world. Torture the data enough, the Nobel economist Ronald Coase once wryly remarked, and nature will confess. It is worthwhile, therefore, no matter how much we enjoy the words, to sometimes take a moment to pause, look past the cadence and rhythm of the carefully constructed syllables, and consider the validity of the arguments being made.[1]

Let's play a game. You live in uncertain times. Property prices are down. You haven't revalued your house in a couple of years and you're afraid to. Asset prices are volatile and the strategy behind your fledging portfolio of stocks has changed from an attempt to time the markets to one of buy, hold, and pray. Your company let 340 people go last week, though, luckily, you were too "valuable" to dispense with—for now. Wages have been frozen for this year and there is growing gossip that next year could be worse.

You've always been careful with credit card debt. But the mortgage, those insurance policies, and the "0 percent APR, nothing to pay for three years" bargains for that car and the new kitchen are weighing more on your mind. A friend jumped ship a few months ago to a better job only to fall afoul of the "last in, first out" dictum. There are some savings built up, enough to sustain your current lifestyle for three months if it all went to the wall and perhaps six months if you were extra careful. You don't want to think about interest rates, inflation, and the like—it all seems a bit arcane and will only likely depress you further. You would rather ponder the timing and size of your next raise, the acquisitions that will give you a better quality of life, and the carefully choreographed steps to fortune and status.

But today money and jobs are scarce. Growth is an impotent rallying cry for ideologues and demagogues. Newspapers are reporting a worsening economy and the growing worries of policy makers. Eighty-three economists wrote an open letter to the *New York Times* last week calling for urgent action to kick-start the economy. The central bank has cut interest rates sharply. The government has extended benefits and unveiled new job initiatives. The opposition has unveiled a radical new plan to reignite growth. There are elections on the horizon. The choice between renewed prosperity and disaster will soon come down to a single, solitary moment in an anonymous voting booth.

This is a recession—like so many others over the years. But this one matters more because it's happening now and it's happening to you.

What do you do?

THE TORTURE OF LOGIC

In troubled times—as in typical times—we make rational choices based on the information at hand. Two common ones are to save more and to look for a better-paying job. The first builds personal security and the second provides the opportunity to earn your way out of trouble.

But from the world of economics, some would argue that you are wrong. The discipline's hallowed halls are riven with paradoxes. Two in particular are worth noting when it comes to dealing with financial crises.

The first is the paradox of thrift.[2] Assuming equilibrium—the notion that the economy or system is stable and unchanging—if everyone saves more during a recession, then they collectively spend less and demand as a whole falls. Firms are able to sell fewer goods and are forced to cut costs, including jobs and wages. This places more downward pressure on a weakened economy as unemployment rises and spending falls, further hammering growth and accentuating the downturn. Subsequent falls in incomes and prices occur, ultimately leading to lower savings across the population. If we individually try to save more, we collectively save less. Therefore, the solution to battling any recession is counterintuitive: spend more as growth turns negative. And if you are in government, be the first to do so.

The second is the paradox of toil.[3] A recession leads to fewer jobs and lower wages as firms look to sell goods more cheaply and pare costs to maintain their profit margins. All other things being equal, if everyone tries to work in this environment, companies will find plenty of desperate takers for their lower wages. At the same time, these lower wages will reduce prices further as people have less to spend and expect prices to be lower in the future. Demand falls and deflation is reinforced. Companies now move to cut costs further, laying off even more employees and reducing employment. Therefore, do your economy a favor and work less. If you are in government, the advice is unchanged—spend more to boost demand. It is one of the few consistent dictums for economic downturns.

What if we all followed this advice to its logical extreme? The theories above tell us that if we spend more all around, firms will see a renewed demand for their goods and services. Banks would see a resurgence in their loan books as all this spending requires further debt. There may be collateral damage in the form of some unfortunate personal bankruptcies at the margins. Still, it would be a worthy sacrifice, as the economy would improve. Asset prices would rise again (we hope), and we would all feel wealthier.

Work less and firms will find themselves competing for fewer workers, resulting in upward pressure on wages. They would have to pay you more for less—a dream come true for many of us. In the interim, the government can step in, spending money to boost demand through unemployment benefits, infrastructure projects, cash-for-clunkers programs, and the like. In time, our collective disposable income would be on the rise (we hope), allowing us to spend even more and grow that notional wealth further.

This, then, is the utopian prescription, couched in the absurd torture of logic: Your reaction to a severe financial downturn should be to work less and spend more. If the hole deepens, then dig harder. In a crisis, redouble your efforts in proportion to its magnitude. To achieve a better outcome, we are asked to exhibit behavior that most of us would term irrational. It's all in a good cause—by beggaring yourself, you benefit the economy.

Unfortunately, if we all choose to follow this prescription, the system changes. Debt balloons and growth has no foundation. Everything can be solved in theory by throwing more money at the problem. In practice, history begs to differ.

This is the problem with logical arguments. Taken to extremes, they tie themselves up into knots and descend farcically into the absurd. An old economist joke illustrates this fallacy of logic particularly well.

The most basic science courses at high school teach us that

$$\text{Power} = \frac{\text{Work}}{\text{Time}}$$

But we all know that knowledge is power and time is money. An economist can now elegantly substitute these into the above equation and rewrite it as:

$$\text{Knowledge} = \frac{\text{Work}}{\text{Money}}$$

A simple mathematical rearrangement now tells us that

$$\text{Money} = \frac{\text{Work}}{\text{Knowledge}}$$

Play around with the above mathematical arrangement—it requires little more than high school math—and you will soon realize something. As knowledge dwindles, money will grow rapidly, irrespective of work put in. The conclusion is simple: It doesn't matter how much you work. The trick is that the less you know, the more money you make.

The theory and its logic are flawed, little more than a stream of carefully constructed words hiding a range of assumptions and intellectual biases. Here, reality is replaced by a faded facsimile thanks to sweeping assumptions of equilibrium and a perverse constancy among all the other variables that go into an economy. Important concepts such as rationality and our collective behavior in the face of these changes are poorly defined and left unexplored. The intricate complexities of the passage of time, economic incentives, the financial system, international trade, and the wider sociopolitical sphere within which economics sits are left ignored. (This is why a truism of financial crises is that economists as a breed fail to either foresee or forestall them.)

Even if the prescription of the twin paradoxes were true, it would be a strange sort of growth and prosperity—hollow at its core, as it represents an increasing indebtedness across society without purpose. We take on debt in the hope that the leverage added will provide greater returns in the future. When tomorrow comes, the pie will have grown larger. The debt is easy to repay and we are still richer. But all this occurs only if the debt is put to productive use, else it is future growth frittered away.

The fetish of GDP (gross domestic product) hangs heavy over these arguments. Long the sacred cow of policy makers and economists, it is deemed synonymous with human progress. Therefore, all increases in GDP are good. Our response to every crisis is painstakingly measured by its impact on falling GDP.

But few ever ask what the concept of GDP means. Not all growth is the same. GDP is a measure of spending. And as any normal person will tell you, there are frivolous expenses and there are useful expenses. A big night out in New York is not a store of capital for future growth in the same way as money invested in developing new commerce. The government produces services that have no market and, therefore, its spending is valued at cost. If it introduces extra layers of bureaucracy, hands out more subsidies, pays all its employees more, and occasionally hosts the odd greenback bonfire, its contribution to GDP will soar. But as the Romans found to their cost, a burgeoning state with no sustainable revenues to meet expenses only hollows out and pauperizes the system in the long run. This is growth that is only borrowed and will need to be given back in the future. If the solution were as simple as spending more, then recessions and crises would not be as frequent or painful as they are.

In practice, the structure and stability of demand in an economy matter as well. Demand can be artificially inflated for only so long. No matter how much the government spends, the baton must pass at some point to the private economy. If the consumer spends, then somewhere down the line, the debt taken on needs to be dealt with and reduced to a more palatable level if consistent sustainable growth is to resume. In this context, savings are a vital part of an economy because they provide the investment that fuels future growth. They are the counterpart to the debt we take on in the present. The tremendous growth in our global economy in recent decades (and the amount of debt we are able to sustain in these strained times) comes thanks to the trillions sitting in pension funds and the savings of countless individuals around the world. Structural reforms beckon that remove the barriers to saving, investing, and producing—the lifeblood of an economy. But the strategy often seems vague, just a hope that the illusory growth born of stimulus will become real once the money wears off.

Otherwise, we only have a final conflagration of growth as the debt in the economy further outstrips the capacity to repay it. The fragility of the system is reinforced. In the future, an otherwise innocuous event—perhaps a corporate default, a rise in bad loans in a niche market, a new regulatory edict, or a natural disaster—would reverberate powerfully through the complex network of debtors and creditors. The house of cards begins to fall again and, shocked, we find ourselves back at the beginning but now with a larger problem than before. At some point, as with Rome, the challenge becomes insurmountable.

We may laugh at the absurdities couched above, but that is the prescription that has driven recent responses to financial turmoil. If you give people a lot of money, they will spend it—or so goes the theory. Spending boosts demand, and demand today equals growth tomorrow. Therefore, governments and central banks have become increasingly fond of unveiling ever-larger stimulus packages. Large deficits have become fashionable in the developed world. "Innovative" strategies such as quantitative easing and forward guidance are unveiled in increasingly rapid succession until all financial literature—business pages and books such as this—is drowning in jargon. In short, we are living through a monsoon of money. The enhanced risks for the future in terms of mounting debts, inflation, impaired sovereign balance sheets, the far more crippling costs of paying for a generally aging population, growing inequality, and the resulting social tensions from all these are of lesser consequence right now.

But there are still small kernels of truth at the heart of this torture of logic. Individual choices have repercussions. Somewhere in that unexpected journey from boom to bust, the seemingly sensible decisions we make as individuals become seemingly irrational outcomes for us all. Second, our decisions are hugely influenced by our subjective perceptions. And it is to these kernels that we must turn to understand our proclivity to financial mishap.

EQUILIBRIUM IS TRANSIENT

History and the financial markets both begin with the same ingredient: people.

"There is a relation between the hours of our life and the centuries of time," noted Ralph Waldo Emerson. To him, a common bond of humanity existed between the present and the past. All history was subjective—a study of our innate human nature with the calming distance of time to aid the lesson.

There is a lot of truth in this. The consistent misperception is that the stories we hear of the past are objective. The emperors, nations, lovers, and wars may be fact, but that is only the superficial detail. Within, the motivations and drivers are all interpretation—psychological guesswork at a distance. The actors on these stages once were living assemblies of hope, fear, kindness, greed, and the rest of that cauldron we collectively designate as human. The people they dragged along on the currents that became the narrative of history were human. Every line we read from Tacitus, Suetonius, Cassius Dio, and their successors is imbued with individual emotion and shaped by individual experience. Today, we view and interpret all of this through the prism of our own experience and environment.

It is this common complexity that makes the past such an object of fascination and debate. Against the grand horizons of evolution, humans have changed little on the inside in the last few millennia. Only a thin veneer of recorded history with its attendant accouterments separates us today from the human of yesteryear. As we grasp for explanations for the events, both major and minor, that punctuate man's sojourn, we unconsciously accept the fact that the impulses of history live in us all to varying degrees.

Economics is, at its heart, a study of human interactions. It is all the more surprising then that our views on financial markets and the economy in the mainstream trade this compelling individuality for sterile omniscience.* In our rush to understand how societies,

---

* It should be noted that the mainstream here is defined as the pool of economic thought and research that has the largest impact on public and central bank policy. There has been plenty of excellent research done in recent years that has begun to tackle many of the shortcomings we lay bare in this chapter, but much of this has yet to permeate through in lasting fashion to policy makers.

economies, and financial markets might function, we remove the human element entirely.

Here we are all rational automatons driven by self-interest, constant in our behavior over time, and blessed with the same perfect understanding of the markets we inhabit. The interplay of supply and demand among these facsimiles dictates that society evolves an economy that optimally allocates resources and maximizes utility—the economist's euphemism for the happiness conferred by wealth.[4] In the absence of external influences, the economy will soon tend to a stable utopian equilibrium. *Ceteris paribus*, the economist would remind us, all other things being equal—the common refrain that allows him to sidestep complexity and substitute myth for reality.

This fallacy extends also to financial markets. Under the so-called efficient market hypothesis, markets embody perfect information. A rational pool of investors aggregates all the known information about a stock and rapidly equilibrates its share price to the "right" value, based on its future prospects. As new information randomly comes to light, they buy and sell shares based on these changed prospects till the market finds its equilibrium again. Consequently, markets move in a random manner, with each move independent of those that preceded it. The volatility that we see every day is a reflection of this assimilation process.

Common sense and history tell us all this is wrong. Equilibrium is transient at best and the exception, not the rule. The constant fine-tuning and firefighting by policy makers and central bankers evidence the dynamic and fleeting nature of any stability that may be found. The rare periods of prolonged relative equilibrium we have produced typically occur when economies die, such as in Europe during the Dark Ages. Here, as money gives way to barter and trade erodes, complexity diminishes. The economy shrinks to ever smaller domains, with each step backward moving it closer to the precision of the models that we champion.

By definition, the more goods, the more people, the more money, and the greater the numbers of interactions and linkages we add on, the more complex an economy becomes. Among all this aggregation, social, political, and fiscal aspects emerge that affect the nature and evolution of the economy and the markets. As in Rome, this complexity and interconnectedness mean that all other things are seldom equal.

People are individuals who value different shares and goods differently, each according to his or her own circumstance and priorities. The common laborer will value the can of baked beans and the venti caramel mint latte differently than the corporate highflier. There may be some commonalities in behavior within social strata, but there are unlikely to be many across them. The repeated appearance of welfare states or subsidies as a means of combating social tensions bears out the lie of maximal utility in practice.

The time horizons of people vary, depending on their age, health, profession, education, and so on. For most investors today, it falls somewhere between the next tick up or down on their market index of choice and the next quarterly report from the latest manager carefully selected from the dartboard. They do not have access to the same information always, nor will they even interpret it the same way. In the financial markets, the existence throughout history of a burgeoning industry of hopeful moneymakers with different strategies that exploit different inefficiencies in the system bears testament to this fact. Most will not make money over the long run, but enough do to tempt the rest of us into believing we can beat the markets too.

Real assets and financial assets can also behave very differently. A rise in commodity prices reduces demand for that commodity—whether it be oil, copper, or coffee—among consumers over time. However, it can also perversely fuel demand for the financial asset as speculative bubbles form looking to take advantage of these higher prices. A similar pattern can be found in rare objects through the ages, such as art or tulip bulbs or red mullets, where price rises and scarcity spur even more demand.

Rational, efficient markets with perfect information do not develop booms and busts—any hints of Alan Greenspan's "irrational exuberance" should equilibrate away to nothingness long before any speculative frenzy becomes tangible. Speculation becomes an aberration under this overly simple worldview, as it requires some people to make more optimistic projections than others about the future and their assessment of risk. Those same bubbles and their painful aftermath also deny the existence of independent prices, with each subsequent movement being fueled by the previous one during the mania and in its immediate painful aftermath.

These are but some of the emperor's new clothes. Still, even a quick rummage through the closet is enough to cast serious doubt on these core economic assumptions that have driven our blinkered complacency toward financial markets and their inherent fragility, particularly in recent decades.[5] It is telling that in the aftermath of the most recent reminder of our limitations, the former chairman of the Federal Reserve, Paul Volcker, wrote that it was clear that "among the causes of the recent financial crisis was an unjustified faith in rational expectations, market efficiencies, and the techniques of modern finance."[6]

The crisis is increasingly clear. The dedicated economist is a learned nymphomaniac in theory, his or her virginity still intact due to never having actually met a real human being in the course of academic travels. It is better that we dispense with what is no longer working and embrace instead the complexity of the markets and the myriad influences upon them. We live in a dynamic world. Like sand dunes, our underlying foundations shift with the changing winds.

Financial markets are not static entities. They are collective nouns for the actions born of the hope, greed, and fear of countless human participants. What they portray is emotion as much as any underlying economic reality, and the volatility we observe is driven by the competition between these emotions. Different worldviews vie for dominance, coalescing into temporary paradigms—transient accepted wisdoms—that ebb and flow over time, euphemistically creating the booms and busts we observe.

Ceteris paribus is passé. A better motto for understanding the real world is *mutatis mutandis*—changing those things that need to be changed.

In short, it is time to put the ego back into economics.

CHAPTER 4

Ego and Euphoria:
A Japanese Interlude

Men, it has been well said, think in herds; it will be seen that they go mad in herds, while they only recover their senses slowly, and one by one.

—CHARLES MACKAY (1814–1889)

When it comes to the all-too-human problem of recessions and depressions, economists need to abandon the neat but wrong solution of assuming that everyone is rational and markets work perfectly.

—PAUL KRUGMAN (1953–)

HUMAN behavior is important to any understanding of the periodic bouts of fragility that seem to afflict financial markets. Nevertheless, it has proven hard to characterize.

Any financial crisis is typified by a multitude of ill-judged decisions. On December 29, 1989, the Nikkei 225 stock index in Japan reached its peak value of 38,916. A month later, the bubble burst and Japan began its journey into uncharted deflationary territory—a journey that is now some two decades old and counting. At the start of 2013, the Nikkei stood at 10,688, a staggering 73 percent off its nominal highs more than twenty-three years earlier.

The beginnings of the Japanese boom lay in Japan's growing technological prowess and dominance, epitomized by household names such as Sony and Panasonic. But behind the numbers were decisions that were hard to fathom. Traditionally a nation of parsimonious savers, Japanese consumers and businesses borrowed money with seemingly wild abandon to speculate in property and shares, driving them to unbelievable valuations in the late 1980s, before rediscovering their frugal inner selves in the lost decade of the 1990s and thereafter.

HUMBLE BEGINNINGS

The Japanese boom and bust were the culmination of a journey begun in the aftermath of the Second World War, as a proud focused population set to work rebuilding a shattered country and economy. Every journey is strewn with choices and, therefore, different. Travelers inevitably encounter forks or obstacles and have to make decisions as to which path to take. To understand the choices that led to the lost decade in Japan, we have to first understand the travelers who set off on this journey.

Japanese history is dominated by a narrative of powerful regional clans, headed by imperious warlords and composed of tightly run feudal hierarchies. These frequently clashed as they vied for political dominance. At the same time, none had the military resources to fight a pyrrhic war of attrition and become sole rulers of Japan. The result was an evolution over centuries of a complex sociopolitical dynamic, with a strong emphasis on social conformity and a strict class hierarchy underpinned by ceremony. That it worked for the Japanese is attested to by the fact that the Japanese monarchy is the oldest hereditary monarchy in the world and claims to have an unbroken line from the seventh century B.C. onward.[1]

By the seventeenth century, Japan had evolved into a federal feudal state, with some 250 warlords. The emperor was a ceremonial figure, akin to the pope, and true power resided in the most powerful warlord, who was known as the shogun. The shogun was responsible for key collective areas such as foreign relations, international trade, and security. The lesser warlords all had their own local spheres of influence with an independent administration and army. Their loyalty was bought through this decentralization of power, coupled with social safeguards. The practice of *sankin kotai* required each warlord to spend alternate years in the capital, Tokyo (then known as Edo), and pursue a lavish lifestyle, both conditions impeding any attempts to foment sedition. The latter also ensured that lower rungs on the social ladder—the warrior samurai, peasants, and merchant classes—benefited from a patronage system that bought their loyalty.

It was an inflexible system where the community was more important than the individual. Social stability was prized, given Japanese history, and the interweaving of people into tightly controlled, tight-knit interdependencies from top to bottom was used to ensure that interests were aligned, engendering trust. This also enabled an efficient command structure, quite deliberately similar to how the military operates. The identity of the individual was subsumed into the clan.

This also had the side effect of making the Japanese a naturally commercial and innovative people, particularly when it came to finance. Money was plentiful thanks to the patronage system and the lavish spending of the state(s). The complex web of relationships provided the bedrock of trust on which all financial transactions depend. The tight control of the state created certainty about the future. As early as the eighteenth century, for example, Japanese rice farmers were selling future deliveries of rice—a futures contract, in today's parlance—and giving rise also to the first derivative traders. One of these, Munehisa Homma, was perhaps the most successful financial trader in history, making as much as $10 billion from rice futures in some years. This was thanks to his perceptive realization that bull and bear markets existed and that market psychology mattered, making him also perhaps one of the earliest value investors.

When Japan began to modernize in the late nineteenth century and become an industrial economy, little changed beneath the surface. There was still a powerful elite directing everything at the top, now known as the government. The clans transmuted into political parties and corporations. The class system with its command structure moved across as well. Peasants became salaried employees with lifetime jobs. A new hierarchy emerged in management, but it was no less strict in its delineation of status and modes of interaction.

The individual emerged somewhat more in that he or she could move up this hierarchy as well as accumulate status through fortune. But his or her efforts were still devoted to the betterment of the collective. In return for lifetime employment and the implicit socialization of risk, people swore loyalty now to their corporate masters and accepted moderate wages. Coupled with the continuation of tight collectives—now composed of corporations—that collaborated and aided each other, productivity and efficiency were high.

Japan boomed in the twentieth century. A bruising set of recessions and a depression in the late 1920s and early 1930s, which was only partly influenced by the Great Depression, reinforced the above model and mind-set. In the aftermath of World War II, the new government made its policies clear. Japan needed a collective economic vision and a concrete strategy that was to be focused on industrialization, technology, and international trade. However, this was not to be the chaotic free market capitalism espoused by the United States and others. Rather, it needed to be directed by the state to key industries. The people had to do their part as well, and therefore consumption had to take a backseat to investment. This command capital-ism—now more recently espoused by China—gave birth to what became known as the Japanese economic miracle. It was aided also by comprehen-sive assistance from the United States, which saw Japan as a bulwark to communism in Asia, particularly as the Korean War got under way.

Large, closely knit groups again emerged. These *keiretsu* were corporate collectives, comprising manufacturers, suppliers, service compa-nies, insurers, shipping, and so on—all underpinned by a major bank that facilitated investment and lent the monies needed. Among their members were all the future luminaries of corporate Japan, including Sony, Canon, Hitachi, Mitsubishi, and Toyota. Behind then stood state institutions such as the Ministry of International Trade and Industry, the Bank of Japan, and the Japan Development Bank, with subsidies, funds, and regulatory barriers to protect and nurture these precious few.

Loans flowed from the Bank of Japan to commercial banks to corpo-rations, often with little regard to the quality of the debtor and ability to repay. It embedded debt deep into the Japanese psyche and corporate landscape. But this was also a way of ensuring influence, much in the same way that past shoguns had kept the warlords in check. There was an implicit understanding—reiterated through constant informal dialogue—that the monies were to be used to grow key parts of the Japanese economy and infrastructure. Profits were not important. Growth was. The members of the *keiretsu* were encouraged to purchase each other's shares, creating a complex web of cross-holdings that deterred takeovers and also bound them even closer. The intention was to align interests on all sides.

The initiative worked spectacularly. Productivity and efficiency soared alongside market share. Growth averaged over 10 percent in the 1960s and over 5 percent thereafter. GDP shot up from $23 billion in 1955 to over $1 trillion by the start of the 1980s. The government and Bank of Japan proved supportive throughout, cutting interest rates, aiding trade, and building infrastructure.

There was, however, a flip side to all this. Continual growth fueled a belief that the Japanese economic miracle was eternal. Property prices boomed all over Japan thanks to a potent combination of demand and limited supply. As Mark Twain advised a century earlier, buy land because they aren't building it anymore. Property was viewed as savings by both individuals and corporations. The *keiretsu* with their enormous holdings had huge pools of assets that could be used as collateral for loans. As these assets grew in value, more money could be borrowed against them.

The Japanese obsession with growth over profit became a mania. As liberalization began to creep in during the 1980s, banks began to borrow more and more money in the international markets and channel these funds to corporations and, increasingly, individuals. The corporations in turn used these for more investment and acquisitions, increasingly of land. Individuals began to use them to speculate on a booming stock market and property market. The close trust between all parties and the implicit backing of the government in case of any trouble created a fertile environment for unbridled speculation.

With every purchase, land prices rose; stock prices followed, collateral improved, and the banks lent even more. Interest rates marched downward through much of the 1980s, making it easier than ever to service the loans taken out. In 1986, for example, prime Tokyo commercial real estate more than trebled in dollar value, from $796 per square foot a year previously to an eye-watering $2,500 per square foot, while the Nikkei increased by 45 percent. Over the course of the 1980s, the Nikkei rose by a factor of more than five, while land prices across Japan quadrupled.

THE HEIGHTS OF FOLLY

The grounds of the emperor's palace in downtown Tokyo became worth more than the whole state of California and even, some claimed, more than the entire continent of South America. The Australian embassy grew so valuable that a foresighted government sold off part of the land it stood on and used the proceeds to repay half its foreign debt. By 1990, the country of Japan's real estate was one and a half times as valuable as the rest of the world combined, despite being only 0.25 percent of the earth's landmass and occupying an area a little smaller than the state of California.

When local land grew too expensive, attention turned overseas. The Mitsui Real Estate Company paid $610 million—almost double the initial asking price—for the Exxon Building in New York in an effort to get into the Guinness Book of World Records for paying the highest price ever for an office building. Exxon was so shocked at the offer that it asked lawyers for an opinion confirming that it was legal to overpay to this extent. Other Japanese businessmen bought up trophy properties such as Rockefeller Center, Pebble Beach, and the Hotel Bel-Air, until 10 percent (by value) of the property in the United States was owned by Japan. Hollywood even paid Japan its highest compliment—Japanese villains became ubiquitous in the late 1980s in movies such as *Black Rain*.

Meanwhile, the banks lent recklessly to feed this orgy. Leading up to the crash, nine of the world's top ten banks—measured according to their loan portfolios—were Japanese. Over a third of global lending belonged to Japan, making the Japanese banking system the largest in the world. Soaring real estate purchases were used as collateral to back stock purchases. As the price of both rose further, they were then used as collateral to back even more purchases. Cross-holdings of bank stocks and corporations became more common as each sought to take part in the success of its peers. By 1989, some 43 percent of all stocks could be classified as cross-holdings between two or more corporations. "Innovative" products were created, such as interest-only mortgages and multigenerational mortgages. The latter allowed buyers to spread payments out over their lifetimes as well as those of their children and even their grandchildren, for periods of up to a hundred years, as the loan amount required outstripped a single generation's capacity to pay.

Policy makers enthusiastically played their part in the drama. The government protected banks and other key industries from foreign competition, while providing benevolent direction. This third way of command capitalism—neither free markets nor socialism but fusing elements of both—was superior, everyone was told. Numerous incentives to expand mortgage availability were unveiled while the Bank of Japan accommodatingly kept interest rates low for several years from 1987 onward. Japanese bureaucrats were hailed the world over for their brilliance and became increasingly sought after for their advice.

As the demand for credit increased, common sense was mortgaged. Many companies fell into the same euphoric trap and began making increasingly large amounts of money from financial dealings.[2] Fueled by their land holdings, companies such as NTT[3] and All Nippon Airways reached individual valuations that exceeded those of entire stock markets.[4] The price-to-earnings ratio of Japanese stocks ran into triple digits and some even crossed 1,000. Japanese dominance of the world seemed ensured. In other words, Japanese growth seemed so certain and its wealth so permanent that people were willing to wait hundreds of years and in some cases more than a millennium to make back their money at current valuations.

Several paper billionaires and countless millionaires were created as portfolios exploded in value. Kichinosuke Sasaki, a doctor, set up a clinic for cataract removals and other geriatric ailments but soon began to dabble in real estate on the side. Within a few years, his sideline had grown into Togensha, an $11 billion conglomerate that was one of the largest owners of commercial property and condos in Tokyo. Sasaki made *Fortune*'s list of the superrich, while his geriatric clinic quietly retired into obscurity.

Speculation eventually reached out to anything remotely material. In 1988, developers began work on Seagaia—a $2 billion indoor water park that, at nearly a thousand feet long and more than three hundred feet wide, with a capacity of ten thousand people, was the largest in the world. It boasted artificial waves up to eight feet high, an artificial beach made not of sand but of crushed white marble, an artificial volcano that erupted in flames every fifteen minutes, artificial clouds that drifted overhead past bathers basking in the balmy 86-degree temperatures, and all just a ten-minute cab ride from the Pacific Ocean. An active trade in private golf club memberships—another derivative of underlying property—reached $200 billion, and the Nikkei unveiled a Golf Club Membership Index.

On September 28, 1989, three months before the Nikkei peaked, Sony paid $3.4 billion for Columbia Pictures. A few months later, on May 15, 1990, Christie's in New York auctioned Vincent van Gogh's *Portrait of*

Dr. Gachet, one of the artist's last works. Bidding began at $20 million and rapidly escalated until an unknown Japanese bidder paid $82.5 million—more than $30 million above the previous record and equivalent to about $150 million today. Two days later, the same buyer reappeared at Sotheby's and paid another $78.1 million for *Bal du Moulin de la Galette* by the French artist Renoir. The buyer was later revealed as Ryoei Saito, chairman of the Daishowa Paper Manufacturing Group, who extravagantly proclaimed that both paintings would be cremated with him when he died.

Behind this mania lay a belief that the Japanese paradigm was permanent. New metrics of valuation were needed, many said, echoing a familiar historical refrain. New terms such as "growth efficiency" and "technology efficiency" took hold. Books such as *The Technopolis Strategy: Japan, High Technology, and the Control of the Twenty-First Century* (1986), *Japan Inc.* (1988), *The Japan That Can Say No* (1989), *Created in Japan: From Imitators to World-Class Innovators* (1990), and *Japanese Technology Policy: What's the Secret?* (1991) trumpeted a growing consensus. One author even suggested that Japanese technological miracles such as the cassette recorder, VCR, and fax machine were ultimately responsible for the Iranian revolution and the Tiananmen Square uprising in China. "The Cold War is over, and Japan and Germany have won," remarked Senator Paul Tsongas in 1992 as he made his pitch to be the next U.S. presidential candidate.

In retrospect, it was collective stupidity on an unimaginable scale. Writing a striking postmortem in 1995, the journalist Christopher Wood noted Japan "became so arrogant in the late 1980s because it really believed it was immune from the natural laws of the marketplace. This really was one of the most astonishing acts of mass delusion ever, and future historians . . . will marvel at it."

THE LOST DECADES

When the bubble finally burst, initial skepticism that the good times were at an end soon gave way to ruin for countless individuals and companies. Land values collapsed and stock markets plunged. By the end of 1990 the Nikkei had halved, and a year later so had Tokyo property. By the end of 1992, it was estimated losses from shares and property were running at $10 trillion. Desperate banks began to offer interest-free loans to homeowners to help them make payments on the mortgages the banks had so effortlessly handed out a few years earlier. The government pushed through reforms that no longer required banks and companies to disclose the extent of their unrealized losses. Consumers and corporations switched into a bunker mentality that prized frugality and saving above everything else.[5] The spending taps shut off. As economic growth reversed course and loans went sour, Japan found itself facing a credit crunch and deflation. Debts grew increasingly insurmountable as the ability to pay them shrank—the familiar debt-deflationary spiral born two millennia earlier in Rome. In 1993, the Japanese government finally acknowledged that the "bubble economy" was no more.

Fifteen years later, prime commercial property in Tokyo's financial districts was going at less than 1 percent of its previous valuation, while residential homes were 90 percent off their peak.[6] In December 2005, the *New York Times* profiled Yoshihisa Nakashima, a Japanese civil servant who had purchased a cramped four-bedroom apartment in a Tokyo suburb for $400,000 in 1991. It was now worth less than half that and he still owed the bank $300,000. "The collapse of the bubble robbed us of our freedom to choose where we can live," bemoaned Mr. Nakashima as he faced the prospect of at least another decade in negative equity.

The Exxon Building still belongs to Mitsui today—an eternity in the real estate world. Meanwhile, other trophies went for a fraction of their purchase price. Sony took a write-down of $2.7 billion on Columbia in 1997, while Mitsubishi wrote off its interest in Rockefeller Center at a loss of $2 billion. The traders of golf club memberships now found themselves buying insurance in case insolvent golf clubs were taken over and the land put to other uses.

Dr. Sasaki found himself a billionaire twice over, the second time in negative territory as Togensha collapsed and his debts exceeded his net worth by $2.4 billion. In May 1996, as public anger grew over "wicked borrowers," police raided his offices and arrested him on charges of fraudulently obstructing his bankers over the auction of some of his land.

Mr. Saito died in 1997; his Renoir was sold privately through Sotheby's by his heirs for $50 million. The van Gogh still remains at large.

Some claimed it was taken by one of the banks he owed money to in the aftermath of the bust. Other rumors placed it with Wolfgang Flöttl, an Austrian hedge fund manager.[7] By 2009, there were only two Japanese left among the world's billionaires.

Bankruptcies rose to a hundred thousand and then to more than two hundred thousand a year. Divorces and crime soared. In a society where personal honor is intrinsically linked to status, suicides climbed as the pain and its attendant ruin became clear. By the mid-1990s, it was estimated that more than thirty thousand Japanese had committed hara-kiri—a ritual suicide—thus far in response to the crisis; by the late 1990s, the annual suicide rate had exceeded this number.

Policy makers were not spared. In 1993, the Liberal Democratic Party lost power for the first time since 1955 as the one-party system fell apart. Thereafter, with one exception, the prime ministership became an annual contest and the finance minister's portfolio a poisoned chalice. The Japanese bureaucrat retreated into caricature, overwhelmed by corruption scandals and paralyzed by uncertainty. "The economic system that has supported the fifty years of economic development following World War II is ill-suited for future growth," noted the Ministry of International Trade and Industry in a 1995 report that was a masterpiece of elegant understatement.

Command capitalists on the way up, the Japanese now became socialists on the way down. The collected $12 trillion household savings of an entire population was put to work. A painful recession and perhaps depression were replaced with decades of stagnation as a generation mortgaged their descendants' future. Banks and, later, governments pumped a steady stream of money into insolvent companies on the grounds that they were too big to fail, creating an economy populated by zombies. Today, only a single Japanese bank remains in the top ten globally.[8] Those that survived became thinly disguised wards of the state, their excessive losses gradually being written down piecemeal.

Interest rates fell to zero by the late 1990s and have hovered there since. Public sector financial institutions were ordered to buy stocks to bolster the stock market. Trillions of dollars were spent on large and expensive public works projects—scathingly dubbed "bridges to nowhere" by critics—in an effort to bring back growth. The Inland Sea, one of Japan's most popular tourist destinations, was graced with two additional bridges to complement the perfectly adequate one it already had. The total cost was $25 billion. More bridges, highways, airports, schools, and so on were built with as much abandon as the speculation of earlier years. Government deficits became *en vogue*.

But relaxed monetary policies and generous government spending in the absence of liquidations and restructuring failed to solve the deeper issues in the economy. Denial, hope, and hubris were the strategies of choice—deny the debt exists, hope the growth returns, and maintain the status quo at all costs. In the end, after all that money was spent, economic growth did resume, but only at a crawl.

As one lost decade stretched into two, Japan had become a nation of depressed consumers, hobbled conglomerates, insolvent banks, and discredited policy makers. Today, more than twenty years later, deflation has scarred the Japanese psyche. Continual failed interventions have left the country with an official national debt of more than twice its GDP. One in six Japanese now lives in poverty (defined as earning less than half the median income), a figure double what it was before the bubble burst, and ranked by the OECD as the sixth-worst in this regard among its members. One-third of the working population is composed of part-timers. Inequality has risen strongly across the board, creating a nation of a few haves and many have-nots.

Generations have turned away from shares and properties en masse, their former optimism and extravagance replaced by pessimism and parsimony. They choose instead to pile their savings into government bonds and various government savings institutions. This hoarding drives both the deflation and finances the debt the government needs to maintain its rearguard action. The National Pension Scheme is now one of the world's largest investors, with assets of over $1.5 trillion, while Japan Post's savings bank and insurance arms have combined assets of more than $3 trillion, dwarfing any sovereign wealth fund.[9] What speculation there is has gone overseas to sow the seeds of subsequent crises—Japan still supplies about 12 percent of the world's capital today.[10]

Wealth may be impaired, but it does not disappear overnight. But, barring a lone rearguard action from a buoyant export sector, Japan's wealth dwindles each year as the rest of the world innovates, a few more zombie loans from earlier heady days are written off, the government's need for debt grows, and the oldest population in the world begins to draw down on its carefully hoarded savings. A once coherent society—though still bound by old feudal ties—crumbles a little more each year.

Like Jay Gatsby, Japan still seeks "the orgastic future that year by year recedes before us. . . . Tomorrow [they] will run faster, stretch out [their] arms further . . . And one fine morning—"

The default strategy of hope lives on.

What is remarkable about Japan's bubble economy and the stories above—as with all other financial crises—is not that some people took a leave of absence from their senses but that so many people did so simultaneously, irrespective of background, education, status, or wealth.

Why did these collective manias—so pregnant with regret in hindsight—take hold?

Part II

Man: The Furnace Within

CHAPTER 5

The Road to Newnham:
The Bounds of Rationality

Life is made up of a series of judgments on insufficient data, and
if we waited to run down all our doubts, it would flow past us.
—BILLINGS LEARNED HAND (1872–1961)

If one is forever cautious, can one remain a human being?
—ALEXANDER SOLZHENITSYN (1918–2008)

IN the ancient university town of Cambridge, England, there is a tiny
semi-pedestrian path that runs between Newnham—one of the only two
all-girls colleges—and Newnham Road. On Friday and Saturday nights, as
the Granta Pub opposite calls closing time, inebriated students haphazardly
navigate past the languid river Cam and the more energetic traffic of Newnham Road with a singular goal in mind. Lovers, singletons, and suitors lurch
down this dimly lit path, bouncing off its narrow walls toward the Holy
Grail beyond. The careful plans of a few hours earlier have now been
replaced with a befuddled mix of emotion and half-formed coherence. But
that only redoubles their hormonal endeavors as the bounded rationality
born of beer and hope takes hold. Firmly focused on the here and now, they
zigzag—one step back, two steps forward—their optimism inversely
proportional to their balance as the cool night air hits their senses. But hope
is not a strategy, and many find the doors of Newnham College firmly closed
when they finally reach the promised land. Ego bruised, they retire
despondent. This humiliation will not go unforgotten. But resolve weakens
with time and memories are carefully pruned until, a week later, the mob
of masculinity finds itself at the Granta again, studying the path across and
devising new stratagems for closing time.

When it comes to our pursuit of money, we are no less rational and
no less easily influenced.

THE NOTION OF IRRATIONALITY

Most analyses of a crisis offer an impressive array of detail about how and when it all went wrong. The historical, economic, and political factors that may have contributed to this particular incarnation of our proclivity to fragility are carefully analyzed. Different economic and political philosophies are brought to bear and their interpretations debated. But when it comes to explaining the human motivations and the escalating layers of personal misjudgment that compounded error into crisis, the attention to detail is suddenly replaced by a uniformly crude pop psychology.

"I can calculate the motions of the heavenly bodies, but not the madness of people," rued the great physicist Isaac Newton following his loss of £20,000—some $5 million today—in the South Sea bubble of 1720. This constant refrain is common to both participants and economists throughout recorded history. Charles Mackay, the nineteenth-century progenitor of the doom-laden niche of financial crisis literature, blamed financial crises on an irrational herdlike behavior in his 1841 catalogue of human folly, *Extraordinary Popular Delusions and the Madness of Crowds*.

A century later, struggling for a more complete explanation, the erudite economist John Maynard Keynes turned to "animal spirits" as an explanation for these episodic reoccurrences.

> There is the instability due to the characteristic of human nature that a large proportion of our positive activities depend on spontaneous optimism rather than on a mathematical expectation, whether moral or hedonistic or economic. Most, probably, of our decisions to do something positive . . . can only be taken as a result of animal spirits.

This catchall psychological pitfall extended to all people in an economy and, for Keynes, was the cause of both speculation and instability. It also drove his belief in the need for a powerful interventionist government that could impose rationality from above, though he neglected to consider that government is also run by people subject to those selfsame animal spirits.

The lexicon of terms bandied about has expanded over the years to include *speculation, delusion, overconfidence, euphoria, denial, groupthink*, and *herd mentality*, among others. When Charles Kindleberger authored the bible of financial crises in 1978—*Manias, Panics and Crashes: A History of Financial Crises*—he placed irrationality at the heart of his argument.

> Speculation for capital gains leads away from normal, rational
> behavior to what has been described as a "mania" or a "bubble."
> The word "mania" emphasizes irrationality. . . . Rational exuberance
> morphs into irrational exuberance, economic euphoria develops
> and investment spending and consumption spending increase.

For Kindleberger, it was time to return to the "musty terms used by earlier generations of economists"—*overtrading* followed by *revulsion* and *discredit*. An otherwise elegant exposition of financial instability and the different stages of a financial crisis had little more to say on the causes of speculation (despite its centrality to Kindleberger's theory) other than unspecified psychological mechanisms couched in the generalities born of Mackay.

It is of little surprise that this notion of collective mania still troubles many economists.

"I do not deny the possible importance of irrationality in economic life," noted Ben Bernanke, the chairman of the Federal Reserve, in a 2000 commentary on the Great Depression. "However, it seems that the best research strategy is to push the rationality postulate as far as it will go."

The reticence is understandable. Irrationality as an explanation by itself is not compelling. To say that people are sometimes irrational and to leave it at that is deeply unsatisfying—the intellectual equivalent of *just because*. It is a linguistic sleight of hand that allows us to sidestep awkward questions and put a safe distance between the madding crowd and our ego.

Part of the problem is that irrationality and rationality are often defined in opposition to each other. The reason is simple: we all instinctively know what the two are. But pressed for a clear explanation, we flounder instead in verbal quicksand.

Even economists struggle. The *New Palgrave Dictionary of Economics* begins its lengthy discussion on the thorny issue of rationality by noting that rationality "is for economists as pornography was to the U.S. Supreme Court, undefinable but nonetheless easily identified; and yet, like the Justices of the Court, no two economists share a common definition." Twenty pages later, it ends with regret as to how rationality has been deployed by the profession and defines the term by noting what it is not.

The problem is one of subjectivity. At the heart of rationality lies the notion of making decisions through the exercise of reason. The problem is that we cannot separate thought from emotion. What we define as reason is colored not only by our state of mind at any given moment but also by our beliefs. The latter is a diverse plethora of mental baggage encompassing religious beliefs, social norms, personal philosophies, key people who have influenced us— parents, friends, talk show hosts, bloggers, pundits—and so on.

Without the subjectivity of reason, debate would not exist. Intelligence is a plentiful commodity not confined to any particular group. This is why, for example, we can have different political leanings— Democrat, Republican, and any other hues—and are capable of coherently articulating compelling arguments for our chosen ideology. They happily coexist alongside each other, both right and at the same time wrong, depending on your chosen viewpoint.

But reason becomes not only subjective but also inconsistent, evolving over time with our emotional state and our environment. We can change opinions—like Wittgenstein, the older incarnation becomes the biggest challenge to the younger one. This is why it seemed perfectly rational in the past to have views that we regard as absurd today.

Eugenics, the improvement of the genetic stock of humanity, is a case in point. Now tainted with the mud of racial supremacy and the Nazi atrocities committed in its name, it was once a respectable and popular philosophy formulated by Charles Darwin's cousin Francis Galton as an extension of the theory of evolution. Early supporters included luminaries such as the future British prime minister Winston Churchill, the playwright George Bernard Shaw, U.S. president Teddy Roosevelt, and the inventor of the telephone, Alexander Graham Bell. Another prominent supporter, Keynes—the same who could not quantify irrationality—wrote as late as 1946 that eugenics is "the most important, significant and, I would add, genuine branch of sociology which exists." Other examples of views that were once accepted wisdom and on which we've changed our minds abound. Women are less able than men. The pope is infallible. There is a market for perhaps five computers worldwide.

Rationality is a spectrum. At one end lies the mythical postulate of rational expectations, touched on earlier, that underpins much of mainstream economics. In this view, we are all little economists, devoid of emotion and overflowing with information, carefully weighing up each decision with cold logic to determine which outcome serves our interests best. At the other end lies equally mythical irrationality, where decisions are based on impulse, with no discernible reasoning behind them and resulting always in us choosing worse outcomes for ourselves and society.

The absurdity of both extremes is plain with respect to financial crises. The truth lies somewhere in between, and like the pining students at the Granta, we need to understand the bounds of our rationality to understand the beginnings of our speculations.

THE INTENTION OF RATIONALITY

As humans, we are all intendedly rational. We make decisions that conform with our self-interests or with social norms, and which often represent reasoned responses to what life throws at us. There may be brief moments of impulse, but all of us would like to believe that our decisions were made on the best available information at the time and with a view to improving our lot in life.

But there is a caveat. There are limits to how close we can get to the ideals of *Homo economicus*. This is a function not of human failing but of the need to live in the real world. Information is not always complete and the time we have is often insufficient for the complex, detailed calculations of theory.

This need to move quickly in the real world and the complexity of analysis lend themselves to shortcuts. The world is a never-ending cornucopia of information, while our brain is a limited resource. Consequently, we invent rules of thumb, rely on past experience, take the advice of others, are prone to contextual interpretations driven by our environment, have hunches, and so on.

Take a look at Figure 2 in the photo insert, and in particular, at the squares marked A and B.

Would you believe me if I told you they were the same color?

Surely not. A is charcoal gray and B is a light gray, you say.

But you would be wrong. Even as I type, I have to remind myself that eyes can lie and this is an optical illusion. Both A and B are the same color, their differing perceptions influenced by the interplay of light around them. This visual sleight of hand is a testament to how easily our environment affects our decisions.

The rational human being becomes bounded on all sides, his or her intentions now limitations obscured behind emotions, words, and assumptions. As the complexity of our world grows, the need to utilize shortcuts increases in proportion. This is key if we are to prioritize information, and often these cognitive biases become an unconscious, unbidden part of our psychological makeup. A gulf remains between *Homo sapiens* and *Homo economicus*.

In 1986, psychologists Antonio Damasio and Paul Eslinger detailed a remarkable case of a patient who appeared to have lost the ability to make decisions. Elliot, as they called him, had suffered damage to the frontal lobes of his brain during the removal of a tumor. Still, he had made a seemingly complete recovery and was able to converse at length about the state of the world, discuss moral dilemmas, and reason his way around problems. As long as these scenarios and conversations remained hypothetical, Elliot was in full charge of his faculties.

Reality, however, was a different beast. A simple decision such as dining at a restaurant became a painful exercise in precision. Menus were studied, ambience evaluated, drive-bys undertaken to ascertain potential hazards, seating plans examined—and yet no decision was reached. Choosing what to wear was a similar nightmare.

Elliot's problem was simple. He had gone from being *Homo sapiens* to *Homo economicus*. Robbed of the ability to use shortcuts, he was now perfectly rational. Every decision was a perfect exercise in rational logic and, ultimately, failed as a result.

Returning to our earlier example in the opening chapter of the nighttime stroll down to the restaurants, our decision was an extrapolation. The one with more people is automatically deemed to be better because we assume that our collective judgment is indicative of quality. But if we go back to the start of the evening, both restaurants were empty until a random couple walked down that street. Assuming the two places were identical in terms of quality, couple A chose one restaurant based on their preconceptions. Perhaps it was the lighting; maybe the menu triggered nostalgia, or possibly they simply flipped a coin. Regardless, they chose, and the next couple that walked down that street would have felt a gentle pressure toward one restaurant over the other. As more and more people end up in one restaurant over another, the pressure to unconsciously correlate the quantity of bodies with the quality of cuisine builds till what we perceive as free will is gently coerced into a herd mentality. There was never a rational reason to prefer one to another—it just seemed better because of all the assumptions we make.

These biases extend throughout every decision we make, whether it is choosing a car, an M&M, or a stock. And the biases come in a host of flavors—from our perceptions of time to our ability to extrapolate to our desire to conform to our unerring ability to cherry-pick those nuggets of information that affirm our preconceptions.

A whole field, behavioral economics, has sprung up in recent years to understand and detail these so-called cognitive biases or heuristics. Embodied in the popular psyche by Daniel Kahneman and Richard Thaler, behavioral economics has mapped out our proclivities in fine detail.[1] They also take us forward from our crude folk psychology to a more empirical assessment of human behavior and the practicalities of economics in the real world.

Kahneman draws a distinction between two types of cognitive processes: those based on intuition and those based on careful reasoning. The former are not thought through but rather result in quick judgments based on the recall of familiar concepts, driven by contextual interpretation, and often colored by emotion. The latter is the domain of rationality, typified by ponderous thought, careful analysis, and a surfeit of time.

To delve into the space in detail would take a book (perhaps, several), and we have neither the pages nor the depth of knowledge to truly do it justice. Therefore, we shall merely limit ourselves in the rest of this narrative to touching on some of the psychological foundations that cast light on our ability to perpetuate these cycles of boom and bust.

CHAPTER 6

The Temple of Janus:
Time, Memory, and Uncertainty

It is notorious that the memory strengthens as you lay burdens upon it, and becomes trustworthy as you trust it.

—THOMAS DE QUINCEY (1785–1859)

People can foresee the future only when it coincides with their own wishes, and the most grossly obvious facts can be ignored when they are unwelcome.

—GEORGE ORWELL (1903–1950)

RETURNING to Rome, you may recall that we talked about how the lack of any long-term planning by Augustus played a key role in the Roman depression of A.D. 33. His chief advisor, Maecenas, was too focused on shorter-term fixes that would boost economic growth, often to the detriment of lasting government infrastructure that might sustain it instead. Additionally, the continual gifts and largesse bankrupted the treasury to the extent where it could no longer fund the economy by itself. The result was a downward spiral and a credit crunch that almost destroyed the system.

Hands up, all those who can point to the behavioral biases on display in the above.

Some of you may quickly be skipping back to the relevant pages to refresh your memories, while the rest have enough meat on the above to form a judgment on my query. I applaud the former for calling my bluff.

The problem is that nothing I wrote in that opening paragraph is actually true. It's near enough, which is why you can remember it. There was plenty of easy money, lots of government spending, and perhaps too little foresight there for the inevitable aftermath, but the argument above was never made by me. Long-term planning—even if misguided—was core to Augustus's policies and the whole Roman bureaucracy stood as evidence to that. Maecenas never made it into my chapter, though he was a real historical figure and an influential advisor. And the treasury never went bankrupt—though it tried to restore fiscal discipline as the coffers grew lighter and inadvertently constricted the flow of money through the economy.

Some of you will now argue that I am wrong. The words I have written before can easily be interpreted on a closer reading to make the above argument, notwithstanding the absence of one Latin name or the other. I am disingenuous or perhaps should have been clearer. Despite my protestations, we are now at an impasse.

This is the fallacy of memory.

What went wrong?

Chances are you will not have stored every last bit of information I imparted. Rather, you will have stored little reminders in your mind that used the words you just read to fill in the blanks and triggered an overarching memory of the chapter you read. This episodic mechanism is akin to a hologram—those three-dimensional projections that we are so fond of as kids. A hologram is nothing more than a collection of bits of information in a two-dimensional setting—a sticker, typically—that encodes a three-dimensional image. If you were to clip a small part of that two-dimensional sticker and shine a light through it, the three-dimensional picture would be re-created, though its quality would be slightly degraded, as the information is patchier and there are more gaps to be filled in.

Augustus is a well-known Roman emperor. The chapter was about the Roman depression of A.D. 33. A large part of the narrative explored the structural weaknesses in the Roman state and how its monetary policies led to recurrent crises. The name Maecenas sounded Latin-like and became just another name lost in the amnesiac forest of ancient names you confronted earlier. Money was restricted and there were lots of detail about people and states going bankrupt.

Most of all, you had an inherent sense of trust in the author to tell you the truth. It's an instinctive assumption that you made on picking up a book. The facts may not always be right and the arguments questionable, but that is a judgment call for you to make after reading. The narration of them was assumed honest and reliable—words and concepts with a powerful emotional import. By breaking that trust, I have crossed a line.

In hindsight, the subterfuge is all too obvious. The chapter title refers to Janus, the two-faced Roman god, and the first quote is as clear an indication of malicious intent as any. But then, things are always clearer in hindsight.

INTERNAL RUMORS

Human memory is not only particularly leaky but also remarkably selective. Further, it is rarely objective and often seems more an evolutionary aid bent to the task of nurturing and protecting the ego. Like rumors, our memories and the experiences, emotions, and biases they convey continually acquire a life of their own, bearing only a passing resemblance to the inputs and influencing the decisions we take.

Are you a better-than-average driver? Your mind quickly remembers all the times you drove to work and on vacation, through good weather and bad; the way you stopped for that old jaywalking couple last month; the remarkable control you showed in swerving to avoid that testosterone-fueled junkie who tore down the highway on Friday; and so on.

Yes, you are better than average. In fact, you're a darn good driver when it comes to both skill and safety.

So too apparently are nine out of ten other Americans.[1]

What your memory quickly glosses over are the near misses, the little scrapes, the poor parking, and the like. You also have little memory of how all the countless other drivers around you drove, save when they got in your way. All this is often deemphasized to the betterment of our own self-evaluation, creating an illusion of superiority and breeding overconfidence.

The same bias toward positive memories is why we hear the constant refrain "in the good old days . . ." in every age and why there is always a reactionary wing in every religion and in each body politic.[2] It is why commentators today sometimes yearn for a return to some fabled "golden age" of banking when the system was trustworthy, genuinely helpful, and honest. If they were to examine the evidence, they would note that it was still just as opaque, riddled with expensive fees and limited choices, and far more exclusionary to large swaths of the population.

The illusion might be seen as problematic. Yet, in contrast, the unfortunate Elliot—forever doomed to rationality—had lost any emotional anchors and the resulting rapid-fire decision making that came from intuition.[3] The result was paralysis. Asked about his driving skills, he likely would have pondered every memory, totting up mental tables of good and bad, till a decision was finally reached at some unknown point in the distant future.

Context is also important, as in the checkered visual illusion seen earlier.

See Figure 3 in the photo insert. How fast would you estimate the cars were going when they smashed into each other?

Perhaps your answer would be different if I rephrased my question thus: How fast would you estimate the cars were going when they hit each other?

In 1974, two psychologists—Elizabeth Loftus and John Palmer at the University of Washington—carried out a similar experiment on people's memories. Forty-five students were split into five groups and shown seven film clips of car accidents. They were then asked how fast the cars were traveling at the time, with one crucial differentiator—the verb.

About how fast were the cars going when they smashed into each other? Variations followed that replaced *smashed* with *collided, bumped, hit*, and finally the anemic *contacted*. The results showed that the more intense the verb used to describe the accidents, the higher the estimated speed.

A second study followed. *Was there any broken glass on the scene?* Almost one in three recalled broken glass when they were told the cars had smashed into each other, compared to only about one in seven when the cars had only hit each other.

In other words, our already leaky memories could be manipulated further simply by asking the right questions. Students of political history will note that this has been demonstrated in mob hysteria and pogroms throughout history, where the selective use of language has succeeded in converting scant suspicion into maddened reality for most people. The witch trials of Salem in the eighteenth century, the weapons of mass destruction secreted in Iraq, the communal riots when India and Pakistan were torn apart in a partition that left over a million dead—these are all cases in point.

There are many other biases associated with memory: the tendency to justify the choices you have made, the projection of your current beliefs onto past memories, the clarity of hindsight, and so on. All of these make recurrent appearances through our journey, becoming familiar acquaintances. But there is one worth noting in particular, which explains why we sometimes miss the elephant in the room.

You are asked to watch a thirty-second video of two teams playing basketball.[4] One team is wearing white and the other is wearing black, with three people on each team. You are now asked to count how many times the basketball is passed by the members of the white team to each other.

Assuming you took a moment away from your reading to surf YouTube, you may be glad to hear the correct answer was fifteen. However, you may also have missed the following. Halfway through the video, a gorilla walks into the middle of the players, thumps its chest, and strolls off—its cameo on screen a lengthy nine seconds. It may seem hard to believe, but when psychologists Daniel Simons and Christopher Chabris conducted the above experiment, they found that half their test subjects were so focused on the counting that they completely missed the gorilla in the room.[5]

Beyond humor, these biases are also a side effect of the need to make up our minds quickly. There are simply far too many decisions that can be debated ad infinitum if there is no gut feeling pointing the way to one conclusion. Chinese takeout or Indian tonight? To buy that new iPad or not? Apple shares or Google shares?

There are economic factors that go into all of these, and when choosing for a hypothetical person X on a piece of paper, it becomes a simple exercise in rational analysis. But when choosing for yourself, the memories and emotional factors triggered are just as important, and any analysis—no matter how momentary—assesses the emotional impact of different choices. Subjectivity, the context, and your past all play key roles, quickly delineating preferences. A more formally reasoned analysis then comes in, if felt necessary, to gently adjust the course already chosen.

There are good reasons for this. We need to make countless decisions every moment of every day, and an intuitive approach has served us well in our evolutionary history to date. Crossing the road, driving a car, tackling my three-year-old son's logic—life is a continual exercise in instinctive opportunism and risk management. Additionally, social cooperation and harmony depend on shared norms, common opinions, and an intuitive grasp of interpersonal skills.

As a former physicist, I was trained to be analytic, Sometimes, however, thinking too much is not ideal. A few years ago, my wife and I went on vacation to a charming part of Italy called Cinque Terre. It is an area of stark beauty, with jagged cliffs that rush toward the sea. Small olive groves and fragile wineries cling to the steep contours of the land, interspersed with wildflowers and manicured Italian gardens. On our second night, we had a private dinner in the botanical gardens. It was a dark night, with the only light being that of a few candles and a beautiful full moon that cut a bright, turbulent swath across an otherwise black sea. Afterward, as we sat on the grass looking out, my wife told me how much she loved the fresh salty smell of the sea. Without hesitation, I carefully explained to her that the smell was actually the by-product of bacteria breaking down dead plankton and rotting seaweed.

I have since learned to be more romantic. It is an intuitive approach that has helped my longevity.

We don't plan out every conversation in advance like some architectural drawing. We talk instinctively, and our biases are often deemed virtues because they are linked in our minds to success. Confidence, drive, eloquence, empathy, relentless focus—these are all qualities we prize in ourselves and our network. Arguably, however, they are also positive spins on the illusion of superiority, the inability to appreciate or analyze potential pitfalls, the manipulation of minds through our words, a propensity toward groupthink, and an obsessive look at details only and never the bigger picture.

Looking through the narrower lens of human speculation, the ability to make quick decisions, and blinkered ones at that—often in unison with our fellow creatures—is key to our repeated economic cycles. Given our obsession with economic growth, we would not want it any other way.

Entrepreneurs and speculators take big chances and are unerringly optimistic. Like the driver in us all, each is convinced that he or she is above average and destined for success. Their hopes are bolstered by all the stories they remember of those who amassed riches and their minds quickly filter out the many more who failed on that journey, inflating a tiny probability of success into certainty. And sheltering the ego behind the internal rumors of memory is important if they are to renew their optimism and try again with each new cycle.

All it takes is time.

EVENT HORIZONS: THE BREVITY OF FORESIGHT

The talented cosmologist John Wheeler was also a talented word-smith.[6] Asked to define space and time, he noted: "Time is what prevents everything from happening at once. Space is what prevents everything from happening to me." The quote encapsulates beautifully both the importance of ego and the perception of time to our navigation of this world.

Time is the great adjunct to memory in the realm of human bias. How we address and incorporate the notion of time into our decision making is key to explaining the psychological mechanisms that underlie financial crises. After all, the one notable feature time and time again in these crises is the brevity of both our horizon and our memory in their aftermath.

Intuitively, the importance of time is self-evident. Time exists first and foremost in our mind, and any relationship between its passage within our internal corridors and that in the physical world is purely tangential. Anyone who has been on a beautiful sun-soaked vacation or had the misfortune to endure an interminably dull date knows this.

Economists have also known for a long time that we discount the future. Their assumption has largely been that we evaluate the future from a rational economic perspective based on grounds of utility, that is, the equal pleasure or pain granted by future gains or losses. Thus, we make consistent decisions at every point in the future, in accordance with our own particular threshold.

But let me ask you the following question. If a complete stranger offered you $1,000 today or $1,010 tomorrow, which would you take? What if you were offered $1,000 one year from now or $1,010 a year and a day from now? Utility theory and its perfect rationality dictate that we would make the same decision in both cases. If you are risk averse, you will always choose the $1,000. If not, you will always pick $1,010.

In practice, however, our more bounded rationality creates inconsistent behaviors in response to simple incentives that make complete sense to us. You are more likely to pick $1,000 today because you do not know if the stranger will be there tomorrow. That uncertainty is enough to bias you toward the here and now. However, a year from now, it makes little difference whether you wait a day or not—the time frames and associated uncertainties are about equal in your mind. Therefore, you are more likely to wait for a year and a day and collect $1,010.[7]

If I change the good Samaritan above to your friend, your answers will change again based on your perception of how reliable that friend is. You are not being irrational. In your world, the context always matters and is a key determinant of your rational choice. The nature of the incentive has subtly shifted and, therefore, so has your response. For most economists, the context is irrelevant. But then, their behavior is consistent over time, unlike yours. They will always tell you tomorrow why what was predicted yesterday didn't happen today.

All humans suffer from a strong temporal myopia that makes lower risks and reward in the near term more appealing than higher perceived risks and potential greater reward in the future. The evidence is overwhelming. In 1972, a Stanford psychologist by the name of Walter Mischel conducted an experiment on six hundred children between the ages of four and six. The results were immortalized as the Stanford Marshmallow Experiment.[8]

The children were each brought into a room and offered a treat: an Oreo cookie, a marshmallow, or a pretzel stick. There was one caveat though. The child could eat the treat right away or wait for fifteen minutes and get two treats. The researcher would then step out, returning fifteen minutes later or earlier if the child rang a bell because he or she could hold out no longer. All the subjects were videotaped.

The results showed that some had eaten the treat straightaway, others after a few agonizing minutes. Some were ingenious, gently nibbling one side of the marshmallow and then laying it down on that side, or twisting the Oreo apart and licking off the cream filling before returning it to its original position. Only about a third survived the temptation long enough to get the second treat, though the steps taken were drastic in some cases. One child reportedly licked the table all around the marshmallow, while others closed their eyes to avoid looking at it.

The aim was to explore when we develop the urge to delay self-gratification. But the abysmal failure of the majority to comply revealed far more about our innate nature. It explains why we find it so hard to diet and why it's so difficult to give up smoking. The long-term rewards are clear in each case and compelling, but the near-term pleasure from that burger or that slow drag is far more appealing, despite its toxicity.

Mischel's experiments were subsequently linked to later success in life, as he and other researchers found the successful children had generally higher SAT scores, suffered less substance abuse, and were perceived as being more successful as adults. The results have also been a boon for the self-help industry, which has used the results to condemn the "irrationality" within us that jeopardizes our future and to tout the importance of goal setting, self-control, and willpower in overcoming these self-destructive tendencies. Who remembers the flood of books regarding emotional intelligence and the Tao/Zen/Yoga/random-generic-Oriental-term method of meditation in the last decade or so?

However, this correlation does not tell the whole story and spuriously leads many to believe that somehow the broad contours of our lives are largely mapped out while still in childhood. The truth, as always, is more nuanced. What may be perceived as an irrational outcome may still have its roots very much in rational decision making, albeit influenced by our environment and the incentives on offer.

In 2012, researchers at the University of Rochester carried out the marshmallow study again, with one important difference. Twenty-eight children, ages three to five, were each given first a blank piece of paper to decorate as part of a create-your-own-cup kit and a container of used crayons. They were then told that if they could wait a few minutes, the researcher would return shortly with a bigger and better set of new art supplies.

The experiment now diverged down two paths. For half the children, the researcher returned after two and a half minutes with an abject apology and helped them open the crayon container. For the other half, a full tray of art supplies magically turned up.

Then a small sticker was placed on the table for decoration. Once more the children were told that if they could wait, the researcher would soon come back with some better ones. Half the children again received an empty-handed apology after two and a half minutes. The other half got a selection of large colorful stickers.

The marshmallow test now followed as before for all the children. The first set of children, who had been continually disappointed by the researcher, lasted only about three minutes on average, with just one child holding out for the full fifteen minutes. In contrast, the second group, who had seen every promise fulfilled, were patient for twelve minutes on average, with the majority going on to receive their second marshmallow.

The levels of trust and certainty played a key role. The first group had every reason to be skeptical that the researcher would return in fifteen minutes with another marshmallow. They therefore made the rational decision under those constraints to take the treat that they knew was there for the taking, rather than holding out some forlorn hope for a better reward in the future. The second group had no such qualms. Both groups exhibited elements of temporal myopia, but it was enhanced or muted also by their perception of the environment and incentives on offer.

Time is the root of uncertainty. What we sometimes despise as temporal myopia is a natural reaction to the fact that there are large unknowns about the future in the real world. From an economic perspective, it explains why we worry more about buying a house today than about saving for retirement. The uncertainty of whether we will make it to old age, what our money might be worth that far down the line, and what the government or some future economic disaster might do to our little hoard, coupled with our innate optimistic bias that there will be ample time and opportunity to make the money later, mean that we are naturally driven to focus on nearer-term needs that can also function as stores of wealth in our perspective.[9]

It explains why we buy expensive items such as televisions, cars, and kitchens now on credit and pay far more over time. We enjoy feeling good today. We expect that credit will always be freely available and affordable—this being another case of where our myopia is enhanced by the economic environment.[10] We may not be around to enjoy these things if we save for years first. We expect that our future income potential and trajectory are exponential. In a worst-case scenario, we think, we can always retrieve some value by hocking our instant-gratification buys on eBay or Craigslist; others do and seem to make quite a tidy living from it. Based on our limited information and positive emotional bias, these decisions make sense to us. Indeed, the larger part of our economy and GDP growth depends on this myopic consumption to drive the demand for mortgages, loans, and credit cards.

It explains why corporations and financial institutions are so focused on near-term returns, for it is those returns that drive share prices this year and the next. The decision makers in those companies and banks know that almost every investor—even purportedly long-term ones such as pension funds—has an actual time horizon that usually spans from today to the end of the quarter or year, depending on reporting cycle.[11] They also know that current models of staff compensation are biased toward returns on equity, that is, returns in the short term. Arbitraging regulation to minimize equity and providing the herd what it demands on the surface are sensible choices that allow you to maximize your return on equity as well as enhance your quality of life and wealth now. If you don't perform, you might lose your job and your chances of success in the rat race. The uncertainty of waiting is deemed too high.

It explains why governments spend today and hope for growth tomorrow. Their myopia is subtly different in that it is driven by the electoral cycle. However, in their case, it always makes more sense to spend today. In boom times, this caters to key groups of voters and demonstrates progress on social and political agendas to supporters. In the bad times, stimulus increases their chances of economic success in the near term and the perception that they are doing something. Both enhance the probability of being reelected. Taking a longer-term view may result in a curtailed career, particularly when they take into account the shorter time horizons of their electorate. It also casts light on their dynamic inconsistency—fancy words for "propensity to disappoint"—as they soon learn that expectations management is far more important than actual delivery. This is one of the reasons the Keynesian prescription of large amounts of fiscal stimuli is flawed. Governments are always ready to spend to mitigate economic downturns, but they are not willing to rein in spending in the good times. It is just not in their nature.

Last, and perhaps most important, it explains why policy makers choose to fight the urgent crisis today instead of the far more important crisis building up in the future. As an example, the last few years have seen trillions of dollars pumped into the global economy to counterbalance the credit crunch. The enhanced risks for the future in terms of impaired sovereign balance sheets and the far larger costs of paying for an aging population are of lesser consequence. This is because in their eyes, the overarching need is to preserve the financial system today. Therefore, like that expensive vacation bought on your credit card, you spend a lot today, cognizant of and yet willfully blinded to the fact that you will pay even more tomorrow. There is also the hope that if this stimulus works, the economy will roar back into life and make those future larger payments eminently more affordable. There is always time enough to plan the deeper structural reforms tomorrow that will make social security, health care, and other spending viable and sustain the fabric of society.

Unfortunately, tomorrow, there will be another crisis and our myopic horizon pushes off the deeper issues for yet another day. Those who made the decision today to postpone, knowing there was still at least a decade or two left to ponder, are also unlikely to still be there that decade or two hence. It is the familiar Roman motif of a vigorous beginning lapsing into a careless end. That is why today we have future government liabilities across the developed world that run into hundreds of trillions of dollars and multiples of our GDP. It is also why structural issues persist and create recurrent cycles of crises throughout history, as noted earlier.

Most of the time, however, it works for all the parties above. Our positive illusions and resultant decisions are based, after all, on the experience that life often seems to work out just fine. When it does go wrong, it is because we have extrapolated too far into the future an illusory certainty that never existed.

THE PAST IS THE FUTURE

The human psyche is defined by its continual battle to reclaim islands of certainty from the turbulent oceans of uncertainty that we inhabit. It is also driven by an obdurate belief that these islands can be grown to encompass the entirety of our existence given enough planning.

Many of the biases we have detailed so far can be understood in terms of this perpetual fight. Our illusions of superiority, our willful optimism, our interpretation of otherwise ambiguous evidence in line with our beliefs, the benefits of hindsight—these are all about projecting a sense of control over our environment. Other biases such as our temporal myopia and the recasting of our memories protect us from uncertainty by instinctively pushing it far enough away so that it sits just beyond our temporal horizon.

The result is a continual search for models and patterns that we can project out into the future. These represent certainties and reliable quantifications that can be used to understand and navigate the world about us. This extrapolation bias is ubiquitous and rooted in induction. Coupled with our failing memory, it means that we not only predict the future based on the past but also emphasize the most recent events when looking ahead.

Some examples are simple. The sun will rise tomorrow, because it has generally been constant every day I've cared to check. The subway ride during rush hour will be hot, sweaty, and overcrowded—the exceptions to this rule are so rare as to be considered urban legends.

Others are less so. The sports gambler taking sure bets on the home team will find himself periodically coming unstuck. The stability of a job and its assumed income growth are rarely questioned, which is why being laid off is often such a psychological shock. Businesses often go out and spend strongly on capital investment only when they have had strong orders for a number of years. However, as seen in countless business cycles, the result is a glut of supply, which may then drive prices down and harm future revenues.[12]

In the financial world, investors are often drawn to those stocks and sectors that have seen strong gains in recent months and years. House prices will always rise. The rule held true for many years but more recently seems suspect.

As manias go, this last one is instructive. The lure of property keeps coming around generation after generation and seems broadly independent of geography. Even when house prices have peaked, the appeal to history and the tendency to extrapolate means that we stubbornly expect values to go up over the long term. The bias is not confined to individuals but seems to broadly apply to economists, policy makers, and lenders—in short, the human race. The reason is that often this bias is accompanied by an extrapolation of recent economic growth well into the future, which in turn fuels beliefs about income growth and future wealth.[13] It is a cascade of extrapolations, each leveraging off the previous one. The pattern is the same, whether it be Japan in the 1980s, the Florida property bubble that preceded the Great Depression, or our more recent history of the subprime crisis and the Great Recession of 2007. Ordinary people itch and fight to get onto the property ladder; lenders yearn and innovate to make ever larger loans of an increasingly poor quality; policy makers laud the extension of housing to all strata of society and plan ambitious new programs; central banks show increasingly confident growth projections with diminishing risks to the downside.

From a psychological perspective, there are two additional lessons to draw from this. First, it explains why, though manias may be typified in popular culture by a few frenzied weeks or months, bubbles take time to emerge and inflate. It is because the stream of supporting data that allows us to extrapolate ad infinitum takes time to build up and reinforce itself in our memory. The longer the bubble progresses, the more people are drawn to the same conclusion, and the risks are magnified to systemic levels.

Second, we have a remarkable propensity to codify and support these extrapolations through quantification and intellectual justification.

Models by their very nature are based on historical data and so are subject to the same extrapolation bias. In the last few years, the outpouring of scorn on the quantitative risk models utilized by banks has stemmed from the fact that they blithely ignored the underlying risks till it was far too late.[14] The same was also true for the macroeconomic models used by central banks and other economic forecasters. The calibration of these models to historical observations and the bias toward more recent data meant that the probabilities assigned to extreme outcomes were far too low. Even worse, as the models made good predictions in the intervening years, there was a tendency to attach ever higher levels of certainty to their predictions—an additional extrapolation.

There is a large, well-known asset management house in the United Kingdom that ran a currency model very successfully for over ten years in the late 1990s and the early part of this century. It had been built by one of the house's senior quants, apparently subjected to extensive back-testing, and eventually incorporated into one of its funds. The unnamed quant moved on elsewhere, but the model stayed on and remained sacrosanct, churning out remarkable returns for more than a decade. After a while, management took a decision to update the model on the basis of new data and to ensure that returns did not degrade over time.

A new team of quants was set to the task. When they took the model apart, they realized—likely with horror—that they had been misinterpreting the results for the entirety of the model's lifetime. When it said buy, they mistook it as a signal to sell; when it said sell, they mistook it as a signal to buy. Idiocy and luck had masqueraded as one of their most successful models all this while.

The perils of overcalibration were driven home for many in 2008 as the perceived patterns transmuted and most models stopped working altogether. I recall that one of my portfolios contained a hedge fund whose manager was almost driven to tears by his continual struggle to find new ways of interpreting data. Different time frames were examined alongside different frequencies of market data, from second by second to daily to weekly. Different emphases were given to different periods: today it was the most recent past, while tomorrow it would be more extreme movements. One of his models—another currency one—proved particularly resistant to intellectual solutions.[15] We could always tell when he used the model because the returns would suddenly get worse. We could also always tell when he took it offline to iterate again because the returns magically improved. In the end, we asked him to remove it altogether and spare us the roller coaster, though it was most definitely not a willing decision for him.

There is always an intellectual argument to justify every number and pattern. In the property market, common ones trotted out are the shortage of available land, demographic changes, and patterns of migration. The presence of mythic new markets will fuel continued growth, while new phenomena such as the "knowledge economy" will enhance GDP.

But much of this is confirmation after the fact. Take a stock such as Apple or Google. If you had the company's entire balance sheet and order book to pore over but did not know either the stock's price history or what price it is currently trading at, could you tell me what its stock price would be in a year's time? Any model you create will capture your biases about valuation, growth, technology, consumer behavior, and so on. Any number can be justified by this model, but only one would be proven correct. In the real world, we often work in reverse. We start by looking at the current price, looking at past history, and then overlaying our opinions. As prices evolve, the process iterates until we are expert stock pickers, albeit for only a moment. That is why prices rarely decouple from "fundamentals" during the bubble. With hindsight, the same spurious process is held to clearly demonstrate that prices had left "fundamentals" far behind long ago.

Incidentally, if you do make a correct prediction, I suggest you go and sell the intellectual property rights to your model immediately to a bank or hedge fund. Despite your astounding predictive power, this is one case where your temporal myopia will serve you particularly well.

ACTUALLY, THE FUTURE IS BETTER THAN THE PAST

The future is more than just an extrapolation of the past. In our minds, it is often a far more alluring place.

Have you ever overcommitted yourself? I do it all the time. When promising something for tomorrow, it's easy to plan ahead. But when you're promising things whose delivery dates are months or years in the future, it seems our ability to overestimate our abilities to deliver and underestimate the time and financial commitment required is remarkable.

Anyone who has been charged with maintaining project budgets will understand. Few ambitious projects ever come in on budget, let alone under budget. It is an inevitable error corrected for by the use of generous contingency buffers.

On October 23, 2012, the U.K. government proudly announced that the 2012 Olympics had come in an astounding £377 million (about $601 million) under budget, costing only £8.9 billion ($14.2 billion) against a budgeted £9.3 billion ($14.8 billion). This delivery of value for money was unprecedented in government history. Mandarins wept and scientists began to search for evidence of parallel universes. The sports minister, Hugh Robertson, happily took credit: "We were lucky to have good project management skills, and a lot of time, attention, and effort has gone into this."

Less noted was the fact that the original budget agreed upon at the time of London's bid in 2005 was £2.3 billion ($3.7 billion). This was then revised upward to £9.3 billion in 2007 when it became clear that the Games were going to cost significantly more. Against the original budget, the Olympics Games came in £6.6 billion ($10.5 billion) over budget, or almost four times more than what had originally been envisaged. That was also likely unprecedented in government history. The mandarins wept again and the scientists returned parallel universes to the theoretical side of the cosmological divide.

The trouble is, we all expect the future to be better in every way—another positive illusion at work. Research indicates the effect is more pronounced for our perception of time. There is always more time tomorrow than today, and even more time the week after. This is the flip side of our temporal myopia. We forget all the little things that fill up our days. In the future, all manners of transport will run on time and the weather will always be accommodating. My three-year-old son will go to bed promptly at 7:00 P.M. and sleep through the night till 6:30 A.M. There will be no illnesses and no domestic emergencies. There will be no hangovers and no wasted afternoons surfing the Web.

We have already noted this mirage of ample time when it comes to our inability to save for retirement and when governments momentarily debate how long it will take to deal with longer-term structural issues. For both, there is always plenty of time tomorrow. In the realm of speculation, this also explains why we always believe we have more time to ride the wave before it crashes. The bursting of a bubble is always a while off until the day it arrives.

THE RISK OF UNCERTAINTY

Much of our discussion to date has been couched in terms of uncertainty. The more common term *risk* has rarely been mentioned. This is because there is a distinction between the two that is little appreciated.

Uncertainty is the scary unknown out there. Risk is a quantitative and mathematical proxy we construct to alleviate its terror. We have a strong aversion to uncertainty, and the notion of risk convinces us that we understand enough to part the curtains and take more informed chances.

The difference may be easily understood through a game of chance. We have before us two jars with twelve balls each. One jar contains half red balls and half white balls, while the other contains one-third yellow balls and two-thirds red balls.

Jar 1: $1/2$ red balls $1/2$ white balls
Jar 2: $2/3$ red balls $1/3$ yellow balls

I now draw a ball at random from each jar. I will give you $3 if I draw two red balls. You will give me $1 if I draw any other combination.

These are simple probabilities. You can consult the laws of probability and work out your expected winnings. You may choose to take the wager if you feel the gamble is attractive enough. Maybe $3 isn't enough, but $10 would certainly do the trick and is worth a quick flutter. You understand the odds and you are quietly confident that you will beat the house on this one over time.

The first ball is drawn and it is red. Your eyes light up.

The second follows but it is yellow. You are disappointed and hand over $1 as agreed.

Shall we go again?

You consult your internal probabilities. There is one less red ball in the first jar, so your chances of drawing red are slightly lower. There is one less yellow ball in the second jar, so your chances of drawing red are higher there.

Why not? It's still an attractive bet and you reckon you're probably more likely to win now.

Unfortunately, I made a mistake and quickly inform you of this. The first jar is correct, but I brought someone else's jar as the second one by accident. I think it contains some red balls, I know it definitely contains yellow balls, and I'm not sure but it may contain another unknown color.

Do you still want to play?

I suspect not. The second is an example of Knightian uncertainty, where the outcomes are unknown. Internally, this is terrifying and something you want to avoid at all costs. You could end up losing a lot of money and be completely deluded into thinking that there is even a slim hope of winning.

This is the game of chance we play every day with the future. The distinctions perhaps are not as stark, but the probability distributions and risk metrics we overlay onto our spectrum of outcomes are always an approximation—sometimes just a guess—and invariably underestimated. If we cannot overlay anything, then we prefer to avoid the speculation altogether. The clearest exposition of this internal struggle was perhaps that given inadvertently by Donald Rumsfeld in his now (in)famous utterance about known unknowns and unknown unknowns at a NATO press conference in June 2002 during the run-up to the Iraq invasion.

As a result, our focus is always on taking those risks we believe we understand. If events conspire against us and show that we were wrong, the result is paralysis. In the event of a financial crisis, unknown unknowns come to the fore, long-held beliefs about "fundamentals" begin to fall by the wayside, and we start to notice risks we had thought were too insignificant or remote to matter. These are the proverbial "black swans": the risk of war, systemic contagion, inconsistency in policy making, and so on. What probability could be possibly applied to any of these, short of throwing darts in the dark?

A contrasting aversion comes through in our differing attitudes to gains and losses. Researchers have long noted that investors tend to sell winning positions too early and hold on to losing positions for far too long. It is important to note first that these are pluses and minuses on the performance of our hypothesized models—internal or quantitative—about the world. The former are confirmations and, therefore, harvested quickly. We played the game, we won, we want to run while the going's good. Losses expose flaws in the model. Emotionally, they wound us far more than equivalent gains bring us pleasure, and therefore we are keen to avoid them. However, rather than admitting that we or our models might be wrong, we instead set ourselves to the task of explaining why it hasn't worked so well in this case and tweaking matters for next time. It is an attempt to protect the ego and our illusions of certainty and control.

Every investor has a losing position he or she held till it was too late. In every crisis, there are large losses sustained, as many refuse to believe the paradigm may have changed. The annals of finance are littered with traders and individuals who tried hard through honest and dishonest means to recover or hide their losses. We have met some already on this journey—Chuck Prince at Citigroup, the Roman emperor Tiberius, the future Pope Callistus, the twice-over Japanese billionaire Dr. Sasaki. Others have entered today's cultural memory: the debacle of Enron, Jon Corzine at MF Global, Long-Term Capital Management, Nick Leeson's escapades at Barings, and so on.

Some take matters to extremes. In 1984, Toshihide Iguchi, a trader at Daiwa Bank's offices in New York, suffered a small ($200,000) loss trading U.S. Treasury bills. Mortified by his failure and terrified of losing his job, he began to place some unauthorized trades to rectify it. Eleven years, thirty thousand trades, and $1.1 billion of losses later, a dejected and exhausted Iguchi finally threw in the towel and sent a confession to his bosses. For his belated honesty, he received four years in prison and a $2.6 million fine. For its own subsequent attempts to cover up as well as its inability to understand and manage human behavior, Daiwa Bank was fined $1.3 billion—later reduced to $340 million on appeal—and ordered to end all U.S. operations. It was an ignominious retreat back into isolation for a Japanese bank once ranked in the top twenty globally.

THE SPECULATOR REVEALED

Just as our memories do, we have cantered episodically through our biases in these pages. The experiments detailed are more than just a WTF look at the "wild and wacky world" of human behavior. They allow us to delve into the psyche of the speculator hiding within us all and paint a portrait of the man or woman who always strives to move purposefully through the world, reaches for something more, and gets caught up in recurrent manias in age after age.

We are likely to overestimate our ability to make money, discount the risks along the way, be driven on in our euphoria or panic by the words of those around us, and be so hell bent on counting the dollars that we miss the big chest-thumping gorilla in the room till it's far too late.

Akin to the three monkeys of proverb, we see no uncertainty, we tolerate no uncertainty, and we speak not of uncertainty. We extrapolate the past and focus myopically on an immediate future that is always brighter. We put our faith in models that repaint the uncertain world in shades of known probabilities, giving us illusions of control and explanatory depth. Often these work well enough that we blinker ourselves to their shortcomings, and where they don't, we calibrate and complicate till they do. And if it all goes wrong, everything is always much clearer in hindsight and, luckily, is also everyone else's fault, ensuring the self-preservation of our egos and talents for the next boom and bust.

There is one final important bias we have neglected to mention, and that is our inability to stand still. Growth is a strong psychological impetus, and if we are not growing in our lives in some way, we feel trapped and miserable. That is why we talk about being stuck in a rut at work, worry about relationships becoming stale, and obsess so much about growth in the economy, in corporate earnings, and in our incomes. A big pay raise today will make us happy but then become part of the status quo tomorrow. No change in our earnings or wealth the year after will make us despondent again, irrespective of where we are. We run on this hedonic treadmill all our lives, and our proximity to others as we jostle for status only accentuates any lack of progress and the associated negative emotions.

The table below summarizes the biases we have mentioned to date and a few others for good measure.

Cognitive bias	Definition	Example
Aversion to ambiguity	Fear of uncertainty; prefer to take only risks that can be quantified or analyzed.	The example of Knightian uncertainty given earlier—our game of two jars—is a case in point. Most investors focus far more on quantifiable financial risks, for example, gains and losses in their investments, rather than qualitative risks, for example, counterparty default, political risks, and so on. Also linked to procrastination.
Cognitive dissonance	When faced with conflicting beliefs or ideas, we unconsciously try to reconcile the conflict and regain our equilibrium though distortion.	The classic case is of someone faced with facts that contradict his or her beliefs. Rather than rejecting the erroneous beliefs, the person instead seeks reasons to reject the dissonant facts. Hence, proponents of efficient markets reject bubbles on the grounds that values never decouple from "fundamentals," while *Homo economicus* endures despite Darwinian limitations. On a more everyday level, the reformed smoker may sneak the odd cigarette and justify it on the grounds that the occasional slip is unlikely to jeopardize his or her health in the same way as smoking regularly.
Confirmation	The propensity to emphasize information that supports your preconceived opinions. Closely related to cognitive dissonance.	We seek out information that confirms our beliefs—a proactive form of preventing dissonance from arising in the first place. The battle lines between proponents of free markets and those of greater regulation are one example. Was our most recent crisis caused by the provision of too much easy money by central banks, by distortions of regulation, or by the greed of bankers? Similarly, people always interpret political events, such as the Iraq war, the state of the economy, health care, etc., and so on, in line with their political beliefs.

Cognitive bias	Definition	Example
Extrapolation	Placing more weight on recent events to predict future outcomes.	Both in Rome in A.D. 33 as well as in the opening decade of the twenty-first century, everyone was convinced that property prices were a one-way trade. Additionally, in recent years, people were typically happy to stretch to take on a large mortgage and buy their home, even though the payments stretched out for many years. This is because again, based on recent evidence, they anticipated having a job in the future and earning more with every passing year.
Framing	The interpretation of events in different ways depending on the context and your emotional state.	You are likely to be skeptical of a car being sold to you by a used car salesman but not of one being sold to you by a friend. This principle of trust is the most relevant example of framing when it comes to financial crises.
Hedonic	Needing to demonstrate growth and accumulate always.	The urban plague of keeping up with the Joneses. There is a competitive tinge to this, as already noted. However, there is also the fact that we quickly accept and adapt to the new status quo till it becomes limiting as well. Thus, your expenses seem to always keep pace with (and sometimes surpass) your income—a bigger house, nicer car, fancier school, and so on, all to reflect that enhanced status.
Hindsight	The perfect clarity of knowing the facts after they occurred and falsely believing they could have been anticipated.	Notable examples include economists and astrologers throughout recorded history. Much of regulation is also founded on this premise. For example, the last five years have seen some thirty thousand pages of new financial regulation emerge, much of it focused on detail and informed by recent events.

Cognitive bias	Definition	Example
Illusion of control	The overestimation of your ability to control your environment or external events.	All investors who make money attribute it to skill rather than luck. They also uniformly believe that you can always exit a stock at the top of the market before others. Equally, policy makers invariably believe they can control the complex flows of money through an economy. The twin decades of the 1990s and 2000s arguably gave central bankers a similar false impression, as the world went through a burst of synchronized growth.
Illusion of explanation	Believing erroneously that your arguments or models explain events. Closely related to the illusion of control.	Millions of dollars and an equal amount of man-hours are spent every year mining the vast tracts of financial data in an effort to identify spurious transient patterns and predict the future path of GDP, stock markets, inflation, interest rates, and so on. Another example is the ever-complex Ptolemaic theory of astronomy in ancient times, which had the earth at the center of the universe, but was still very successful at predicting the movements of the stars.
Loss/gain asymmetry	Giving a greater weight to losses over gains.	We seek to avoid losses where we can, which is why financial manias do not end gradually but rather in a panic as people attempt en masse to avoid losses. When losses emerge, we suddenly become more open to taking risks to get back to profit. Individual investors are far more likely to hang on to a losing stock position, because they feel it is possible somehow to trade or wait their way back into profit. Many fraudsters, such as Bernie Madoff, started off with small losses and then invented increasingly grandiose lies in an effort to cover these up.

Cognitive bias	Definition	Example
Overconfidence	Overestimating the likelihood of positive outcomes and the accuracy of your predictions.	Entrepreneurs are the perennial example, as they always believe they can succeed despite the clear statistical odds against them. Within the realm of financial speculation, during the dot-com boom of the late 1990s, people talked of hypergrowth as companies suddenly had potentially global client bases. During the 1980s, Japanese domination of the world led to similarly rosy predictions. Both led to dizzyingly high valuations that made little sense in hindsight, particularly given the serendipities required for them to come true.
Temporal myopia	The ability to discount the distant future far more than the immediate future.	The brevity of financial memory is well noted throughout. We also like to make money preferably in the here and now. If I offered to buy your car and pay you either $1,000 tomorrow or $2,000 in five years, you are more likely to settle for the former. Another example is finding it hard to stick to a diet when you're overweight. That doughnut today is a lot more alluring than the six-pack you might have in a couple of years if you skipped eating it.

In an entrepreneur, all the above are virtues that grow economies, pioneer advances, and take the human race forward. In a speculator, these are all vices that cause financial contagion, strain societies, and periodically take us to the edge of imagined disaster.

In truth, these are just cognitive biases common to every human. They are present in all of us to varying degrees, giving us the distinction of personalities. The above delineation is merely the result of taking snapshots of the same person at different points in time and in different environments. If we focus on the speculator here, it is only because we have chosen to examine those occasions when the system proves fallible and understand why.

When we mingle with our fellow creatures, these simple proclivities soon become hostage to an increasingly complex environment, sometimes transmuting into collective delusions and abdications of judgment. Nowhere is this truer than in the world of finance.

CHAPTER 7

The Greater Fools:
A Personal Interlude

A wealth of information creates a poverty of attention.

—HERBERT SIMON (1916–2001)

Most men, including those at ease with problems of the greatest complexity, can seldom accept even the simplest and most obvious truth if it be such as would oblige them to admit the falsity of conclusions which they have delighted in explaining to colleagues, which they have proudly taught to others, and which they have woven, thread by thread, into the fabric of their lives.

—LEO TOLSTOY (1828–1910)

IT was mid-July 2004.

I had recently joined a small fund that invested its assets into a range of hedge funds—a hedge fund of funds, in industry parlance. My research for my Ph.D. in cosmology had come to an end, and I had quickly realized that getting a tenured position anywhere decent required a nomadic decade of international wandering. Suddenly, the surprisingly high proportion of bachelors among all the male physicists I knew made a lot more sense. It was celibacy enforced by incentive rather than intent. Meanwhile, my friends from university (and my girlfriend) had all gone on to work on Wall Street and in the City of London. They had money, office ski trips to Switzerland, coolness, and status. I was a perpetual student, with an allowance, a fascinating line in cosmological small talk, and notions of a higher altruism.[1] Upon more careful consideration, I became the latest brain drain statistic, fleeing science for money.[2]

My first boss in this new world, a brusque social animal whose chief skills resided in his ability to read a Rolodex and update our performance database, had given me a hedge fund to analyze for the portfolio. An innovative proprietary arbitrage strategy, with an amazing track record and great pedigree—well worth a look, he said. I opened up the summary and began to read.

KINGATE GLOBAL FUND, LTD. CLASS B

KINGATE MANAGEMENT LTD

STRATEGY	ASSET CLASS	COUNTRY
ARBITRAGE	Equity	U.S.A.

INVESTMENT OBJECTIVE

The principal investment objective of Kingate Global Fund Ltd. Class B (the "Company") is to achieve capital appreciation of its assets through the utilization of nontraditional options trading strategies: split strike conversion.

INVESTMENT PHILOSOPHY

The Fund's investment objective is long term capital appreciation with low volatility. The Fund currently has investments with only one Investment Manager and while it does not foresee adding additional managers at this point, the Fund does reserve the right to do so.

The Company has established an account for Kingate at an Investment Securities, a registered broker-dealer in New York, who utilizes a strategy described as "split strike conversion" and invests exclusively in the United States.

The "Investment Manager" and "registered broker-dealer" in question was Bernard L. Madoff Investment Securities LLC, owned and run by one Bernie Madoff.

THE BABELFISH IS ALIVE AND WELL IN FINANCE

Bernie Madoff created and oversaw the largest Ponzi scheme in history, which defrauded clients of $65 billion over a period of some twenty-five years. His returns had been astonishing. The Kingate document I was looking at was a year old then but showed that he had made over 13 percent a year with a volatility of less than 3 percent since 1995. To put it in perspective, his performance was about five times better than that of the global stock indices over that period and about the same as the general hedge fund index but with less than a third of the risk.

Bernie's pedigree was impeccable. He had founded his firm in the 1960s and grown it into one of the leading market makers on Wall Street. He had helped set up the NASDAQ and served as its nonexecutive chairman. His clients included large foundations, funds, endowments, and well-known individuals, all of whom had extrapolated the above into an abdication of judgment. Many could tell you happily that he had been probably their best investment for the last five, ten, fifteen years. The Kingate Fund alone had some $2.4 billion invested with him.

Madoff's modus operandi had always been never to take any money directly. Rather, funds such as Kingate that allocated exclusively to him through a personal managed account functioned as feeders, funneling ever-increasing amounts of money into the Ponzi scheme and reaping rich fees in the process. They provided a necessary veneer of credibility—the Kingate analysis came from the Hedge Alternative Advisory Group at HSBC Republic and the auditors were Coopers and Lybrand, soon to form part of PriceWaterhouseCoopers, one of the "Big Four" accountancy firms. In later years, as I saw materials from other Madoff feeders, the descriptions of the strategy, analysis, and accouterments of respectability were so similar as to be almost cut-and-paste jobs across the industry.

Meanwhile, the money came in, went straight into a Chase Manhattan bank account, and stayed there. Fictitious trades were created and executed, and profits (invariably) were entered into fictitious accounts. If anyone wanted any money back, Bernie simply withdrew it from the bank and wired it over. Luckily, not many people ever did, as his performance was so stellar. Instead, they further increased their allocations to his fund, as the ease of access to their money confirmed their view that Bernie was a reliable cash machine.

Madoff's reputation, pedigree, and returns combined in the alchemy of investor psychology to make him gold. He was also aloof, rarely meeting people and refusing to even attend conference calls. Investing in Bernie was a privilege extended only to the chosen few. He was one of those mysterious all-important hedge fund titans whose returns needed no explanation. Michael Bienes, who ran one of the feeder funds, noted in the aftermath of Madoff's downfall, "Doubt Bernie Madoff? Doubt Bernie? No . . . You can doubt God, but you don't doubt Bernie."

The Ponzi scheme only fell apart following the credit crunch in 2008 as cash-strapped investors desperate for liquidity went to the only functioning ATM many of them knew: Bernie Madoff. But $7 billion of redemption requests later, Bernie threw his hands up in the air and the authorities promptly handcuffed them on the way down.

In hindsight, the signs were very clear to everyone. He was secretive and refused to discuss his strategies. The numbers were too good to be true. The investment advisory business ran alongside a major broker-dealer—a clear conflict of interests. The auditor was an unheard-of firm, Friehling & Horowitz, with precisely three employees and only one accountant. All the entities involved in the strategy were directly or indirectly controlled by Madoff. Trades were always provided to investors in paper format only, with no access to electronic files. The days on which the trades were reported to have occurred did not show the required liquidity to execute the strategy. Madoff only registered with the Securities and Exchange Commission in 2006, despite having run his strategy for many years previously.

Shortly after Madoff's fall I was e-mailed a long list of these red flags by a hedge fund manager who proudly proclaimed that he had already positioned himself to respond to the new challenges faced by the hedge fund industry. He clearly didn't do a very good job—he was fined $5 million by the Financial Services Authority in the United Kingdom and banned for life in May 2012 for concealing losses of $390 million from his investors in late 2008.

Back in July 2004, I did not have the hindsight of experience, only the rube's privilege of no preconceptions. A simple analysis showed that the numbers were remarkably distributed. The losing months over all this period from March 1995 onward could be counted on the fingers of one hand and the first one ever had occurred in January 2002, eighty-two months into the fund's history. The probability of his being so good was so remote that you felt perhaps you were doing Bernie a disservice by suggesting that such laws of nature might apply. Bernie was the Babelfish of finance.[3]

I've learned over the years that good due diligence comes down to asking three fundamental questions about fund managers: How do they make money? Why do they make money? How do they avoid losing the money they've made?

In Bernie's case, the answers were: I don't understand. He must be blessed by God. What's "losing money"?

Mystified, I turned in my preliminary analysis, albeit with more words and numbers than above. I clearly had a lot to learn about hedge funds.

Talking to others, I got a slightly different perspective. Some thought he was engaging in insider trading, and many couldn't understand how the strategy was so profitable for him. Certainly, when they tried to back-solve from the rare materials they could lay their hands on and juice their own, more mediocre returns hadn't worked for any of them.

Too risk-averse, we passed on the opportunity and never made it to the next, more detailed round of due diligence. Would we have picked up on the red flags everyone identified afterward? I'd like to hope so, but it's hard to say. Back then, if anyone took a fund forward, the second round was seen as largely confirmatory, as opposed to a genuine investigation. Many managers were big swinging dicks, their strategies were black boxes, and you were buying into the club.[4] The gut reaction for most investors was to just say yes and pony up, because you wanted those returns, particularly in the aftermath of the punishing equity losses caused by the bursting of the dot-com bubble.

A FOOL AND OTHERS' MONEY

A few months later, in early 2005, Madoff turned up again on my desk. This time it was an existing investor who brought him to us. We had formed close links with some of the Swiss private banks, and one of our contacts had decided that now was the time to spread his wings and take the next step in his career.

For an investment banker, the next step was invariably to join or found a hedge fund. For a private banker, the next step was invariably to join or found a hedge fund of funds.

François was an impeccably groomed Swiss-French private banker from Geneva who had risen to the upper echelons of his bank and was now gently bumping his head against the glass ceiling that separated employment from equity.[5] Like many of his breed, he had superb marketing skills that were steeped in charm and flattery as well as a long list of clients with deep pockets and an appetite for hedge funds. However, he also lacked the actual skills that one needed to play in the financial markets—trading, stock picking, fundamental analysis, and so on.

Unfortunately, he also lacked the basic knowledge to analyze and choose the best hedge funds. The industry had evolved past the days when you simply bought the same hedge funds that all your other friends owned and recommended. Some rudimentary quantitative analysis and an attempt to construct sensible portfolios had begun to creep in as the industry professionalized, though they were still decades behind the rest of finance.

François was not mathematically minded, but he did have a salesman's eye. The great demand at the time was ever more diversification, as investors worried about having too much risk in any one fund. Spotting an opportunity, François decided he was going to do a different and innovative fund. First, he would have only two funds—our humble fund of funds, returning some 8–9 percent a year, and a Madoff feeder fund. Our fund provided diversification, and the remarkable Madoff fund made money in every financial circumstance. Second, he would leverage the fund up by about two times by going to some of his banking contacts. That would boost returns—after our fees, the bankers' fees, and his own fees—to a level that would keep his clients happy.

As it turned out, the model worked extremely well. Madoff only ever went up, we muddled along, and the leverage ensured that François was able to return 10–12 percent annually to his investors. It was, on one hand, depressing. He made more than we did in good months and was usually up in months when we were down, which was hard to explain to our investors. However, as his fund began to find a receptive audience, we also benefited as his assets grew and more allocations flowed our way. Inevitably, tensions began to emerge toward the end of 2006 and in 2007 as our performance continued to lag Madoff's. François began to complain that perhaps the allocation to us was too large, given our poorer risk-reward ratio.

I left shortly afterward to join another fund. I don't know what became of François, but I know that the Madoff feeder he chose is in liquidation and litigation. I know that my old firm was bought by another firm in 2009 and no longer exists. I know that leverage is rarer and a lot more expensive these days.

And if I do my quick analysis again today, as Madoff went to zero in 2008 the leverage would have begun to work backward, the losses would have been magnified, and François's fund would have seen its assets rapidly diminish to zero—another victim of innovation and the hopeful optimism of extrapolation.

FONZIE JUMPED THE SHARK

In 1969, Edgar de Picciotto founded Union Bancaire Privée (UBP) and over the next four decades grew it into one of the largest private banks in Switzerland. At the start of 2008, assets under management stood at 135 million Swiss francs ($119 billion). Almost half of this lay in the hedge fund of funds division, where UBP had established itself as one of the best and largest players in the world. Its teams worked hard, played hard, and, most important of all, made money year in and year out.

A few years ago, their research team had gone to see Madoff. After careful due diligence, they overwhelmingly rejected him. There were too many unanswered questions, too many rumors, and too many areas of doubt. It was the right and prudent course of action to take.

However, in finance, you do not get paid for being right. You get paid for making money—every year. In the world of hedge funds, that translates into an annual management fee on the assets you manage and an annual performance fee, which is a proportion of the gains you made over the year. Your temporal myopia is set to a very short-term setting.

As Madoff continued to deliver stunning numbers and investors began to query why UBP was missing out, senior management began to fret. Eager clients could go to Madoff through other players. It could be the thin end of the wedge that could soon lead to whole accounts being moved to other funds of funds. Additionally, these were valuable fees that UBP were missing out on, particularly given the growing demand for Madoff.

Ever since the Roman emperor Vespasian's father became the first to provide them with private banking services, the Swiss have had a long-standing reputation for being careful and cautious investors. They are far more focused on the preservation and careful nurturing of wealth than on risky speculation. But care and caution can easily be put aside if the returns are attractive enough and the perceived risk low enough. Madoff had produced excellent returns with low volatility for at least a decade. As his track record grew, investors globally—including the Swiss—found it easier and easier to extrapolate those returns out into the infinite future and assume that Bernie had mastered uncertainty. In this grown-up version of the two jars game, why miss out?

In haste, UBP made a fateful decision. It decided to set up its own Madoff feeder. Now, it could keep its clients, provide the services it prided itself on, and make some money doing it all. The sales team made their pitches and nearly $1 billion flowed into the feeder.

Bosses were delighted. Strategically, the bank was making great strides in providing comprehensive investment solutions for its clients. Teams and expertise were built up in larger traditional areas such as equities and fixed income. New offices were leased in 2007 in St. James's Square in London to accommodate all the extra staff, both current and anticipated. It was rumored that UBP had paid a record £140 (about $220) per square foot.

But in late 2008, as the Madoff scandal erupted, UBP found itself badly exposed as investors collectively felt angered. They were not alone, but unfortunately, UBP became a public face of the collective failure of the fund of funds industry to look under the veil of trust and judge if Madoff was too good to be true. Years of careful messaging, trust, and reputation all went down the drain. Many funds of funds were punished severely for their lapses in the aftermath, as it exposed the flimsiness of their due diligence and the naive optimism of their assumptions. This, coupled with poor performance in 2008, led the whole industry to implode and it was forced into a careful, soul-searching introspection that is still far from over.

The anticipated growth now went into reverse as clients fled en masse. Over the next three years, the hedge fund of funds industry shrank in size from $1.25 trillion to $910 billion. UBP's assets fell by more than half to just 65 billion Swiss francs (about $70 billion).[6] Today, UBP continues to painstakingly rebuild trust and acquire new businesses in an effort to turn the ship around. It's a much harder journey.

In many ways, investors were just relearning the lessons imparted by Ivar Kreuger, the infamous Match King, who had a mansion in every major city in the 1920s and swindled his investors out of billions during the Great Depression. Madoff was but the latest incarnation to demonstrate our ability to cherry-pick and interpret facts to suit our views of the world. He showed the pitfalls of blind optimism and willful extrapolation, particularly when we are jostling to get to the front of the crowd. Most of all, it was a powerful demonstration of our recurring ability to reduce the complexity of finance into simple mental shortcuts that engineer manias when enough of us get together.

The most important shortcut: trust.

CHAPTER 8

The Madding Crowd:
Crowds, Confirmation, and Confidence

The greater part of men are much too exhausted and enervated by their struggle with want to be able to engage in a new and severe contest with error. Satisfied if they themselves can escape from the hard labor of thought, they willingly abandon to others the guardianship of their thoughts.

—FRIEDRICH SCHILLER (1759–1805)

Human beings are quite simple. The apparent complexity of our behavior over time is largely a reflection of the complexity of the environment in which we find ourselves.

—HERBERT SIMON (1916–2001)

ARGUMENTS are like corsets. We manipulate the body of facts till it fits our purpose. And more often than not, we take a helping hand from others.

> Bellingham, a trim little city of 34,000 people in northwest Washington, danced like a man beset by bees. Someone was cracking auto windshields; in one short week, 1,500 of them plus assorted store and house windows had been pock-marked. The magnitude of the shenanigan—whole parking lots splattered at a time—dwarfed the known destructive capacity of the small boy armed with a slingshot, the normal suspect in such cases.

Thus began a short write-up in the April 12, 1954, issue of *Life* magazine, the faithful paparazzo of American history and society in the twentieth century. Accompanying the item was a two-page photo spread showing cracked windshields, baffled security guards peering out over a store parking lot where a dozen windshields had fallen victim under their watchful eye, windshields covered with protective layers of plywood or newspaper, and contraptions purporting to solve the mystery. This tragic episode was one of the week's key events, second only to the newly declassified images of the United States' first-ever detonation of a hydrogen bomb.

The story had begun innocuously a few weeks earlier. In mid-March, some angry residents complained to Bellingham police that tiny holes and pits had suddenly appeared in their car windshields. A vandal armed with a shotgun or BB gun was suspected. The number of reported cases grew daily and rapidly till there were dozens of complaints. As police grew increasingly frustrated, the story assumed sufficient importance to make its debut in the local papers on March 23.

Within the next week, the complaints numbered in the hundreds. It was also no longer just Bellingham's problem. Nearby towns began to find damage to their windshields. As the affected area widened southward, worried police set up roadblocks and carefully screened every car in the hope of apprehending the mysterious vandals. It was to no avail.

> With ghastly regularity the tiny pellets flew through the air and glass cracked, sometimes as cars were in motion. But drivers failed to see how the deed was done. The phantom respected no one. Jagged, ugly scars appeared in the windshields of police cars. Angry businessmen stalked one another, but glass kept breaking.
>
> In calmer moments the police, who made tests of presumed weapons, were sure that someone using a scatter air gun from a moving car was the culprit. But as the damage mounted, Chief Bill Breuer was close to muttering officially a word that unofficially was on everyone's lips—ghosts.

On April 13, mysterious pits and dings were found in two cars at the high-security Whidbey Island Naval Air Station. Marines conducted a meticulous five-hour search but found nothing. Doubts now began to emerge that vandals were the cause. As some two thousand new reports piled in that day, these doubts were reinforced.

The following evening, the epidemic hit Seattle. Isolated reports soon gave way to a flood. Local papers such as the *Seattle Times* found space for little else on their front pages. Within twenty-four hours, pit marks had been reported on more than three thousand vehicles, including those in parking lots and used car lots.

Hoodlums were now ruled out. Police said they had found "black or gray particles resembling soot or graphite . . . [on] windshields and car hoods." A growing number of people, including several policemen, claimed that they "had seen bubbles form within the glass, expand to the bursting point and leave the glass pitted, much as though it had been hit by a B-B or shotgun pellet."

Thirty law enforcement officials from across Washington gathered together on April 15 and agreed that "some form of ash" was responsible. Some hypothesized that radioactive fallout from the recent H-bomb tests might be responsible. Experts and the media provided additional suspects for the lineup: cosmic rays, a new million-watt radio transmitter installed by the navy, shifts in the earth's magnetic field, or perhaps eggs laid by sand fleas in the glass that were now hatching.

In desperation, the mayor of Seattle, Allan Pomeroy, telegraphed both the state's governor and President Dwight D. Eisenhower that evening asking that "appropriate federal (and state) agencies be instructed to cooperate with local authorities on [an] emergency basis." An interdisciplinary team of scientists was quickly assembled by the authorities and set to work.

The next day, the number of new reports in Seattle dramatically dropped to forty-six. Suspicions lingered, but the first skeptics now began to emerge. Sergeant Max Allison of the Seattle police crime laboratory declared that the damage reports were composed of "5 percent hoodlumism, and 95 percent public hysteria." He also noted that new cars were undamaged and the only observable pitting had been found on cars that had been driven on the roads.

The scientists concurred. It was most likely "the result of normal driving conditions in which small objects strike the windshields of cars."

The pits, dings, and other defects that constituted the epidemic had always been there. It was just that people had always looked through windshields and never at them. As rumors and then media reports spread, more began looking at their windshields and noticed for the first time all the defects accumulated through a lifetime of driving. But they couldn't see the obvious. Instead, they were bound by the easier ties of gossip and society. They were blinded by myopia and the fallacy of their memories. They chose not to think and imagined patterns where none existed. Once minds were set, a complexity of false explanations abounded, fed by an environment composed of one part Cold War paranoia and one part new curiosity about the mysterious universe.[1] All of this was reinforced at every stage by confident pronouncements from those they trusted: friends and neighbors; the media and its touted experts; and authority figures at every level from the police to the mayor to the governor. In short, it was a mass delusion, pricked only when the harsh light of scientific reason sifted through all the words, emotions, and biases to unearth the bare facts.

And the mysterious black "ash"? That turned out to be the fine dust formed by the incomplete burning of coal. Again, it had been a part of the local atmosphere for many years, but no one had ever paid attention until now.

As with many manias, once begun, the Seattle windshield epidemic gave way only grudgingly to skepticism and growing evidence that the dings had always been with us. The will to ignore fact and nurture the illusion of knowledge is a hard flood to stem. On April 17, three counties in Ohio fell victim to the mysterious marauders. By the end, reports had come in from as far afield as Los Angeles, Chicago, and Canada before the notorious Seattle windshield epidemic of 1954 was finally consigned to the microfiche archives of history. As Charles Mackay had noted sagely over a century earlier, "Men, it has been well said, think in herds. . . . [They] go mad in herds, while they only recover their senses slowly, and one by one."

WHOM DO YOU TRUST?

I talked earlier about the influence of the environment in bounding our rationality, and the mental shortcuts that we all use every day to make decisions. By far the largest part of our environment is other people, who subtly bias our decision making. The most common shortcut we all take is to believe the word of others and trust them.

In the complex world we inhabit, trust becomes a necessary survival mechanism to navigate the everyday world and make quick decisions. Careful analysis often takes too long, and the information needed may not be immediately to hand. At the same time, the excess of information confronting us on a daily basis needs to be carefully filtered if we are not to be overwhelmed and our decision making paralyzed.[2] There are too many variables, too many iterations, too many uncertainties—in short, too much complexity in our environment—for our brains to take in.

Other people provide valuable algorithms for making timely sense of all this complexity. As a child, you look to parents and friends for guidance in keeping yourself alive on a daily basis. As an adult, you consult friends, strangers, so-called gurus, the Internet, self-help books, and the like to inform your views of the world and direct your actions in a timely manner. All over the world, humans place abstract faith in social groups, impersonal institutions, and distant dogmas.

The people and ideas that resonate with our emotions and support our preconceptions become initial receptacles of our trust. Thereafter, like all heuristics, they grow or shrink in our estimation based on performance and reliability. Over time, this accumulated mental baggage contextualizes all of our dealings. If you recall the marshmallow experiment from chapter 6, the children more likely to eat the marshmallow immediately were those who trusted the experimenter less, based on his or her failed promises. Their temporal myopia was in part a reasoned response, not merely greed or a desire for short-term gratification.

The original marshmallow experiment spawned a self-help industry when researchers looked at the children years on and found that the ability to resist temptation was linked to higher achievement and better social skills in later life. The assumption drawn was that the ability to delay gratification and display self-control was the key to success. That may be true in a sterile theoretical vacuum. In the real world, what it also represented was the distinction between having a stable world that incubated trust versus an uncertain environment that challenged your trust regularly.

One group of children relied increasingly on the happy heuristic called trust and used it to filter the world to their advantage in later years. The second group increasingly questioned this haphazard heuristic called trust and found themselves struggling to handle a complex world on their own in later years. After seeing the stark effects of perceived reliability on the results, Celeste Kidd, one of the researchers in the updated study, noted, "If you are used to getting things taken away from you, not waiting is the rational choice."

Trust is one of the fundamental underpinnings of society. Without it, society would rarely extend beyond a handful of people. Every decision would need to be carefully measured. Every person would become a stranger whose intentions need to be examined. Without trust, our horizons would become limited—looking farther into the future needs the aid of other eyes, and extending beyond our threshold needs the efforts of other people.

Introduce trust into the picture and the possibilities expand. We become interlinked through mutual pacts of cooperation. Our dizzying array of choices now simplifies into a manageable few, filtered through the words and actions of others. Trust between and among groups of people leads to the division and delegation of tasks. What we call society begins to emerge. The belief underlying the decision to trust is we all benefit. A bridge begins to be built from the certain shores of today, reaching across the uncertain tomorrows to some distant shore that houses the goals this new society has chosen for itself.

As more people enter the fold and society becomes more complex, trust expands to encompass religions, institutions, scientific theories, and other abstractions in addition to the people we actually know. At every stage, complexity is counterbalanced to make the world simpler for each of us and still accessible within the bounds of our rationality.

We have many flavors of what we term trust. At one extreme, there is blind faith—in a god, in a leader or in a parent. At the other end, there is an unconscious acceptance of reliance on other people and institutions, that some may term the "fabric" of society—whether it is relying on a taxi driver to get to you from A to B unharmed, on a police officer to come to your aid when you are mugged, or on the Java-powered cogs of some online retail store to process the purchase of that last-minute anniversary gift in time. Somewhere between, there is an emphasis on reliability and competency—in a handyman, a manufacturer, an employee, or a fund manager. All of this is a continuum of mobility. A fund manager, for example, can rapidly ascend the heights of blind faith—deserved or not—if performance is good and sustained for a long enough time. Warren Buffett is one case in point. Bernie Madoff is another.

However, as history and our experience bear testament, the descent can be vicious. The more you trust someone, the greater your emotional investiture and the more you rely on that person to sustain your worldview as well as your status therein. That is why we punish so brutally those we trust most, if that trust is betrayed. The loss of such a deep trust leaves a vacuum that threatens to destabilize the equilibrium we have created. It breaches our illusions of control and certainty. Many once-charismatic leaders have ended up on the metaphorical and sometimes real funeral pyre as a result. Empires and nations have descended into obscurity through losing the trust of their people, as we have already seen with the Roman Empire. The harsh treatment meted to loved ones who betray our blind faith through infidelity, abuse, deception, or otherwise is another familiar example throughout history.[3]

It is only natural that money and trust are closely intertwined. Like trust, money also helps to bond a society. It records our status relative to our peers, and acts a psychological buffer of resources squirreled away against the vagaries of uncertainty. Both necessitate trust that the coin or notes will be honored at some future date. Similarly, any exchange of goods or services requires trust; as noted earlier, the word *credit* itself is derived from the Latin *credere*, "to believe." This is all intrinsic to the confidence we need in business partners, counterparties, and institutions if we are to take a speculative leap into what is otherwise uncertain. Only then can a boom build. The weakening or loss of that selfsame trust destroys confidence and sows the seeds of panic.

FROM EGO TO GESTALT

A few years ago, I had the (mis)fortune of designing and building the regulatory capital model for a large financial institution. For the uninitiated, a regulatory capital model is how banks, insurers, and others steeped in the economic infrastructure assess their risk and quantify how much additional money needs to be held in reserve to cover the losses from adverse events. As with all models, a hodgepodge of assumptions and "expert judgments" goes into this careful exercise, all overseen by numerous levels of internal and external bureaucracy.

The model took months of work, painstaking analysis, and protracted agonizing over ifs and buts. The model was presented to senior management, who responded with generic praise, as the complexity and numbing sweep of numbers on display provided them with the emotional reassurance that all the risks had truly been captured.

Afterward, one of the senior board members pulled me aside. "Love the model," he said, "but here's a word of advice. Make sure that our numbers are the same as everyone else's. You don't want to stray too far from the pack."

It took a while to appreciate the wisdom of what he said. When you've spent so much time building something, the emotional investment means that egos can be easily bruised, particularly when the inference is that it is where you stand in relation to your peers that really matters, not the rigorous assessment and estimation of your risks.

But with the benefit of experience, I can see he was right. His judgment was driven by what he had seen.

No one really understands complexity. So they rely on the aforementioned shortcuts. Regulators cannot use blind trust, and assessing every firm from first principles is an intensive and cumbersome process. So they substitute rules of thumb and benchmarking instead. This allows them to reduce their universe to a few outliers, which they can then scrutinize in greater detail.

No financial institution wants to be an outlier. A closer look inevitably means more questions and a higher probability that it might be judged to be inadequately assessing its risk. This translates into having to hold more capital, along with a higher risk that returns to shareholders might be lower. That means lower compensation and greater job insecurity for its executives and employees.

Further, if an institution is an outlier, it probably has a very different profile from its peers in terms of the risks being taken and the assets being bought. There may be good reasons for this. A cautious man does not want to be holding the same assets as everyone else. In a downturn, that differentiation from your peers can be a powerful protection as everyone runs for the exits. But there is a problem. If the institution in question should ever get into trouble, the chances of it being bailed out are slim. The virtuous heterodox approach to investments means that any problems are likely not shared with the wider industry. The institution is not the harbinger of some systemic risk that could crash the system. There is actually a greater risk to the business's longevity.

Therefore, the dictum becomes simple: don't stick your head above the parapet. Run with the pack. There is safety in numbers, especially in the bad times. It may not be the rational human's choice, but it is the sensible human's choice.

There are two points to be noted here. First, the notion of inclusivity is powerful and can create perverse economic incentives that encourage crowding. Second, having decided to go with the flow, we are very good at convincing ourselves that there are strong rational bases for what is essentially a primal urge to belong and conform.

Both are evident in the behavior of people in the financial markets. A friend of mine—let's call him Fred—manages a book of investments for a large European institution. He has a simple compensation structure. He is paid a base salary of $250,000 and has an annual bonus that is between 20 percent and 28 percent of his base. If his performance is okay, he gets 20 percent. If he shoots the lights out, he gets 28 percent. If he tries to shoot the lights out and screws up, he gets fired.

If you were in his shoes, how would you invest?

Fred only gives money to the largest managers because they are deemed to offer the lowest risk. He also knows that most of his peers also invest with these people, which gives him comfort. If anything goes wrong, he can always point to the fact that everyone else was invested in them also. Any loss becomes due to some exogenous event out of Fred's control, rather than any endogenous failure. Any gains are due to his having called the markets right.

Fred is unlikely to ever achieve his 28 percent bonus. His performance will largely be in line with that of his peers. The managers he chooses to invest with are also subject to the same pressures. Most will slavishly follow an index and try to ensure that their performance deviates only in some limited fashion from it. This is why so many investment managers fail to outperform the financial markets. But, bound together in this pack, Fred will get his 20 percent bonus most years and his investment managers will collect the management fees on their substantial assets every year. Everyone is happy and gets to make money over an extended period. Fred's employer also benefits by staying in the pack. Any reputational risk from trying something new is muted, and regulators and stakeholders are unlikely to single you out.

If you were to ever question Fred, he would deny all of this. He isn't lying. Fred genuinely believes he is making good investment decisions. His investment process has simple flags for perceived risks, such as fund size, length of track record, and so on.[4] He has a mountain of research pouring into his inbox most days to help him understand the complex world and make the right decisions. But much of this is just Fred's confirmation bias at work. Through it all, *ceteris paribus*, everything is carefully filtered to cherry-pick those nuggets that support his preconceived worldview and shelter his career.

The same dynamics can be seen at work in the most recent crisis. Some of the biggest losers in Bear Stearns and Lehman Brothers were their own employees, who had put large parts of their net worth and bonuses into company stock. Contrary to popular portrayal, few were sharks looking for unsuspecting victims among the wider populace. Rather, they actually believed that they understood and were managing the risk of their products. It was this fervent belief that drove them to sometimes even borrow more so that they could ride the "smart money."

Even when things began to unravel in 2007, few of these bankers believed they could be wrong. The firm where I worked at the time invested in a new fund that was acquiring positions in "distressed" leveraged loans. A fall of about 10 percent in the values of these distressed loans was seen to be an unprecedented opportunity to buy good paper at compelling "once-in-a-lifetime" valuations. Keen to maximize the opportunity (and fees), the fund also had borrowed money from a large U.S. bank to leverage its position (and gains) up by four times. The fund was run by an old friend of one of the senior management of my then employer with a great track record. Trust was masquerading for analysis.

In more benign times, the old friend might have been proved right. But they misread the gravity of the situation badly and were far too early in investing. Within a year, values collapsed and the leverage within the portfolio meant that every loss was magnified. The fund fell to about 1 percent of its original value. The bank that was providing the leverage seized control. Investors were eventually told that if they were lucky, they could recover up to 70 percent of their investment after a long, painful process lasting an as yet unknown number of years. Yet I distinctly recall that when the question of purchasing the position in question went to the investment committee, its two biggest proponents happily proclaimed that they were so confident of the strategy and its success that they would gladly take their bonus in the form of stakes in the fund. Luckily for them, the committee didn't take them up on the offer, and their mortgages rested a little easier in future years.

THE REINFORCEMENT OF OTHERS

The above experiences are not born of stupidity, even if they sometimes lead to unfortunate outcomes. Rather, they are born of the knowledge that the herd is a good place to be most of the time. Capitalism as a philosophy is founded on the principle that our selfish desires unconsciously meld into group behaviors that benefit us all. Similarly, democracy is deemed to be a superior political system because it empowers a majority to drive social and political change to the betterment of everyone. In general, both have served us well. The pace of technological change, the reduction in poverty, the rise in literacy, the rapid and sustained economic growth around the world in the last two centuries—all are strong points in evidence.

Trust is key to the functioning of both capitalism and democracy. It acts as an economic and social lubricant, engendering cooperation. By funneling us down into a narrow set of agreed outcomes, it creates focus and allows us to leverage off each other, creating powerful forces that can drive progress and growth. By involving more of us, it shares the benefits of growth, mitigating envy and imparting cohesion—all vital for sustaining society.

But embracing the benefits of groupthink, of course, means that we are also exposed to its flaws. Our individual temporal myopia and propensity to extrapolate the recent past means that collectively, we can come to rely on others to the exclusion of analysis as the good times roll. Growth and prosperity are seen as a given and the risks flickering on the horizon become too distant to be spotted, save for a few Cassandras. Our capacity to cope with uncertainty and unexpected outcomes diminishes, leaving us badly prepared and disbelieving when things go wrong.

Additionally, trust is not evenly distributed throughout a society but resides in varying degrees in individuals that we interact with or see at a distance. And this inevitably leads to social influences that can change our herd mentality for better—or for worse. We are drawn to people who display conviction and strong opinions. They help to conquer the fear of uncertainty that resides deep within. Additionally, as we see others drawn to the decisive among us, it also appeals to our need to belong and we find ourselves—consciously or unconsciously—trusting these strong voices and parroting their opinions as our own.

In extremis, large swaths of society can fall in thrall to what is effectively a gigantic pyramid scheme. History identifies the top of the scheme as statesmen, leaders, prophets, and gurus of various inclinations. By buying into these cults of personality, people feel their own status is further enhanced and that they are somehow a part of grander events. As more and more acolytes fall into place, a herd mentality can easily build and blind trust eventually trumps fact. Note that in the Seattle windshield epidemic, the overlapping influences of politicians, trusted authority figures such as the police, and so-called experts convinced entire populations that their own cars were a threat.

Finance is no exception to these dynamics. Growing economies make politicians, policy makers, and regulators look good. They make people feel happier and wealthier. Continued growth inevitably leads to a surge of pundits and investment gods, who hold the answer to more riches. In short, a boom enhances everyone's status. There is, therefore, little rationale to look for problems. Being a naysayer often only makes you an irritation and a party pooper. There is always social pressure to conform to the overarching mood of those around you.

As we saw earlier, what is remarkable about financial crises is that so many miss the signs that are all too obvious in hindsight. Complexity is one part of the answer. The search for belonging and status is the other part. This also casts light on why our faith in experts and leaders can so often be misplaced. In the corporate world and in finance, there are some who have reached the top of the tree through sheer ability. But these are rare. The vast majority are proof of the Peter principle, namely, that everyone rises to their natural level of incompetence. Ill-prepared to effectively handle the responsibilities they have been given, many are there thanks to their mastery of the arts of flattery and politicking, with a dash of serendipity. We also often make a specious association of longevity of employment with seniority and ability.

As an example, the vast majority of CEOs within investment banks and asset management firms come from areas that generate the highest revenues, be it trading or corporate finance. For most people, high revenue equals intelligence. The human propensity toward extrapolation means that their specific success is assumed to qualify them for the broader and more challenging stage of running a whole business.

The "front office" roles within a bank are always the most sought after, so intelligence is also taken as a given. Certainly, personal experience tells me that the best and most ambitious at Cambridge University during my time there—as with any top university these days—almost universally applied to work in the financial sector. The crowing order of job offers was clear:

- Corporate finance, trading and private equity: dealmakers and moneymakers, with the highest potential for fortune as well as name-dropping.[5]
- Quant finance and structuring: fewer social skills but still wanted to make money, though they rarely got to do "iconic" deals that might grant them the odd mention in the middle pages of the *Financial Times*. They would have their moment in the sun in later years.
- Other front office jobs in investment banking (e.g., fixed income, sales, emerging markets): get a foot in the door and make some

decent money. If you were lucky, one of these areas would "break out" during your time.

- Middle office jobs (e.g., risk management, derivative pricing, model validation): work here and hope to transition to the front office down the line. A classic example of hope over experience, as it almost never happened.
- Asset management (larger is better): regarded as second tier to investment banks and alternatives, with lower bonuses and kudos all around.
- Accountancy: the lowest rung of the ladder. Little money and no respect from your peers, though you could always try to cross over into finance later in your career.
- Avoid small investment firms, back office functions such as IT, and regulators like the plague. These were seen as dead ends.

Once you're in, the rest of your career is determined less by merit and more by your ability to play politics. As one of my first employers told me, the golden rule in finance is to always "manage your managers." Many finance professionals get culled within the first couple of years, and the best of those who survive usually move on after the first few years in an effort to jump rungs on a slippery career ladder. No one wants to hang around in a firm for more than three to five years at most, else it might be perceived as career-harming. As another of my mentors noted, the trick is to continually fall forward. If you are particularly talented and loyal, and if you survive to senior level within an investment bank, the probability is high that you will leave in any case to set up your own hedge fund or private equity firm.

This same dynamic of jostling ambition juxtaposed alongside our spurious extrapolation is at play in most other spheres of human competition, whether it be politics or the corporate world. The end result is a self-selecting subset of potential experts and leaders, many of whom are talented at human interaction and mediocre otherwise. Nevertheless, having drifted up to the pinnacles of their respective organizations, they now become senior luminaries, whose intelligence is unquestioned and who are blindly trusted by many of us. Their success is proof of their ability in our minds, and their opinions now more easily mold ours. After all, books are rarely written about those who failed.

The correlation of criminal fraud with financial crisis also has its roots in the above. In every population like this one, there will be those who realize that flattery and words alone are an effective way of making your fortune and cementing your status. They arbitrage the mechanism of trust to gain people's confidence and create a faster route to success for themselves. Additionally, this route also saves them the awkward ego dynamics of admitting that they just may not be that good at making money. Madoff, for example, did trade in his early years. It's just that he wasn't very good at it. A few lies to cover early losses soon blossomed into the largest pyramid scheme in history.

In a boom, as more and more people look to make money, their critical senses are dulled by success, and the words of these experts resonate all the more. Those words provide comfort, stroke egos, and guide increasingly large numbers of us down some "guaranteed" path to success.

Fear, greed, and hope are all powerful motivators. In the scramble for primacy among our peers, what we call money is just an abacus of social status. It is no different from children in the playground playing with marbles in past decades and trading Pokémon cards today.

Part III
Money: The Catalyst Without

CHAPTER 9

Man, Meet Money:
The Bank Run

In reality, money, like numbers and law, is a category of thought.
—OSWALD SPENGLER (1880–1936)

Money often costs too much.
—RALPH WALDO EMERSON (1803–1882)

O N July 27, 2007, Ginko Financial—a small nondescript bank of insufficient standing to grace the broadsheets—suspended cash withdrawals abruptly. The head of the bank, Nicholas Portocarrero, made a statement announcing that Ginko's "reserve has been depleted" and that he had been forced into drastic measures because as soon as he replenished the reserve, people emptied it again almost immediately. "It's a bank run in essence," he concluded.

A per-day withdrawal cap was introduced, though that fell by the wayside within hours. The next day, allegations of fraud began to make the rounds, despite Ginko's claims that it had total deposits of $192 million. In retrospect, the interest rate of 61 percent promised on the account looked a bit too good to be true.

On July 30, the bank's main ATM started working again. Word spread like wildfire and a disorderly queue of people formed to withdraw the $10,000 they were allowed per day. In desperation, Ginko launched an unsuccessful IPO to raise further equity, with the aim of making an ambitious acquisition—a large stock exchange named AVIX.

It was a bailout by any other name. Tragically, the IPO raised just $25,000 and was abandoned shortly afterward. Portocarrero took to the airwaves to reassure investors, asking them to be patient. "We have both tangible and intangible assets we have spent money to acquire or develop," he said. "But they cannot simply be turned into cash for people to withdraw."

On August 6, Ginko offered depositors two choices: either continue to wait to get their funds back, or take the equivalent amount in perpetual bonds that might someday be tradable. Three days later, the choice was made for them. Ginko stopped taking deposits, froze all withdrawals, and converted all its deposits into perpetual bonds. Anybody who wanted to get cash was still free to ask but would get back only a fraction of their claim. Ginko had collapsed.

The chances are you will never have heard of Ginko Financial. The numbers above are paltry compared to some of the other numbers thrown about at the time. And there was a lot else going on in the real world for it to register on a crowded horizon.

And that is what makes Ginko remarkable.

This was a bank run not in the real world of flesh and paper but one in cyberspace. The numbers above were all virtual dollars—so-called Linden dollars—in an online world called Second Life. However, there were real losses. The Linden dollar, named after the company that owned Second Life, was convertible into U.S. dollars, and the nearly two hundred million Linden dollars lost equated to $750,000 in cold, hard cash.

MAN CREATES MONEY, AND MONEY INNOVATES MAN

Money is a testament to human ingenuity. Second Life is proof that we can create an economy and speculation out of thin air if we want—as long as there are other people to participate and transactions to be done. Ginko Financial proved that where you have people and where you have money, our natural biases and yearning for status will lead inevitably to speculation and its critical consequences.

Second Life began in 1999 as an extension of the obsession with virtual reality. Rather than a game, it was an online world with no limitations. People were free to interact with each other in any way they chose through their digital avatars. The complete lack of restrictions or some overarching purpose has meant that over the years, Second Life has become a bazaar of human interactions.

Second Life includes the inevitable multiplayer online games, teeming with residents fighting off dragons, saving the world, or exploring distant stars. But many also just talk to each other, forming friendships, having casual cyberflings, and even getting married. Some use it as an educational tool, hosting online classes. Others are artists, putting on exhibitions of abstract works of art or re-creating historical wonders in the digital sphere. Companies use it for virtual meetings and brainstorming sessions. There are churches, bars, theaters, little communities of scientists and philosophers, shops, political movements agitating for change, traveling entertainers, sporting events—in short, shades of everything that we see in the real world. There are even virtual embassies from countries such as Sweden and the Maldives.

The richness of this interaction has been aided by the creation of a virtual currency in the form of Linden dollars. The result is a virtual free market economy that allows goods and services to be bought and sold freely. All that is required is to match supply and demand as in any economy. If you have a service or good that someone wants and is willing to pay for, you have a transaction that makes you that little bit richer and enhances your status that little bit more.

Try something, anything—be a wandering minstrel, an escort, a dragon breeder, or an artist. Be an entrepreneur and you may make your fortune. But that is not all. In Second Life, you can also buy and trade virtual real estate. Linden Laboratories will sell you large plots—each corresponding to a physical server in our world—and you can then do what you want with the space: keep it digitally pristine, build your own fantasy, parcel it up and sell it on, rent plots out, build malls. It's all up to you.

But freedom becomes boring without purpose. If the only point of Second Life was to accumulate points and advance up the leaderboard, people would eventually reach a saturation point. The complexity described above would be hard to sustain if people dropped out of the digital ecosystem or ceased to interact frequently enough with it. Transactions are the lifeblood of an economy, and if these dry up, the economy begins to collapse—as we saw in ancient Rome.

But add in the capacity to convert Linden dollars to U.S. dollars and the whole equation is transformed. Those digital points now become a substitute for money in people's eyes. They become enhancers of status not just in Second Life but also in our nonvirtual lives. The complexity born of humble transactions now becomes sustainable and grows rapidly as more and more people flock to take part in this new meta-market, attracted by the gains of the few.

In December 2005, CNN's *Business 2.0* magazine published a piece entitled "The Virtual Rockefeller." It profiled Anshe Chung—the online avatar of one Ailin Graef, who had built up a huge real estate empire in Second Life and was now earning $150,000 per annum. A series of articles in other publications followed as others jumped on the news story. In November 2006, her company, Anshe Chung Studios, put out a press release stating that Anshe was the first person to become a "virtual" millionaire thanks to her online businesses. The rapid growth in her fortune would not have been entirely unrelated to the growing coverage that Second Life was now receiving.

Alongside, a financial industry had sprung up in Second Life. This was and is a natural consequence of commoditized exchange, that is, money. Before, we might have just bartered within Second Life, exchanging dragons for favors. But with the introduction of money, we have a common medium that we can both use to purchase other items or services of interest. It is a simple step from there to realizing that it is the accumulation of this new commodity that grants you convenience and societal advantages compared to your peers.

By creating money, we have at once and paradoxically both bound society closer and created tensions within it. Transactions are easier because we no longer require direct exchange. You may want one of my horses, but I may not want your weird sculptures. But as long as you can find someone to pay you money for one of your monstrosities, I am happy to take this new agnostic medium in exchange for my horse. I can now use this money to acquire any good or service I want—as long as I have enough. The paucity of items to barter is replaced with a multiplicity of goods and services to buy.

And therein lies the tension. I can now compare my pile of money to yours and determine where we rank against each other. In a world where more money implies a greater ability to interact with others and acquire goods or services, this confers on me some perceived higher social status than you. And though you may have a better education, be happier in life, or be a more Important Person for other reasons, I feel comforted by the competitive satisfaction of being better than you at something, namely, at getting rich.[1] Money may not buy you love, but it does get you a whole lot of attention. It gives you a greater variety of options and some perceived additional influence in your dealings with the world, which also appeals to our innate desire for greater certainty over future outcomes.

Once these genies of money were unleashed, Second Life's economy evolved the way any other economy does. Instead of making cute animations or providing a comforting shoulder, people realized that they could make money by facilitating and leveraging off others.

At the most basic level of this economic interaction, you can employ people to work for you, provide them with some certainty of income, and sell their services on at a premium, retaining the uncertain difference as profit for yourself. This is commerce. In Second Life, some users employed teams of fellow programmers to create new alluring digi-luxuries for sale, from furniture to clothes to transportation, or to set up sports events, wrestling promotions, and so on.

Or you can take it one step further. Promote the ambition of others by lending them money or assets. They will pay you a premium for the privilege, whether it be as a regular cash flow (yield) or as part share of the profits (equity). This is finance, and if you indulge in this, you are a rentier. You generate economic rents by allowing others to make productive use of your wealth, and thereby further enhance your dragon's hoard by leveraging off their efforts. In Second Life, these were the people who, for example, bought tracts of digital land and became large landowners, renting out idyllic beachside huts or nostalgic medieval castles. Some built large digital malls and rented out the space inside to companies—both virtual and those in the real world. Others set up banks to finance these hopeful land barons or stock exchanges, where companies could float and everyone could theoretically get a piece of the leveraged action.

MONEY SPECULATES

At the apex sits speculation. Working for yourself is too slow and organic a growth. And making good money through financing others, though faster, can often take time and dedication. For those of us with myopic leanings, both are agonizingly slow in building our pools of status. So we speculate to accumulate. You borrow money from a financier and launch a new business to tap into the consumers around you. If you have called their need and psychology right, you will see powerful growth and a fortune soon. This is entrepreneurship.

Or you look to play the changing emotions, the ebb and flow of business confidence, and the flows of money around you. You dart in and out of the markets, grabbing little economic rents and gains here and there, as you quickly buy and sell land, equities, goods, debt claims, and any other commodity that can feasibly be exchanged between two parties. This is arbitrage and trading, where the financial speculator resides.

The collective hopes, greed, and fears of these entrepreneurs and speculators form the financial markets. Their flitting emotions provide liquidity and grease the wheels of commerce, allowing individuals to tap into the power of the crowd. Sometimes, however, individuals become part of the crowd. Drawn by the strong-willed or fluent-tongued, they form themselves into powerful psychological waves we call manias that value assets far above their true worth. In time, these turn into panics and crash spectacularly, leaving broken balance sheets and egos in their wake.

Rampant speculation is the domain of an advanced and complex economy that has realized—even if subconsciously—that money is a fluid concept and can be manufactured readily in arbitrary quantities by the confluence of human ingenuity and mass belief. As long as there is confidence and trust, there is money and status to be minted.

The economy of Second Life eventually gave birth to speculators as well—including Ginko Financial. Linden Labs originally had converted Linden dollars to U.S. dollars at a fixed exchange rate through its own currency exchange, LindeX. However, the dynamics of supply and demand meant that the exchange rate soon began to fluctuate. Alternative currency exchanges sprang up, offering different rates and better delivery times.

Some people began to trade U.S. dollars for Linden dollars, taking advantage of the currency fluctuations and multiplicity of exchanges to generate incremental trading returns. However, turning incremental returns into meaningful gains requires large pools of money. It was a simple step for the first companies to be set up that took money in from investors to indulge in currency trading. These soon diversified into other areas of speculation such as land development and online gambling.

Some styled themselves as investment banks and began to offer savings accounts with attractive rates of interest in an attempt to capture pools of money for these speculations. Ginko Financial was simply one of the better-known of this breed. It began by offering interest rates of 100 percent per annum, though as demand for its deposits rose, this interest rate fell steadily until it was paying a more modest 40–60 percent just before its collapse.

As discussed earlier, crises occur when the system's capacity for dealing with shocks becomes increasingly limited, often because of leverage. In 2007, the proliferation of banks meant that plenty of money was being lent out for all manners of speculation. In other words, leverage was rife. The shock to the system was the decision by Linden Labs at the end of 2006 to ban online gambling within Second Life to avoid falling afoul of U.S. laws.

Unfortunately, Linden Labs had birthed a complex economy unbeknownst to itself. The unintended consequences of its business decision to manage its legal liability in the real world soon rippled through the virtual economy of Second Life. Ginko Financial and its peers found themselves deprived of a valuable source of revenue and thus of the ability to pay the promised high rates of interest. They began to drop rates further.

Some people grew impatient and moved their money elsewhere. Meanwhile, others ran to bank profits and deal with other monetary needs back in the real world. A few began to speculate on online bulletin boards about the financial health of these so-called banks. The withdrawals gathered pace, and in the absence of much tangible income, Ginko's reserves—the cash it held back for short-term liquidity needs—soon melted away. On July 27, 2007, it stopped honoring withdrawals. The rest of the story you already know.

In the aftermath of Ginko's collapse, Linden Labs awoke suddenly to the realities of regulation as an angry digital population demanded compensation. Five months later, in January 2008, it passed the buck and banned all banks that were not already regulated in the real world.

Despite the stutter, Second Life's economy has continued to motor along. The volume of transactions increases every year, though its growth rate is not as spectacular now in the absence of so much hot money. But dig a little deeper and you'll find plenty of people who will gladly sell you a piece of digital real estate at a knockdown price. For them, the financial stress and psychological trauma are still real.

Meanwhile, the seeds of future crisis are germinating beneath the surface. Linden Labs is a central, albeit digital, bank. The currency peg it has created for the Linden dollar is given some form of stability by its ability to create as many Linden dollars as required. This becomes little more than money printing if the new dollars are not matched by Linden's own revenues within Second Life from its customers. As the money supply in the system grows, the money finds new avenues for its expression and the economy booms in sympathy. If it ever reverses course or if people begin to value it less due to its pervasive availability, Second Life will find itself living through a second financial crisis.

In the real world, things are not so different.

CHAPTER 10

Life After Debt:
Credit and Currency

The study of money, above all other fields in economics, is one in
which complexity is used to disguise truth or to evade truth, not to
reveal it. The process by which banks create money is so simple
the mind is repelled.

—J. K. GALBRAITH (1908–2006)

Nothing sedates rationality like large doses of effortless money.

—WARREN BUFFETT (1930–)

A financial crisis may be said to last approximately twice the professional tenure of a credit officer, the hapless individual charged with
assessing borrowers and making loans at a bank. I had this statement on
good authority from a wise old man early in my career. Right after a financial crisis, the incumbent is fired, flayed, or generally kiboshed in some
unsavory way. The replacement is cautious and lends money prudently,
taking care to make sure the balance sheet is protected at all times.

Unfortunately, after seven years, the replacement is fired because he
isn't making enough money. His successor comes in, sees a pristine bank
balance sheet, and immediately begins to leverage up, lending more
money at looser standards to get profits up. He has no memory of what
happened a few years ago, as it was too far back and he wasn't in the job
then. All he knows are the recent good times, and his risk appetite is
calibrated by these.

Seven years later, the leverage comes back to haunt them as some
loans go sour. The balance sheet begins to blush, then bleed, and the bank
is forced to raise additional money, cut costs, ask for a bailout, and so on.

The guilty credit officer is fired, flayed, or kiboshed. A cautious replacement, eager to protect his career, comes in, and the cycle starts again.

A SOCIAL CONSTRUCT

Money and financial crises are inseparable. As discussed, money accentuates human biases. However, the nature of money and its counterpart,
debt, also increases the fragility of the economic system, creating booms
and busts even in the absence of overt human psychology.[1] At the heart of
every financial crisis lies too much money and, often, also debt.

This is because money is at its heart a social construct. Conventional
history has money evolving from bartering in a linear fashion much as
humans evolved from apes in the ubiquitous, erroneous graphic that
adorns countless classrooms. Fishermen trading seashells, farmers trading
cows, and bards trading songs soon gave way to the simple exchange of
coins and precious metals as a portable universal store of value and medium
of trade. Kings and states came in as facilitators and arbiters, adding
authority and catalyzing trust. Soon banks sprang up, taking little hoards
from individuals and lending them out repeatedly to a wider group,
thereby creating credit, and allowing the many to leverage off the fortunes
of a few. The complexity soon permeated through society, creating what
we term an economy and fueling the engines of trade that enriched us all.
The growing demands for more money and credit drove innovation, leading to more and more new species, from paper money to fiat currency to
bills of exchange to public markets in credit to derivatives today. Tomorrow,
who knows where we might yet evolve?

It's a nice story, with an inexorable tide of progress taking us from the
village-bound savages of yesterday to the suit-wearing educated masters of
today. Underlying this history is the observation that we all appear to enjoy
trading with one another from an early age (slaps and blows exchanged
giving way to marbles and trading cards as age mimics evolution). Money
is a utility in this narrative, a facilitator of human trade, that accelerated
growth and aided in the creation of modern society. It is an abstract, devoid
of social connotations, giving expression to every conceivable human good
or service that we see about us.

Despite the many grains of truth in the above, this fable does a
disservice to the real story. We now know that human evolution was not a
linear path. Instead, branches sprouted off the primal ape tree, exploring

new possibilities of evolution. Multiple species of human-like apes and ape-like humans coexisted alongside each other. Through a process of elimination, we finally ended up with *Homo sapiens*, that is, us.

The history of money is no less nuanced. It is not some natural phenomenon waiting to be birthed ex nihilo by the miraculous growth in our brain capacity. That is a misconception that emphasizes our superiority by belittling the past. Trade carried on between individuals, villages, and nations quite happily without any side feeling the imperative to create a portable medium of exchange. The first coins we know of were issued by a small Greek kingdom, Lydia, and the issuing authority—a certain King Croesus—earned a place in mythology as the richest king in the world. But Croesus was a small king, and all around him, far larger empires with far more extensive and sophisticated trade networks such as the Egyptians and the Asian kingdoms saw little need for small bits of metal (other than for adornment). Rather, the Egyptians wanted silk, dyes, and precious metals, while their counterparts in Asia wanted wheat. Long before coins, the earliest proto-currencies we know of were staples such as wheat and cattle that represented durable stores of sustenance and were of use to virtually everyone. Their influence still lingers in the use of terms such as shekels, grains, and non-metric units of weight.

Money retains its meaning through the social interactions that it encodes. The interplay of status, social conformity, and human behavior are key for money to exist. Without the trust born of these, no medium of exchange can exist. When two people trade, the use of any medium outside of goods or services being exchanged relies on trust. I cannot invent the Bob dollar and use it as a proxy in my interactions with the world. In the eyes of strangers (and even friends), it would lack credibility, and its potential acceptance by others would be even more suspect. Even when two nations trade, the money exchanged needs to be credible and convertible. That is why countries use U.S. dollars rather than their own currencies for many transactions, conferring trust and, therefore, reserve currency status on a trusted third party to stand behind it all. Where they choose to use something else, it is often more an expression of geopolitical power than trading convenience—consider the recent emergence of the renminbi as the underlying currency in some regional transactions.

Money as coin and paper exists only when lots of people accept it. That implies the presence of society and the overarching institutions it creates. In other words, it presupposes the existence of a dominant state that can influence the behavior of individuals. Historically, kings and nations had large armies that could extract taxes from citizens or tribute from vassals. However, a state consumes a lot of goods and there are inefficiencies in directly collecting what you need (e.g., weapons, wheat, and horses), notably a lack of control over the means and timetables of production.

People are also not specialized out of the box. In the absence of anything but limited exchange, self-sufficiency is the norm, not the exception. Only a foolhardy person would choose to specialize, as that way might lie starvation and death. Therefore, it serves the state to incentivize speculation by giving people portable stores of value in the form of metal trinkets and, later, paper that they can exchange among themselves and utilize to enhance the duration of their specialized existence. Once the state begins to collect these trinkets as taxes or tribute, you also drive individuals to find new ways of acquiring this new medium called money. They now work for others, exchange goods or services, and, in an important shift, begin to exchange money itself as a social hierarchy begins to emerge from these humble beginnings.

Money as a unit of account has a longer history than money as some medium of exchange, emanating again from relationships of power, though this time between individual debtors and creditors. The first written records were not love letters or divine commandments from on high, but rather long tables of debits and credits, and notes on the social morass about these. Ancient legal codes such as Hammurabi's Code, from the eighteenth century B.C., as noted earlier, prescribed the treatment of debt and debtors in extensive detail. Money did not birth credit, as the standard history would have it. It was very much the other way round. Money was not the natural evolution of bartering but rather the convenient medium of borrowing, lending, and taxing. Once money was discovered, trade became far richer and pregnant with new possibilities. But that was a consequence, not the cause.

OF SONS AND GOLD STARS

I have a three-year-old son, Maanas. A few months ago, in an effort to incentivize good habits and following the advice on numerous online parenting forums, I bought a reward chart. The idea is simple: We agree on a series of simple tasks like tidying up his room, going to the toilet, saying please and thank you all day long, finishing all his food, and so on. These are all noted on the reward chart, and every time he does one of these, he gets a gold star. Once he has collected enough gold stars, he gets a treat.

Initially, we had a deal whereby if he collected a total of ten stars in a week, he earned a choice of social outings, such as going to the zoo or to see dino bones. But our interaction soon became more complicated. Having quantified the impact of following social norms, this new medium soon began to ripen with potential.

Maanas and I began to debate what merited a gold star and what did not. Having a set number of gold stars to earn rewards meant that inevitably there were weeks when he did not achieve the required number of stars and was left disappointed. That created tensions between us and, over time, began to lessen the incentive created by the stars to "behave," as the rewards were occasional.

We evolved the reward system, therefore, to a new level. Whatever stars Maanas collected over the week could now be accumulated and exchanged for different rewards. It's good for teaching delayed gratification and promotes independence, I am assured. Three stars got him an hour of TV, five stars got him a chocolate or lollipop, ten stars earned him a trip to the British Museum, and so on. These were arbitrary rewards but, I hoped, ones that led him to realize that there were advantages to sustaining good behavior. Bad behavior inevitably had its own consequences through the lack of treats and, if terrible enough, sanctions such as the dreaded naughty corner.[2]

We have now created a currency that encapsulates within it the to-ing and fro-ing, the cajoling and scolding, the promise of reward and the threat of punishment found in human interactions. Within this limited universe, I can already see evidence of other complications and emergent phenomena that remind me of the monetary dilemmas we face in the grander theaters of society and economy.

Sometimes we may have a family trip already planned, such as the vacation we took to New York a few weeks ago. The trip had been long in the making, though Maanas never knew that. In an effort to get him to be super good, I told him that if he collected thirty stars, we would go on a plane, he would get a chocolate *and* a lollipop, and we'd all enjoy a *reee-aally* long vacation.

A few days to go and we were still a distant twenty stars away from the finish line. That created a quandary. I had no intention of cancelling the trip to New York, but in the interests of good parenting, I could hardly pretend that the stars were irrelevant. If I let him go regardless, we risked breaking the credibility of our little currency and sowing what central bankers call moral hazard.

Two choices were open: I could start handing out stars for the smallest glimpse of good behavior, or I could tell him that we could go but that he needed to make up any remaining stars once we were back. Both avenues were fraught with difficulties.

Offering more stars cheapens their value in his eyes over time. I have a limitless supply of stars in any case—I can always go out and buy another packet if needed. He can now collect twenty, thirty, forty stars easily in a week. Every "thank you," every "please" gets him one. He is a clever kid. He will soon realize the new incentives and bend over backward to accommodate. There is a small fortune to be made. Extrapolation soon fills his thoughts with visions of Hansel and Gretel's cornucopia of sweets and the saccharine blare of Baby TV.

But in our little world, the supply of lollipops and TV time is limited, thanks to parental paranoia. My son may now need to pay me five stars rather than three for that half hour of *Charlie and Lola*, perhaps more. Prices have gone up and we have effectively created a little domestic inflation. The number of stars needed will only grow over time as we struggle to find a new balance. If this is left unchecked, I might well drown under a hyperinflationary ocean of gold stars when I open my wardrobe. I could always revert to the old methods of earning them—a whole day of "please" and "thank you" for a single star. That will allow me to maintain the old exchange rates, but its deflationary impact will create resentment as his hedonic urges kick in and he feels poorer.

The alternative is to allow him to go to New York and repay me the extra stars at a later date. That makes sense. The stars don't really have any meaning in and of themselves. They represent a unit of account for credit I extend to him for services of good behavior, and which he can trade for childhood essentials and luxuries. Because I am the authority figure, my ability to procure these as I want and give him the goods he desires in return means our little Swarup Star currency has considerable credibility, as it's backed by the Bank of Daddy.

However, lending him more of these stars for purchases, secured against future acts of behavior, changes our relationship subtly to an overt one of creditor and debtor. We now have leverage in our little household and an increased money supply. I have strict lending stand-ards (to avoid the aforementioned inflation). Being a generous soul, especially to my own spawn, there are also no rates of interest in the Swarup household. But having opened the spigots of credit, I will find them hard to turn them off again. The more I lend, the more risk I am taking on his future ability to be consistently well behaved and the greater the demands on him. Should I tell him that if he borrows ten stars, he will have to repay me with twelve? Do I just let him accumulate, realizing that we run the risk of borrowing ad infinitum and overreaching till the debt can never realistically be repaid? Our unequal status is also emphasized as the gulf grows, though, as with the banker who loans $100 million versus $100, the problem is very much mine. In the end, I may simply just have to write off the number of stars Maanas owes me and reset the counter to zero.

In practice, I have tried both methods with little consistency as I seek a stable equilibrium. Unfortunately, there doesn't appear to be one, and we have had minor crises of authority and confidence en route.

Now that there is a daughter joining the family, my mind boggles at the unknown complexity I may face in a couple of years. The children will have information asymmetries, with Maanas far more versed in the illogic of his central banker. They may evolve their own relationships of pseudo-money, exchanging favors and sweets and childish trinkets that each values differently—collaborating to leave me with even less control (and hair) than I already have.

I am birthing an entire economy in this house, and like Newton's dawning realization that his theory of gravity was solvable for two bodies but not when he introduced a third, I am fast learning that this may be completely insoluble.

FLAVORS OF MONEY AND CREDIT

Money evolves naturally, wherever people need a medium to keep account and signify status. Once birthed, the complexity of exchange is impossible to unravel and quickly takes on a life of its own.

In this sense, money and credit are largely interchangeable, particularly as economies grow larger and more complex. Very often, what we call money is simply a set of debt claims on other people. The deposits we see in our checking accounts are actually the *mutuum* of Roman times— money given to others to lend out repeatedly and generate additional returns that are shared between us (in the form of interest) and them (as profits). What we get back are not the physical manifestations we handed over but a facsimile. Often, there is no physicality, only entries moved from one part of the balance sheet to another.

The actual base amount of money in a system may be very small, compared to the notional amount sloshing around bank accounts and the financial markets. As an example, the United States had a monetary base of about $3 trillion at the end of 2012. This was the sum total of all the coins, notes, and reserves that banks held with the Federal Reserve. By one measure known as M1, this represented the total money supply in the United States. Alongside this, there are different monetary aggregates that can be measured, which include the totals of various other forms of money that exist in the system. Thus, M2 is the sum total of coins and notes in circulation, current accounts, savings accounts, money market accounts and funds for individuals, and traveler's checks. This is $10 trillion. If we now add in all other certificates of deposit, Eurodollar deposits, repurchase agreements, commercial paper, and Treasury bills, the number balloons to $18 trillion. If we expand to all the credit that is out there in the

United States—corporate loans, mortgages, credit card debt, and so on—the number is $51 trillion. Throw in all the derivatives and you are looking at numbers that are an order of magnitude larger.

How is this possible? In short, through the miracle of fractional reserving. When you deposit money into a bank, it does not stay there. The notional numbers may still appear in your bank statement or on a computer screen, but the money has quickly been lent out to other people. This is how banks make money—by effectively borrowing money from you (what did you think that low interest rate they paid you was for?) and lending it out to other people at higher interest rates. That difference in interest rates in the middle is their revenue. Banks only have to retain a small amount of money on hand—regulatory capital, in financial parlance—in case any of the loans go sour or in case anyone asks for his or her money back.

If I deposit $1 million into a bank, the financial institution can lend most of that money out and keep only a small amount in reserve for potential losses. The money lent out soon appears as someone else's asset in another bank account. The bank overseeing that account can now take this new asset and lend it out again, keeping back, as before, a small amount to cover losses. The new amount lent out is now a deposit in a third account and can be lent out again, with a small proportion kept back for future losses. Before you know it, we have an infinity of loans and the money in the system is multiplied many times over, the multiple depending only on a combination of institutional prudence and regulatory prescription. One person's loan is another person's asset, and much of what people view as safe money in a bank account is actually a set of uncertain debt claims on other people.

But this is only the most basic level of the flows of money and credit in our economy. There are banks, and there are shadow banks—financial entities that may not be regulated but which also borrow and lend money in much the same way. Money market funds, for example, control large pools of money, which they use to purchase short-term pieces of debt that are backed by secured assets. Those loans are similarly multiplied as above. I can take any financial security you care to name and borrow money against it to use for my own ends. Before you know it, we have a highly leveraged system that can rapidly transmit booms and busts.

The confluence of all this money with the human need to seek out status is a heady mixture. As noted before, speculation needs money. As investors bid up the prices of commodities, property, gold, stocks, bonds, and other assets, it becomes easy to imagine ourselves rich. This nebulous creation of wealth means we can borrow more against this growing pot and funnel it into further investments, leading to an explosion of money and debt. Where there is insufficient money, people find ways of creating proxies. The history of finance is replete with innovations such as bonds, derivatives and asset-backed securities—all ways of leveraging upon leverage. And when the money flows reverse course and people want their money back, the cycle turns equally vicious and confidence crumbles as people realize that not all money is equal.

This provision of money is necessary for the economic growth we crave. In this sense, it is a public good. However, it is impossible to precisely adjust the supply of money to the uncertain needs of an economy. Rather, how much money courses through the veins of an economy depends far more on the demands of human nature. Like the Swarup Star, a single authority—a central bank in today's world—often controls the monetary base. However, the really large pools of money in any economy, ancient or modern, are created out of thin air and the catalyst of credit by lenders. These are much harder to control and lie at the heart of crises, because they represent a leveraging of human emotions and interactions.

Anything can be money, provided humans are there to lend it existence and value through the medium of trust. In prisons, cigarettes have evolved into a clichéd currency, and in parts of the United States, drugs are traded using boxes of Tide detergent rather than dollars. But money only has value as long as it is traded. Without transactions, value is meaningless.

The shifting sands of perception lead to their own bubbles. Bitcoin is a case in point. Akin to Second Life's Linden dollar, it is a digital currency created by the mysterious Satoshi Nakamoto, and limited to a maximum supply of twenty-one million units. New Bitcoins can be "mined" by solving increasingly complex mathematical problems till the digital wildcats finally unearth the last Bitcoin and the seam is exhausted. This is a game with not even a shred of physical backing. But that has not stopped it from becoming a store of value, or people from using real-world resources such as huge computer servers to solve the mathematical puzzles at the heart of Bitcoin and create virtual currency.

Since its advent in 2009, it has become a medium of exchange, first online and more recently, in real-world transactions. Its limited supply and perceived freedom from human interference in a recent era where trust in the traditional monetary system has been shaken are powerful assets that have transformed an interesting intellectual experiment into a living economy.

Notably, from January to April 2013, the exchange rate shot up from $13 per Bitcoin to $266 per Bitcoin. The Winklevoss twins—more famous for suing Mark Zuckerberg over the creation of Facebook—announced that they had purchased large amounts of Bitcoins as a store of value. Then, on April 13, the value collapsed from $266 down to $105 before jumping back up to $166, all in a single day. A confluence of participants all began to pull in the same direction and fed off each other into a frenzy of emotion. As doubt began to creep in, the process began to reverse rapidly.

Whether Bitcoin is a bubble is too early to tell. It does demonstrate, however, that anything can be a currency and that emotion can overload even the most mathematical of formulations.

Before we convince ourselves that this easy assumption of monetary guise is just a modern phenomenon, it's worth noting that medieval England used wooden sticks as a proxy for money for more than half a millennium and evolved a sophisticated system of government financing based around these humble instruments. The story of tallies is one of the clearest expositions of money's evolution as a unit of account for credit, legitimized by authority.

Notches were cut into a wooden stick known as a tally, with the sum of money in question being represented by the size of the notches in a simple abacus-like methodology. As the *Dialogue Concerning the Exchequer* laid it out in 1180:

> The incision, moreover, is made in this way. At the top, they put a
> thousand pounds, in such way that its notch has the thickness of
> the palm; a hundred pounds, of the thumb; twenty pounds, of the

ear; the notch of one pound, about that of a swelling grain of
barley; but that of a shilling, less; in such wise, nevertheless, that, a
space being cleared out by cutting, a moderate furrow shall be
made there; the penny is marked by the incision being made, but
no wood being cut away.

The tally would then be split down the middle with the creditor keeping
half (the stock) and the debtor keeping the other half (the foil). Both
parties had a record and forgery was prevented by the fact that the notches
on both halves of the stick had to line up perfectly. It was an elegant solution to the lack of coin in medieval Britain and the need for people to have
some medium of exchange.

The tally was granted widespread legitimacy by Henry I in 1100
when he decided to accept taxes only in the form of tallies. This gave
people confidence and created a natural demand for tallies. The need to
acquire the sticks for taxes soon meant that all sorts of transactions began
to be done using them.

Money is always in short supply. Successive kings soon found that
they could issue tallies in advance of taxes being paid, in order to raise
funds for emergencies, wars, and the other perennial concerns of nations.
These were sold at a discount to their face value, effectively representing
a rudimentary form of government bond that paid out the equivalent of
interest.

This innovation was a huge success, and it wasn't until seven centuries later, in 1826, that wooden tallies were finally removed from circulation.
By then, the volume of tallies had grown so large that in 1834 it was
decided to burn all these infernal antiquated sticks to make room.

Thousands of tallies were pushed into a furnace in the basement of
the Houses of Parliament. But the fire soon proved impossible to manage.
The furnace set fire to the paneling; this spread to the House of Commons,
and a day later all of Parliament had gone up in flames and been reduced
to a smoldering wreck.

It was not the first nor the last time that money had destroyed the
system, though it's unlikely that it had ever been so literal.

CHAPTER 11

All That Glitters:
Tulipmania

Dutch tulips from their beds
Flaunted their stately heads.
—JAMES MONTGOMERY (1771–1854)

It is when money looks like manna that we truly delight in it.
—J. B. PRIESTLEY (1894–1984)

WHEN money is plentiful, trust is cheap. The seeds of a future crisis find a fertile economic environment. A steady sprinkling of monetary rain aided by a mild clime of political and social stability means that ideas and innovation soon germinate. There is a reason why explosions of mass human creativity—medieval China, the Renaissance, the Industrial Revolution, and so on—are often associated with periods of wealth. An excess of money is like a flooding river, covering the land in a rich alluvium. Speculation in all its forms flourishes and prosperity emerges seemingly without effort.

Unfortunately, flowers and weeds often grow together. The seductive ease with which money begets money (and status) means that caution soon falls by the wayside. Our proclivity to extrapolate the recent past into the infinite future captures one mind, then another and another, till eventually large swaths of impressionable gray matter labor like galley slaves under the illusion of intelligence. Belief becomes blind, and credit permeates throughout the system. Malinvestments begin to appear as capital is leveraged and put to increasingly unproductive use.[1]

The most infamous and clichéd example is the obsession of the seventeenth-century Dutch population with the tulip, a pretty but common flower today, which you can buy a dozen of in my local supermarket for about $8. The Dutch "tulipmania" became so legendary that it has entered popular parlance as a description of irrational exuberance, where prices disconnect completely from the fundamentals. In other words, it is the archetypal bubble that many accounts erroneously refer to as the first recorded financial crisis.

Tulipmania was not irrational—a point sometimes erroneously used to argue that this was not a mania at all. But it is a potent reminder of how human bias and money can react together explosively and birth an alchemy of speculation in almost anything. The facts of the case are slightly different from the legend and all the more educational for it.

AN OBJECT OF DESIRE

Speculation always begins with something that promises to enhance our life. It may be an advance in productivity or technology, such as the advent of the railroad, the development of the Internet, or the promise of renewable energy. It may be the discovery of entirely new markets such as the Indies and the Americas. It may be something that advances the quality of life, such as a new drug, or a time- and labor-saving innovation such as the car. It may just be a shiny, sparkly distraction that whiles away leisure time and makes you feel happier on a primal level, often coupled with the knowledge that others envy your possession. Diamonds, trading cards, and iPhones are but some examples.

The tulip belonged to that last category. When Ogier Ghiselin de Busbecq, a Flemish diplomat, stumbled across the tulip in the Ottoman Empire in the late 1550s, he was astounded by its beauty and also by the fact that it appeared to be flowering in midwinter.[2]

> As we passed through these districts we were presented with large nosegays of flowers, the narcissus, the hyacinth, and the tulipan (as the Turks call this last). We were very much surprised to see them blooming in midwinter, a season which does not suit flowers at all. . . . The tulip has little or no smell; its recommendation is the variety and beauty of the coloring. The Turks are passionately fond of flowers, and though somewhat parsimonious in other matters, they do not hesitate to give several aspres [a currency unit] for a choice blossom.

Tulip bulbs—completely unlike anything in Europe—soon found their way over to the aristocratic gardens of Vienna and from there to all the corners of the Holy Roman Empire. The bloom's status as the preserve of the very rich is evidenced by the fact that the first recorded appearance of a tulip in Europe was in 1559 in the gardens of the Fugger family—then the richest family in all of Europe—in Augsburg, Germany.[3] By 1593, the tulip bulb had made its way over to Holland, thanks to Carolus Clusius, a noted botanist, who established one of the finest botanical gardens in Europe at Leiden. The plant was an instant hit with the Dutch, who found the tulip well suited to the harsher climes of their land.

Holland at the time was on the cusp of its golden age—a beneficiary of the largesse coursing through Europe thanks to the discovery of the New World and new trade routes to the Orient. Over the course of the sixteenth century, the money supply in Europe had grown rapidly as large amounts of gold and silver—the base currency of their day—flooded into Spain and Portugal from the Americas. From there, the money went down two routes. First, it led to an explosion of conflicts as Spain notably began to use the increased monies to wage wars against its neighbors and establish a religious and territorial hegemony.[4] Second, a lot of the money quickly leaked out in search of better opportunities elsewhere as the escalating conflicts threatened to confiscate these new found riches through either taxation or debasement.[5]

Holland was well placed to benefit. Its low-lying landscape made it prone to flooding and therefore had incubated a population that was far more urban. The country had become a major trading hub, and its commercial attraction was boosted further by a revolution in 1572 that established a republic and removed many of the imperial shackles that had restricted trade elsewhere. Alongside, the religious wars sweeping Europe led to a huge influx of Protestant immigrants into the country, who enhanced both the intellectual and commercial credentials of the state.

Much of the gold and silver flowed to Holland. There, it met a growing mass of humanity looking to gain and regain their share of this growing economic pie. The confluence of so much money and so many people led—as it so often does throughout history—to innovation. Amsterdam soon became the leading center of commerce in Europe, with a firm focus on shipping and international trade.

Meanwhile, a sophisticated financial industry sprang up to manage all the complexities of this new world and provide the leverage needed for growth. For the first time since ancient Rome, Europe saw the widespread reemergence of trade credit, marine insurance, and the creation of proto–stock markets, where the all-important economic activity of price discovery could take place. In other words, people could get information on the supply and demand dynamics of different goods. Previously, this had only been the limited private preserve of individual merchants. The wider dissemination of this information enabled a better judgment of business and investment risks, the generation of more trading opportunities as well as the rise of speculators, who sought to profit from fluctuations in these dynamics over time.

Inevitably, the pools of money also sought new ways to demonstrate their wealth and trumpet their growing status. Lavish properties, precious stones, and fine artwork were some of the expressions. The tulip became another. With its beauty, scarcity, Oriental origins, and imperial heritage, it was well placed to pander to inflating egos. Paintings such as Rembrandt's *Tulips* emphasized its desirability and scarcity.[6] Additionally, in the absence of their own gardens, a highly urban population turned to the humble window box—now a staple of urban habitats everywhere—as flowers became a particularly visible sign of status. With its rare midwinter blooms, a new luxury good was waiting in the wings to make its debut.

AN OBJECT OF SPECULATION

By the late 1590s, the tulip had crossed from Clusius's horticultural world into private hands. Some of those transmissions would have been lucrative sales. Others were thefts born of economic incentive. Regardless, the flower had crossed over, and its unique biology emphasized its scarcity. Tulip seeds took up to a dozen years to become flowering bulbs, and once there, they had limited life spans.[7]

Additionally, European gardens were infested with green peach aphids, a parasite that over time infected many tulip bulbs with the mosaic virus. The virus gains its name from its distinctive symptom—a breakdown of the monochromatic expression seen in normal tulips. Instead, the flowers born to infected bulbs display vivid streaks, scattershots, and fractals of

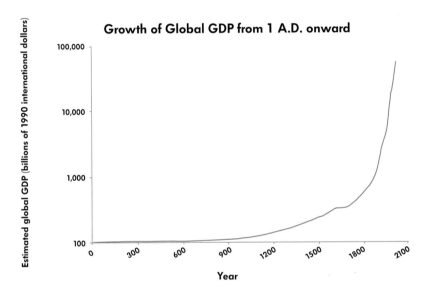

Plot of estimated global GDP over the last two millennia in millions of 1990 international dollars. (Angus Maddison, University of Groningen, the Netherlands; Image: Camdor Global)

Optical illusion created by a shadow on a checkerboard. (Image © 2013 by butisit, http://butisit.deviantart.com/art/Checker-shadow-illusion-263331875)

A head-on collision between two cars. (kadmy/123RF)

Panoramic view of the Milky Way from the Quiver Tree Forest near Keetmanshoop, Namibia. (© 2012 by Florian Breuer, www.floriansphotographs.blogspot.com)

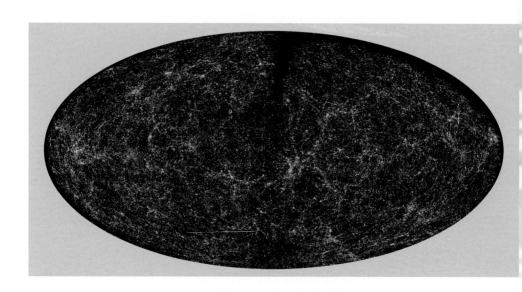

A panoramic view of the universe, containing over 1.6 million galaxies beyond the Milky Way, as observed by the Two Micron All-Sky Survey. The universe emerges as clumpy and uneven, with vast "voids" and "walls" forming a complex large-scale structure. (Atlas Image mosaic obtained as part of the Two Micron All-Sky Survey (2MASS), a joint project of the University of Massachusetts and the Infrared Processing and Analysis Center/California Institute of Technology, funded by the National Aeronautics and Space Administration and the National Science Foundation. 2MASS / T. H. Jarrett, J. Carpenter, & R. Hurt)

 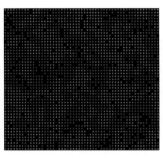 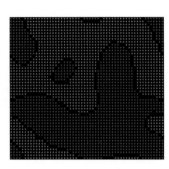

Schelling's evolution of segregation from simple individual biases. The three pictures represent from left to right: a) a starting random arrangement of red and green "individuals"; b) the evolution of distinct clusters, when individuals have a preference for at least one third of their neighbors being of a similar color; and c) the stark delineation into clear red and green zones, when individuals have a preference for at least two thirds of their neighbors being of a similar color. (Images produced using NetLogo Segregation model, Uri Wilensky, Center for Connected Learning and Computer-Based Modeling, Northwestern Institute on Complex Systems, Northwestern University, Evanston, IL, 1997 and 1999. http://ccl .northwestern.edu/netlogo/models/Segregation and http://ccl.northwestern.edu/netlogo/)

A map of the internet at the end of 2003. The dense patchwork of lines represents the links between different networks, with the colors representing different geographies. (Image courtesy of Barrett Lyon and the Opte Project)

intense color. Only pink, red, and purple tulips are affected, which enhances the visual appeal as, for example, white juxtaposes starkly against rich purple or yellow fire erupts against a red backdrop. The effect differs from flower to flower, in the same way that no two snowflakes are quite alike. But it still masks a disease. Infected bulbs produce fewer clones (and fewer offsets) and die sooner.

The Dutch had little knowledge of botany, so this all escaped them. Instead, all they saw were intensely beautiful and fragile variations that were much harder to cultivate. Their scarcity made them a far more potent symbol of wealth and status than the common varieties.

Where there is demand, speculators will always step in to provide supply. As noted earlier, the entrepreneur and financial speculator are just two facets of the same human nature.

The first—the entrepreneur—speculates by attempting to directly fill a need for a good or service today. In seventeenth-century Holland, a number of these quickly sprang up to develop the tulip industry. They cultivated bulbs, acted as merchants and exporters to meet growing demand in different places, and facilitated the trade in other roles, such as assessors and brokers, as the market grew in complexity.

The second—the financial speculator—speculates by greasing the wheels of that trade, through financing or liquidity provision. It is an arbitrage of time and of emotion, which takes a bet on the uncertain path of future supply and demand. Initially, collectors traded with each other as they came to see their tulips as stores of wealth to be crystallized for future profit or need. In time, merchants began to hoard bulbs to sell for higher future prices as they extrapolated out a growing demand and limited supply. As more and more people began to clamor for tulips and especially the rarer varieties, more speculators of both ilks joined the fray and the market grew.

The tulip was what economists call a Veblen good—demand grew all the more as the price increased. It was an aberration to the "normal" laws of supply and demand, which dictated that demand should fall as the price grew. But "normal" laws often ignore human emotion and social norms. Tulips had transitioned into symbols of status and stores of wealth, a pseudo-money status seen today in goods such as classic cars, fine art, and good wine. Thus, as the value grew, they became all the more desirable. They demonstrated wealth, and the demand meant that a tulip speculator knew that others existed who would likely pay more tomorrow.

VEBLEN GOODS AND RATIONAL JUSTIFICATIONS

Every speculative bubble has a Veblen good at its heart. This is natural within the bounds of human rationality. Such a good demonstrates a track record of growing in value and enhancing your wealth. It always seems to have willing buyers. Whether you believe in the worth of that good or not, somebody else does and will always buy it from you. There is liquidity and for the skeptical, there is always a greater fool out there. The risks are fewer and the rewards are greater. There is also status associated with it—both that born of increased wealth and the veneer of intelligence conferred by success.

The last is more often than not guesswork. Rational arguments can be made for almost all outcomes in every case. The only reason we choose one is because we are already biased to one outcome above others in our minds. Everything else is cherry-picked confirmation. If we are correct, then we are immediately visionaries. In hindsight, it is always easy to attribute intelligence as well as inevitability to the gamble—educated or otherwise.

I come from a family of lawyers. My sister is a lawyer. My parents are lawyers. Both my grandfathers and several generations before them were all lawyers. All of them were versed in the art of debate and can make an argument for any set of facts. Nearly a half century ago, my maternal grandfather—a particularly eminent lawyer in his time—arrived late at the Supreme Court in New Delhi, India, for an important case. He grabbed the legal brief quickly from his junior and immediately began to argue his case. I am told by those present it was a masterful argument, which painted a convincing picture as to why the defendant was completely and utterly guilty. As he finished thunderously and paused for dramatic effect, his agitated junior whispered quickly in his ear that he had just spent the last hour arguing against his client.

Your Honor, my grandfather continued seamlessly, I have just painted the prosecution's case for them and as you can see, it appears very black. I shall now demonstrate why they are completely and utterly wrong. He then proceeded to speak for another two hours.

He won the case. Good lawyers are also Veblen goods in their own right.

Tulip growers multiplied over the early part of the seventeenth century. The random impact of the mosaic virus meant that anyone could transform overnight into an expert gardener and ensure a fortune. Bulbs were dubbed "Admirals" and then "Generals" to demonstrate their relative worth. The most expensive on record was imperially christened the "Semper Augustus," as it came with rich purple streaks.

Merchants and traders multiplied alongside. The rarity of many tulips meant that there was an active trade in sourcing fine specimens as well as controlling the future supply. At a time when the ordinary Dutchman earned a few hundred guilders in a year, bulbs went for multiples of that. The Semper Augustus rose in value from 1,000 guilders per bulb in 1623 to 3,000 guilders per bulb in 1625. Accounts relate how the original owner held on to his bulbs for years as the price appreciated and even held veto rights over all future sales by future owners. Other, lesser blooms still fetched prices comparable to those of small houses.

Tulipmania was about to emerge.

A BRIEF ASIDE ON THE
FUNDAMENTALS OF BICYCLES

Bubbles and crises take time to gestate before they accelerate into frenzied action. Tulipmania was no exception. Yet some economists have pointed to the above dynamics to argue that it never did. A bubble is conventionally defined as a sharp deviation from fundamental valuations. The argument against a tulip bubble goes that at no stage did valuations deviate from what people might have rationally expected from the information at hand.

There is a fallacy of logic and language here. No bubble ever deviates from the "fundamentals" at the time. Naysayers are few and it is often judged a bubble in hindsight. But "fundamentals" is a loaded notion. It implies some absolute independent assessment when actually the very concept of fundamental value is determined only by the biases we bring to the valuation of an asset and our beliefs about what the market will pay. These are constantly changing with the environment we find ourselves in, the people we surround ourselves with, and the passage of time. The example of how to price Apple, given earlier, is a case in point.

In a bubble, people will justify the prices they are paying today and expecting in the future. This is human cognitive bias in its many flavors at

work. There are issues of status, conformity, groupthink, endless extrapolation, emotional confirmation, and a misplaced sense of superiority, to
name just a few.

The "fundamentals" justify a high valuation in these times. The
1890s saw a tremendous boom in bicycle shares in the Birmingham
stock exchange, not dissimilar to the dot-com boom a century later. The
bicycle was a technological marvel and a revolutionary new mode of
transport, made easy to ride on hard roads with the invention of the
pneumatic tire in 1887 by one John Boyd Dunlop. A bicycle was cheaper
to buy and maintain than horses, more durable (hypothetically), and
ideally suited for the narrower bounds of urban life. A growing affluent
society meant a deep pool of future buyers, making bicycles more than
just the latest playthings of the rich. Even women could ride one, so the
market was instantly twice as large. As cycling organizations grew in
number, they began to lobby for a network of good roads to connect
cities and rural communities. The first roads were built for commuters
and travelers on cycles, not in cars. With every success, the pool of
consumers and their need for a bicycle grew. Innovation followed—you
could buy a bike on credit and pay in installments over time. Predictions
of hypergrowth abounded.

As fortunes were made overnight, more and more people flocked to
marvel at these fundamentals and get a slice of this future growth. By
1895, as the bicycle transitioned into a statement of feminine independence, a wave of financiers—the venture capitalists of their day—hit the
markets in both the United States and Britain. Bicycle companies were
bought up, money borrowed to invest in increased production, balance
sheets enhanced with vast amounts of intangible goodwill and patents, and
the results floated on the stock exchange to great success as people ran to
load up on bicycle shares.

As all this growth permeated outward, a swath of businesses and
manufacturers focused on mail-order bicycles, bicycle parts, bicycle tires,
and so on developed rapidly. The Wright brothers—better known as the
inventors of the airplane—funded all their work through the profits of the
bike shop they set up in 1892. New areas such as the nascent magazine
industry and the advertising industry hitched a ride on the industry's

coattails to help bicycle companies spread the good word to consumers and fulfill all these promises. The "fundamentals" were sound.

After a boom, biases reset to new paradigms. Suddenly our definition of what constituted the "fundamentals" changes. Now, the high valuations justified previously are immediately suspect because in hindsight the "fundamentals" justified a lower valuation. In the case of the bicycles, cycles were made not just in Birmingham but also in the United States. Advances in manufacturing and competition soon drove prices down. Profit margins invariably fell. The future growth in the market did not necessarily translate into the same growth in profits—any extrapolation that thought profit margins could be maintained in the face of so much competition was naive. The bicycle companies themselves were overleveraged or spending vast amounts of money to fill a hypothetical growth vacuum that did not actually exist today. Vast orders were anticipated that may or may not have come through. The bicycle itself was a more durable innovation. Therefore, there was limited capacity for people to continually keep purchasing these in the same numbers year after year. A saturated market in time would have led to a fall in sales growth. As technology advanced, competitors inevitably emerged such as the automobile that wrested the roads away from the cyclists and proved far more of a convenience. Profit margins shrank and with them, the fortunes associated with future hypergrowth dissipated rapidly. The fundamentals born of hindsight clearly pointed to a bubble.

The only conclusion to be drawn from the above is that we are very good at justifying the outcomes we want. Any set of so-called fundamentals we choose is just an ex post expression of collective optimism or pessimism about what others will pay.[8] Booms are driven by the intoxicating mix of human bias and leverage. Where there is growth and money, people will pay any price for it. As more come to the mix, an avalanche effect is set in motion where rationality becomes increasingly bounded. Our decisions come to rely almost solely on shortcuts and a self-affirming groupthink rooted in blind trust. An illusion of stability means that whether you are an avid cyclist or merely a cynic hoping to arbitrage those who are, you implicitly assume that the dynamics you observe are unchanging. The fundamentals are deemed sound, and what observers have so often termed a mania is born.

AN OBJECT OF MANIA

In the 1620s, tulips were still the preserve of a few. The traders of these flowers were largely avid and affluent collectors who obsessively studied the variations produced each year and bid up the prices of whatever caught their collective fancy. Buying and selling took place when bulbs were in bloom, so that quality could be assessed and verified.

The high levels reached thus far were more a reflection of the growing prosperity and sense of wealth permeating Dutch society in this golden age. It was the same dynamic we observe today or during the late 1980s in Japan in the fine art world, where the auction prices of Van Goghs, Pollocks, and others reach new heights as wealth surges and seeks new expressions of status. Like offsets, these smaller bubbles bud off a larger bulb.

In 1602, the Dutch East India Company—or the VOC (Vereenigde Oost-Indische Compagnie), as it was known in Dutch—was set up to facilitate trade in spices with Asia and expand Dutch influence over this lucrative area of trade. Its charter laid the foundations for colonialism by granting it a monopoly over these regions, giving it the power to raise armies and conclude treaties, allowing it to establish trading colonies that were subject to Dutch law and thereby Dutch sovereignty, and authorizing it to wage war where necessary to further and protect its economic interests.[9]

The VOC was spectacularly successful. It soon established trading outposts with China, Japan, and parts of modern-day Indonesia—many of them exclusive monopolies on desirable goods such as nutmeg, cloves, porcelain, and silk. These all had a ready market in Europe, thanks to the large inflows of precious metals in Spain and Portugal. Alongside all this trade, a healthy business also developed in piracy, as Dutch ships intercepted and looted Spanish and Portuguese ships with regularity and supplemented the national income further.

The commercially minded Dutch made several innovations that further drove Europe's money to Holland. The VOC was a joint-stock company that distributed profits and would eventually pay dividends for two centuries. Other companies soon followed this example, and a stock market, where large numbers of people could fund and share in the profits of private enterprise, was born. In 1609, the Bank of Amsterdam was set up to ensure the quality of money in the Dutch system. Its independence from sovereign interference and the issuance of a standardized bank money that was far more resistant to counterfeiting and clipping made the bank popular across Europe. Anyone could deposit gold and silver and receive paper against it. Its credit notes soon traded at a small premium and began to be used in transactions widely.

Over the 1620s and 1630s, the trends in money supply accelerated further. Records indicate that the total mint output of the South Netherlands, for example, grew from 2.8 million guilders in 1628–29 to 9.2 million guilders in 1630–32 to a peak of 23.1 million guilders in 1636–38.

Over the first half of the seventeenth century, the Dutch economy entered a golden period. Fortunes were made, growth permeated society, and a sizable middle class came into existence with money to spend and a hunger to make more. As noted earlier, the money flowing in from East and West found expression in many different forms. The excess of money led to a general inflation in the prices of almost all assets. This created a positive feedback loop where wealth needed to constantly grow to satisfy the hedonic biases of its owners or at the very least, find stores of value.

A wider population soon turned its attention to the alluring tulip. The boom of the 1620s and early 1630s had established the tulip as a luxury good par excellence with wide appeal, strong demand, and an excellent track record of consistent gains. Additionally, the botany of the plant—notably offsets—meant that it was a good that could potentially multiply over time and return multiples of the original amount paid, so it was an attractive investment. As the tulip industry had grown, the number of varieties and therefore opportunities to profit had also grown rapidly.

The perception of risk was set by the hitherto easy success of commerce and the stock market. People felt comfortable speculating on the future and adding leverage as they extrapolated past their myopic horizon. By 1634, sales were taking place outside flowering season as more buyers began to buy on spec with a view to avoiding the greater interest and run-up in prices that a bloom naturally created.

The transformation of tulips into an asset class and a form of pseudo-money led to a financialization of the market. In other words, the tulip as a financial asset took on a life of its own separate from the tulip as a horticultural object of beauty. Now that you could buy the bulb in advance, you could also sell it in advance without actually taking ownership. A futures market began to emerge unbidden. Like any asset, measurement and division became part of the trade. Future bulbs were now sold by weight, in fractions, and by bulk. A derivatives trade began in the offsets of future bulbs—effectively physical options that were cheaper but represented a bet on the uncertainty that the offset would survive to flower into the same beautiful patterns as its progenitor.

Financial markets increase scale but also lead to a loss of informational resolution. Macro replaces micro. The new buyers and sellers were no longer necessarily tulip cultivators, merchants, and collectors with an expert knowledge of the bulbs. Instead, these were replaced with people trading trends of supply and demand that they saw around them, and the information pertaining to these became more important: who was buying, who was selling, what were the hot predictions for the coming season, how much was being exported, and so on. The actual foundations of information—climate, soil, bulb quality, what techniques were used, what genuine collectors might value, and so on—that underlay all these dynamics were becoming increasingly taken for granted. That was the preserve of the tulip experts, who fast became a repository of blind trust.

The transformation here was accelerated by the potentially vast rewards on offer. Additionally, the market was boosted—as happens throughout history—by the (un)happy coincidence of exogenous events. In 1635, Holland suffered a terrible plague. Over the next two years, large cities such as Amsterdam and Haarlem lost a fifth or more of their population.

Economically, the plague boosted the money supply per head. As an impartial arbiter, it felled rich and poor alike, and many people suddenly found themselves wealthier as inheritances were accelerated, riches were shared between fewer people, and competitors literally fell by the wayside.

Psychologically, time horizons shrank alongside the population. Life was measured day by day, then month by month. Next year might never dawn, and with that, investment horizons became more immediate. The uncertainty drove a greater search for security and stability. Religion and money were the chief beneficiaries.

Socially, travel was restricted. People gathered together locally to drink, and social conversation gave way to economic posturing. It created a fertile environment for groupthink and for the words of an expert to carry a crowd that had little place else to go and more limited choices for speculation.

The phenomenon that would come to be known as tulipmania developed quickly. Colleges of traders began to meet on a weekly basis or more often in local inns and taverns. A set of rules evolved whereby purchases could be made on the strength of a small deposit up front and the balance of the fee due on settlement. This was a futures market in all but name, where no one intended to actually deliver the bulbs on settlement. Rather, payment on the difference in value between prices at contract and settlement respectively was to be made in either direction. The fact that these bets could be backed by pieces of bank paper that everyone accepted at face value and which represented security elsewhere meant that people heavily discounted the possibility of contracts not being honored.

Additionally, the network included tulip growers and collectors, who were immediately perceived as experts. The close social ties among the participants—many of whom belonged to heterodox religious groups, notably the Mennonites, that were bound all the closer by the wider tensions of the era—meant that market participants were more susceptible to the influence of their peers. These were not just anonymous market counterparties in some sterile trade but rather social connections and people of note. It was easy to take their advice at face value.

The trouble with older manias is that they often lack the bureaucracy to maintain the detailed records historians and economists love to analyze. Beyond the steep rise in prices of a few tulips, it is hard to map out finer details such as the volume of transactions, the evolution in different geographies, who the individual buyers and sellers were, and who won and lost in these economic games born of human nature. Tulip prices were sporadically recorded, often in court cases over disputes or in cautionary pamphlets in the aftermath of the crisis. The stories associated with tulipmania are also often inflected with legend.

However, we do know the financial values of bulbs soared in late 1636 as the mania gathered pace. Bulbs were planted in October, and by November prices started to rise steeply as people actively began to buy and sell contracts for future delivery. As prices of the rarer varieties outstripped the ability of most to purchase, attention shifted to the more common varieties. Individual bulbs rose tenfold in price over three months, while bulk orders increased by multiples of twenty or more. According to reports, the common Witte Croonen bulb rose in price twenty-six times in January 1637 alone.

A week later, on February 3, 1637, a public auction of bulbs in Haarlem failed to find buyers. A second auction on February 5 produced higher prices again, but it was too late. Market confidence had been shaken, and trading came to a rapid halt as people no longer knew what price to value tulip bulbs at. On February 23, the colleges all gathered together in Amsterdam to find a solution and salvage the market. Contracts till November 30, 1636, were to be honored while any thereafter could be annulled for a fee of 10 percent of the contract value.

The agreement failed to hold as different colleges and authorities alternately demanded all contracts be honored to maintain confidence or voided to avoid widespread ruin and disrepute. Meanwhile, prices began to collapse. Within months, the Witte Croonen bulb was at less than one-twentieth of its peak price, while bulk orders of common bulbs were allegedly going for less than 1 percent of their previous valuations.

In the end, the Dutch authorities deemed the contracts to be little more than bets and allowed them to be cancelled for a payment of 3.5 percent of the contract value. The financial pain was short-lived—a small rise in bankruptcies—but the wider economy was spared, as most of the money owed was effectively written off. It was a bold step but also meant that the Dutch golden period continued untarnished. The VOC became one of the two dominant forces in Asia and began the first of many wars over control of the colonies with its chief rival, the British.

People may have felt a lot poorer, but that was only in comparison to a few months earlier. The wealth built up elsewhere was largely untouched. Still, the psychological scars remained and came to the fore in the form of urban myths of excess and shrill pamphlets on the evils of speculation that would come in later years to birth the legend of tulipmania.

As financial crises go, the economic aftermath of this one was not lasting, with the horrors and regret being confined largely to the mind. This was because the complexity of the Dutch economy was still modest. The financial system was yet nascent, and debt was limited. Much of the speculation had taken place through derivative contracts, not by borrowing, so little money had actually exchanged hands. When contracts were annulled and values collapsed, the losses were to the quantification of personal ego and did not propagate through the economy via a network of debtors and creditors, spreading panic. The plague had also helped, as the travel restrictions meant that each town and community was largely self-contained in its speculations.

However, it bore all the hallmarks of its predecessors and successors in lurid detail, enough so as to enter our cultural memory and unleash a thousand future books on the perils of speculation. Money and finance are a heady cocktail. The other lessons of tulipmania—that crises have deep, complex roots and the bounds of our rationality are easily altered—went unlearned.

Part IV

Complexity: The Alchemy of Crisis

CHAPTER 12

A Universal Truth:
An Aside on Paradigms

Though analogy is often misleading, it is the least misleading thing
we have.

—SAMUEL BUTLER (1835–1902)

I read, I study, I examine, I listen, I reflect, and out of all of this I
try to form an idea into which I put as much common sense as
I can.

—MARQUIS DE LAFAYETTE (1757–1834)

IF you ever get the chance, take a trip to the South Luangwa nature
reserve in the north of Zambia. It is a rare, beautiful, and unspoiled
corner of the world, some thirty-five hundred square miles in size with just
fifty miles of dirt tracks that masquerade as roads. The locals have a laissez-
faire amiability when it comes to nature, something that comes from an
acceptance of their limited control over it. For the rest of us, this attitude
is highly disconcerting at first, particularly when your trip requires you to
sign a seemingly endless number of waivers excusing your host's culpabil-
ity in all possible loss of life and limbs.

Thereafter, the amiability becomes terrifying. The jeeps everyone
travels around in have no doors, windows, or roofs—just metal bars to
hang on to as you go hurtling around the rough terrain. The guides all
radio one another to find where the lions are. As soon as they locate a
pride, they drive straight into its midst and park the jeep so you can enjoy
the view. The first time this happened, a lioness nonchalantly strolled over
and began sniffing my leg. It all takes some getting used to, particularly
when the leopard tree outside your hut turns out to have an actual leopard
in it and the idiot next door gets his hut demolished by an elephant because
he unthinkingly brought some sugar along.

A few days in, however, and you've imbibed some of the local airs. You tiptoe carefully around the elephant's favorite mango tree and make sure the baboons don't jump you in the shower. Even the sound of hippos making love in the watering hole outside becomes just another part of the ambient white noise.

Evenings take on a special charm of their own. You sit on rickety chairs in the dry riverbed with a lantern and sip a gin and tonic or beer as the other denizens of South Luangwa take their nighttime strolls. Occasionally, a pride of lions or some hippos pass by. They look at you, you raise your glass to them, and they walk on uninterested.

When you've reached that point of detachment, lie back and gaze up at the night sky. You will see the Milky Way as never before—a thick river of bright white sparkling stars overflowing its cosmic banks as it runs across your vision, its grandeur now no longer dimmed by the light pollution that permeates everyday urban environments (see Figure 4 in the photo insert).

As order goes, this is the grandest exposition of it in the universe. Ever since man first learned to use that most primitive of astronomical instruments—the eye—and gazed upward, we have strived to re-create that perceived order here on earth and in our lives. Religions have incorporated the night skies into mythology and countless religious shrines, be it Stonehenge or the pyramids. Movements such as the Enlightenment embraced Newton's perfect clockwork universe run by immutable laws and unleashed the hounds of rationality that have shaped modern society. Even today, the ennui of our hectic, pressured lives leads many of us to search for answers in the perfect harmonious arrangement of our living spaces or in the hidden patterns of runes, crystals, the zodiac, and the like.

But there is a deeper, more troubling eternal question that you should ponder as you stare up at this beautiful superstructure of island universes laid out above you in the Zambian night sky. Where did all this order—not just in the sky visible from earth but throughout the universe—come from? (See Figure 5 in the photo insert.)

FROM SMALL BEGINNINGS . . .

Analogies are tortured beings, but they have their uses.

Leaving God on the philosophical shelf, the picture above is troubling to (former) cosmologists such as myself. We believe in the Big Bang, namely, that the entire universe came about from a rapid explosive expansion of an infinitesimally small point in all directions. But instead of the homogeneous random structure that one might expect, the night sky indicates a richly structured universe, where galaxies tend to lie on vast sheetlike structures surrounding large empty regions. These arrangements seem nonrandom, and there is no answer in standard cosmology as to how and why they may have arisen.

The universe is much like a street party of many thousands of people. It may have started out small with a few particles here and there, but over time it rapidly and exponentially grew ever larger as more and more joined in. The problem is that there was no grand plan, no open invite on Facebook, and no flash mob hiding behind the scenes biding its time. None of these people initially knew what the party was about—they all seem to be there just for the hell of it—so how did they get to hear about it? How did a uniform sea of quantum particles birthed in the instants after the Big Bang aggregate together to discover common laws of physics and form the stars and galaxies we see about us?

This is not a primer on cosmological problems and their hopeful resolution. But the answers to the above are educational when we come to consider the more ordinary problem of how financial crises originate and evolve. The resolution to our quandary lies in some key insights.

1. THE ABSENCE OF ACTION DOES NOT MEAN NOTHING IS HAPPENING

We often talk of the vacuum or emptiness of space. But the term is disingenuous, implying an absence of everything. Today, we know that empty space is not really empty. Instead, it is a invisible reservoir of unimaginable energy, far fuller than any overstuffed closet that we could imagine, where invisible subatomic particles play a constant frenzied game of creation and annihilation. However, all this action lies hidden beneath the surface, masquerading as emptiness. But it is from these infinitesimally small quantum fluctuations that our universe and the structure within was born.

Even in the absence of great booms and busts, our human emotions always lie beneath the surface, sweeping through the palette of extraordinary emotions from hope to fear to greed to envy. The dullness of the commuter train, with every actor steadfastly avoiding all human interaction, masks a roiling sea of emotions, no less powerful when muted as when they find expression and come to the fore. Under that placid exterior, we are always speculating, always running, always reaching.

2. EQUILIBRIUM AND ITS ASSOCIATED STABILITY ARE AN ILLUSION; CHANGE IS THE NORM

Rewinding the cosmological clock, the very early universe in the moments after the Big Bang was an unimaginably hot place. It was also uniform as matter and energy interchanged at will and flew about in all directions. Physicists cling dearly to a principle called symmetry—the belief that a system at some level is uniform and agnostic about changes in its environment. For example, it could be symmetrical with regard to time. Thus, you could run the system forward in time and expect the same pattern of behavior if you were to run it backward. In the immediate aftermath of the Big Bang, everything was perfectly symmetrical—the cosmologist's way of saying that the behavior and evolution of the universe could be described by one simple theory.

Unfortunately, the elegant simplicity of theory is not the sole rationale of reality, which seems to naturally evolve complexity. The universe was not static and this perfect equilibrium was only transient. As the universe expanded, it cooled down. It went through so-called phase transitions, that is to say, the properties and even the forms of matter changed. Thus, much like steam condensing to water and then freezing into ice, the universe transmuted as it grew colder. All this perfect symmetry fell away strand by strand as atoms, then stars, and eventually galaxies were born.

Elegance in theory is prized, but more often than not it refers to an idealized state. It rarely corresponds to current reality except transiently.

In economics, the equivalent to the beauty of symmetry is typified by the use of *ceteris paribus* and the focus on perfectly rational actors who seek to maximize their lot in life dispassionately and whose perfect equilibrium is disturbed only by outside events. But we are not *Homo economicus*. As detailed elsewhere, we have cognitive biases inherent in us all and are captive to the incentives born of our environment.

If there is one clear parallel that emerges above all else, it is that our history of speculation and crises is birthed from within, never without. The wider world influences and external events punctuate the arc of boom and bust. But it is the sea of emotions within us that make us *Homo sapiens*. It is always waiting to find an expression.

The making of a bubble, its pricking, and the accompanying bust are as much a phase transition as any that occurred in the early universe. New innovations and opportunities become certainties signposting the road to status and prosperity. A dogma is created that more and more of us buy into, though as it ages, the flaws and contradictions gradually pile up beneath the surface. Still, the established theory moves on relentlessly, thanks to its momentum and the inertia granted by its many followers even as its foundations and arguments become assailable over time. Soon, the weight of argument, evidence, and reality pile up till a tipping point is reached. The now shaky paradigm is replaced instead with a new knowledge, often in a disorderly manner. This is our version of a phase transition, as emotions and ideas transmute. In the financial sphere, this is typically the gently nuanced retreading of a cyclical theory, namely, that we know far less than we think.

This is not a new idea. What I have outlined above is little more than Thomas Kuhn's theory of how scientific revolutions occur, which is where the well-worn phrase "paradigm shift" originates from. Kuhn realized that even a supremely rational pursuit such as science was practiced by people, not by automatons. Progress came not through the diligent mining of knowledge—though that myth is still around—but through successive waves of social acceptance and rejection. As noted earlier, the need to conform is a powerful primal driver in us all.

3. THE PATH OF LEAST EFFORT IS
ALWAYS THE MOST POPULAR

How does a phase transition happen? When and how does the placid vacuum erupt into visible frenzied action?

What we term a vacuum is simply a mass decision by the particles in the universe to congregate in the lowest possible energy level. It is the path of least effort that all particles will search out. This general rule is a powerful motivator in the universe. As the universe cooled down after the Big Bang, it took just a few random particles to realize that lower temperatures implied lower energy levels and hurtle down to a more comfortable state of being. A new lowest common denominator—a new vacuum—was born.

Bubbles of the "new" vacuum began to simultaneously form within the once stable "old" vacuum. Several different upstarts competed for dominance as different particles took different paths to the same end. These grew exponentially as more and more denizens of the universe rushed through to find a promised lower energy state and expanded like ink diffusing through water. The different vacua competed for dominance till the "old" vacuum ceased to exist and the universe reached a new transiently stable state of lower energy. The fast and chaotic pace of change also meant that no one state necessarily dominated, and the boundaries at which they met their peers would have produced defects—relics of the old universe forever preserved in an eternal limbo caught between two or more clashing bubbles.[1]

We are always striving in an eternal race, and if an opportunity presents itself to get ahead, we seize it. If it is successful enough, then others will rush to copy us. More money for less work is always a popular mantra. We do not see epidemics of Michelin-starred chefs or seasoned value investors. This is because honing the needed skills and learning the necessary lessons take years of hard work and require far more from us than most are willing to give.

If it involves minimal effort and little thought, then so much the better. As in the Seattle windshield epidemic, the Birmingham bicycle boom, tulipmania, and their siblings, these are the paradigms that take hold from innocuous beginnings and then grow exponentially as others jump on board.

There are always multiple bubbles forming at any given moment. An environment of money leads to many paths to prosperity. This is why stocks zoom up in value as "savvy" investors pile in, why an economic boom crosses boundaries between asset classes and across geographies, and why money rushes from one bubble to another in search of opportunity. Japan in the 1980s transmuted into Southeast Asia in the 1990s as that paradigm took hold, only to be superseded by the dot-com boom and so on. Each bust ushered in a new transition and the capital fled to find new homes where money might yet be multiplied.

The bust is the same in reverse. As trust fades from one party, then another, a third, and so on, an exponential fear takes hold. Bubbles of panic occur in different areas and grow exponentially till the euphoric boom is left decimated and a bust is born. A new stability—equally precarious—of cautious fear and regulation now exists.

One could argue that even these transitions of money and emotion create their own socioeconomic versions of the "defects" hiding in our universe. Where different bubbles meet each other, we find new exotic financial instruments to fulfill the need for leverage, intermediaries to facilitate the path to prosperity for a price, and grandiose social promises made in throes of euphoric prosperity. Where busts meet, we find bankrupts, defaulters, regulators, and central banks.

4. CHANGE SOWS THE SEEDS FOR FUTURE CHANGE

We now begin to reach an answer to our original question of where the complex structure of the universe came from. The phase transitions in the early universe were not gradual. Their disorderly uneven journey altered the very fabric of space and time. As different bubbles clashed, the defects produced became further distortions in the environment that influenced the particles around them.[2] As the universe grew rapidly to many times its original infinitesimal size, the tiny fluctuations in the original pea now became vast perturbations. Surrounding particles flocked to these growing nodes of influence in greater numbers. They became the primordial seeds that created future stars and galaxies, much as a piece of grit in an oyster sows the seed for a pearl.

We live in a world of disequilibrium, where change is a constant. This is by choice, as can be seen by the emphasis placed on innovation as a driver of growth throughout history. As waves of emotion unfurl and crash, the debris they leave in their wake can become seeds for future phase transitions. They also change the fabric of an economy and a society, creating new linkages and complexities. New incentives are born, and the simpler mind in us all responds in sympathy.

This is not just for economics. As an example, tribal societies evolved cities and created armies in response to the need for common protection from other marauders, which turned out to be best done from a single well-defended vantage point. They developed linear hierarchies because an efficient operation needed a clear chain of command. These proto-cities drew people to them in search of protection. As more gathered together, they formed new social, political, and economic linkages. The simple actions of actors soon iterated and blended to create a complex whole that was far more than the sum of its parts. Cities developed ambitions of becoming nations, and commanders dreamed of becoming kings. Some succeeded, others did not. Irrespective of the outcome, cities were here to stay once they came about, and they have influenced the course of human nature since.

As for the empires, none of them lasted. They were always political paradigms, growing to the extent they captured hearts and territories, but ultimately they were always destined to be replaced by some other. Take any country in the world and you will see over its history a series of expanding and contracting hegemonies. There will be local kings and warlords, external conquerors, rebels, insurrections, political movements, and so on. Every one was transient but almost all also had their birth in the actions and decisions of their predecessors.

In the world of money, innovation and creation march on hand in hand. They cannot be controlled. Paper money, bonds, the joint-stock company, derivatives, financial mathematics—all were here to stay once they came about. They also provided the instruments we needed to leverage the emotions beneath the surface at every stage and drag others along in our wake. Legislation, regulators, and central banks in most cases came from the aftermath of our booms—hopeful antidotes for our hangovers. But as we see, they create their own distortions of incentive.

Through it all, capitalism evolves from complexity to increasing complexity. And boom and bust become part of our socioeconomic DNA.

CHAPTER 13

Birds of a Feather:
The Ecology of Capitalism

The world is a big place and our brain is only three pounds.

—R. SCOTT BAKKER (1967–)

Capitalism ... never can be stationary. [It] incessantly revolutionizes the economic structure from within, incessantly destroying the old one, incessantly creating a new one. This process of Creative Destruction is the essential fact about capitalism.

—JOSEPH SCHUMPETER (1883–1950)

O N June 9, 1772, Alexander Fordyce—speculator extraordinaire with trophy aristocrat wife and the principal partner in the banking house of Neal, James, Fordyce, and Down—left his London home for France. He did not return. The next day, on June 10, Black Wednesday struck.[1] Neal, James, Fordyce, and Down stopped all payments as soon as it became clear that Fordyce had absconded following a ruinous set of speculative losses that he had unsuccessfully tried to cover with customer deposits. Within hours, as the prominent Scottish banker Sir William Forbes was to recall in his memoirs years later, panic set in as "this bankruptcy set fire to the mine, which at once blew up the whole traffic of circulation that had been carrying on for a number of years."

Banks in Edinburgh—a burgeoning financial center in the eighteenth century—were greeted on June 12 by a lone horseman who had ridden forty-three hours from London to bring them the news. The same day, word also reached Amsterdam, London's great financial rival. It became clear that Fordyce had short positions in the shares of the East India Company and the Bank of England, then a private entity. Both were in the futures market and had been put on through the well-known

Anglo-Dutch banking house of Hope & Co.[2] Fordyce's default left Hope responsible for the positions and the losses.

Speculation ran rampant as to what the sums involved might be. "It is said that the banker, who absented, had a difference of 10 percent to pay on a million and a half of India stocks, of which he had been a bear for many months past," reported the *Middlesex Journal* on June 13, 1772. In reality, the numbers were much smaller, though still large by the standards of the time—£57,000 for the East India Company (about 1.7 percent of the company) and £22,000 for the Bank of England.

Within three days, the first of several Edinburgh banking houses suspended their payments. The share price of the Bank of England and the East India Company began to climb rapidly as the market became convinced that Hope would need to buy the shares in the open market to cover their losses. Contagion spread rapidly. By the nineteenth of June, ten banks had shut their doors.

Meanwhile, it turned out that the Scottish banks all had bills of exchange from the Ayr Bank, a Scottish bank with an impressive share-holder register of the great and good as well as ambitions of becoming a Scottish version of the Bank of England. As the bank runs now spread to the Ayr Bank, a deputation was sent to the Bank of England to ask for a bailout. Unfortunately, the Bank of England was less than accommodating. It had been troubled by the rampant growth in speculation in recent years and already held in its books some £150,000 of the Ayr Bank's paper. Additionally, it had already given selective bailouts to some of the banks in London. A loan of £300,000 was offered but on stiff terms that were unpalatable. Rumors began to circulate that the bills issued by the Ayr Bank had been refused in London. On June 22, Ayr closed its doors as well.

The situation was as unbelievable as it was unexpected. Britain had just gone through three decades of economic and geopolitical prosperity. A successful end to the Seven Years' War in 1763 had reiterated its status as the world's leading superpower. The country was rapidly growing a global colonial empire matched by strong growth in trade, thanks to the mercantile approach favored. Mercantilism was essentially a form of state capitalism, where the merchants explored and colonized new territories on behalf of the state with its full political and military support. In

particular, trade with the colonies in the Americas was thriving, notwithstanding political tensions. Coupled with the technological advances of the
Industrial Revolution that was unfolding, this was spurring a rapid
economic expansion. But all that seemed at risk as a general credit crunch
suddenly took hold.

"One rascally and extravagant banker has brought Britannia, Queen
of the Indies, to the precipice of bankruptcy," thundered Horace Walpole,
the elderly statesman of British politics, on June 22. "It is very true, and
Fordyce is the name of the caitiff. He has broken half the bankers."

"We are here in a very melancholy Situation: Continual Bankruptcies,
universal Loss of Credit, and endless Suspicions," complained the philosopher David Hume in a letter dated June 27 to Adam Smith, the father of
modern economics.

The ripples spread outward. British merchants had lent heavily to
the farmers in the American colonies. All that money needed to be repaid
urgently. Meanwhile, the lack of credit meant a general fall in the prices
of tobacco, corn, and other crops as demand dropped. The deflation was
only exacerbated by the attempts to liquidate holdings by debtors to
meet their obligations.

Among the worst hit was the British East India Company. A month
into the crunch, the surge in the share price had turned into a steep drop
as the economy went into recession. At the same time, the company had
heavy debts, notably an annual payment of £400,000 to the British government for its trading monopoly. These debts were proving increasingly hard
to service, and in fact, the company had been unable to fulfill the last obli-
gation for a number of years. A heavy-handed approach to the newly
acquired province of Bengal had unleashed one of the worst famine disasters in history and destroyed tax revenues. Meanwhile, the company was
also banned by law from exporting tea—one of its most lucrative monopolies—and instead had to sell it wholesale at auctions in Britain. But high
tea taxes had led to falling demand and the company's warehouses in
Britain were rapidly becoming a compost heap of tea leaves that were
earning nothing.

The crisis gave the company an opportunity to lobby for a bailout as
well as for the government to exert more control over the territories that

the East India Company was expanding in. A deal was struck. In return for accepting regulation by the British government, the East India Company was allowed to export tea directly to the lucrative market of the American colonies—hitherto dominated by smuggled Dutch teas—and exempted from all duties barring the Townshend duty of three pence per pound.

This deal, codified as the Tea Act of 1773, was greeted with agitation in the American colonies. The Townshend duty was a sensitive issue, viewed by colonials as an attempt to assert Britain's sovereign right of taxation through the back door. They were right—Britain had huge government debts in the aftermath of the Seven Years' War and viewed the colonies as its domain. The refusal to let the colonies trade with other countries ensured a healthy smuggling industry, particularly in Dutch tea.

Now, by shipping all this excess tea over to the colonies within the Trojan hold of the East India Company, the British hoped to undercut the price of smuggled tea and advance their political agenda.[3] It was a miscalculation. Political resistance found common ground with merchants, who were still reeling from the credit crunch unleashed in Britain and were worried about the impact of all this excess supply on their business.

In September 1773, seven vessels bearing nearly six hundred thousand pounds of tea set sail for Boston, New York, Philadelphia, and Charleston. All were turned back except for those heading for Boston, where a tense standoff developed between the authorities, who refused to let the ships leave the harbor, and the local populace, who refused to let them land. On December 16, 1773, a group of colonists disguised as Mohawk warriors boarded the ships under cover of dark and dumped all the tea overboard into the water.

The incident would be immortalized in history as the Boston Tea Party, an iconic milestone en route to the American Revolutionary War and Britain's loss of the American colonies. Meanwhile, back home, Adam Smith would publish his seminal work, An Inquiry into the Nature and Causes of the Wealth of Nations, in 1776. The book would attack mercantilism, espouse free trade, and talk of the "invisible hand" that guided markets. The Wealth of Nations birthed a new field, economics, and its principles of individual self-interest leading to collectively positive outcomes would morph over the years into the mantra of free markets that fueled modern capitalism and the specter of *Homo economicus* that still deludes us today. The influence of the forgotten credit crunch of the 1770s was clear, for example, in Smith's long description of how bills of exchange worked, and the impact of all this credit on the Scottish economy. But nowhere were the ramifications born of the actions of one man—Alexander Fordyce—more explicit than in Smith's closing words as he urged Britain to give up its colonial ambitions and focus on setting its financial house in order:

> The rulers of Great Britain have, for more than a century past, amused the people with the imagination that they possessed a great empire on the west side of the Atlantic. This empire, however, has hitherto existed in imagination only. It has hitherto been, not an empire, but the project of an empire; . . . a project which has cost, which continues to cost, and which . . . is likely to cost, immense expense, without being likely to bring any profit. . . . If the project cannot be completed, it ought to be given up. If any of the provinces of the British empire cannot be made to contribute toward the support of the whole empire, it is surely time that Great Britain should free herself from the expense of defending those provinces in time of war, and of supporting any part of their civil or military establishment in time of peace; and endeavor to accommodate her future views and designs to the real mediocrity of her circumstances.

It was an extraordinary chain of events. The beatings of a butterfly's wings had led to an economic hurricane that paralyzed one nation, assisted the birth of another, and spawned a powerful new ideology. Yet how could the flight of one rogue have brought an entire economy to a standstill and, a continent away, influenced events that would shape the course of history?

SIMON SAYS

Previously we have talked of human bias, incentives, and the psychology of crowds. We have debated the nature of money and the role of credit in leveraging human emotion. We have spoken of how bubbles form and paradigms shift, and the relics they leave behind to seed the next generation of crises. These are all ingredients of the fragility of capital-ism—booms and busts by any other name.

But through it all, capitalism itself has been an enigmatic goddess on a pedestal. Few question how individual self-interest morphs into the marvel of free markets. For whether we designate ourselves as *Homo economicus* or beings of bounded rationality, we all believe that our indi-vidual actions lead to outcomes that are far more than the sum of the parts. Yet all too often, free markets are treated as a miracle, much like Jesus turning water into wine. Our focus shifts instead to whether they are a good thing or not for society—the answer more often than not already predetermined by our political bias.

Miracles are the preserve of religion. Despite its enduring success, capitalism is not one of those miracles. It is an aggregation of human behavior that appears to evolve an order and direction, which is often not present at the individual level and which is not directed by some central body or individual. Even more remarkably, that common purpose is usually directed toward the efficient utilization of resources and the maximization of economic benefit for society as a whole.

The noted economist Friedrich Hayek—Keynes's great rival and bugbear of the economics establishment during his lifetime—wrestled with this topic during his career. Searching for the words to explain, he noted that the "peculiar character of the problem of a rational economic order is determined precisely by the fact that the knowledge of the circumstances of which we must make use never exists in concentrated or integrated form but solely as the dispersed bits of incomplete and frequently contradictory knowledge which all the separate individuals possess."

Hayek's conclusion that the markets were far more efficient than individuals or institutions at setting prices was arguably his most lasting contribution. His great leap forward was to appreciate that in the real world, people were not rational actors with perfect knowledge but indi-viduals with varying degrees of competency and knowledge. Moreover, no one expert or body of people was capable of overcoming this fundamental shortcoming and knowing everything. Therefore, the only way to make informed decisions was to act on the limited knowledge—rightly or wrongly—that you had at that time and place. However, the existence of a free market where people could trade based on their perceptions ensured that there would be prices that reacted continually to both these biases as well as the underlying dynamics of supply and demand. These prices encapsulated within them more of the diffuse knowledge from across society than any person or institution could ever hope to have on its own. The result was a spontaneous self-organization of coherent economies, seemingly full of purpose and despite the lack of planning.

"The marvel is that in a case like that of a scarcity of one raw material, without an order being issued, without more than perhaps a handful of people knowing the cause, tens of thousands of people whose identity could not be ascertained by months of investigation, are made to use the material or its products more sparingly; that is, they move in the right direction," Hayek noted.

In other words, the market was essential to the efficient allocation of resources and superior to any central authority, because it aggregated and communicated information far more effectively and dynamically.[4] Any attempt to restrict this market exchange would inevitably lead to lesser degrees of knowledge and poorer outcomes for society as a whole.

Free markets are still a theoretical construct in that they are a limiting, idealized view of human interaction in the economic sphere. In practice, we have our biases and perceptions, which affect the quality of information provided and lead to inconsistent actions emanating from that information over time. There is an external environment of social norms, noneconomic relationships, laws, institutions, and vested interests that will always impact the availability and exchange of information as well as the implementation of actions in response. Money and credit can overwhelm thought and amplify some bits of information above the aggregate. There is also a time lag associated with all of the above, which means that important pieces can take time to come through and become assimilated. We can see the ebb and flow of information across this network of human actors and institutions, and how it can lead to occasionally flawed mass perceptions and their associated bubbles of speculation.

Capitalism is a complex system. Its structure and behavior spontaneously evolve from the simpler uncoordinated actions of individuals. We are all pragmatists at heart. With the rare exception, most of us spend our lives in a never-ending search for enhanced status. Social popularity and the pursuit of power are two common expressions of this inner drive. The accumulation of wealth, as noted, is another. In this sense, capitalism evolves naturally from human interaction.

SOCIAL NETWORKING

We talked earlier of how flocks of geese move and change direction with purpose, despite the lack of a central leader. The movement of individual geese may be viewed as random movements. However, adding a few simple rules results in a powerful feedback loop that soon coordinates the actions of all these geese into a flock. At its most basic, one could outline the following rules in order of priority for any given bird:

- All motion is autonomous.
- Avoid getting too close to your immediate neighbors.
- Don't get too far away from them either.
- Aim for the general direction of movement of your immediate neighbors.

As one bird randomly changes direction, it impedes the flight paths of its neighbors. They accommodate the change by altering their direction in accordance with the above rules. This then impedes the paths of even more geese in their vicinity, who respond accordingly. An exponential cascade rapidly develops—first one, then five, later twenty or thirty birds, and eventually the whole population of birds there. Iterated repeatedly, the result is an emergent complex behavior that creates the flock we perceive. In practice, there are subtler rules that impact as well, involving obstacles, the presence of food, occasional dangers or predators, and so on. But all this behavior is rooted in simple actions and feedback loops.

    This spontaneous organization and demonstration of complex behavior is seen throughout nature, for example, in how ants and termites create complex hierarchies and colonies. We find it in the history of the universe, as already discussed. We find it in theories of how life emerged. We find it in ocean currents and weather patterns. We find it in chemical reactions. And we see it in human context from the behavior of simple crowds to the evolution of societies and empires.

Networks of individuals always interact dynamically. Their interactions often lead to unplanned outcomes. One famous example is provided by how distinct neighborhoods evolve in cities. In the United States, housing segregation was outlawed in 1964, at the height of the civil rights movement. Yet neighborhoods are still highly monoracial and monoethnic in their composition. In cosmopolitan cities such as London, it is common to see areas dominated by different nationalities, linguistic identities, religious leanings, and ethnic profiles emerge rapidly within a number of years. Anyone who has seen the profusion of Polish shops in certain areas, the radical Islamism associated with Finsbury Park, or the colonization of Fulham by the French will instinctively know what I mean.[5]

This is because segregation can emerge spontaneously even in the absence of any central planning from above or individual personal bigotry from below. All it takes is an individual preference for friends or family over strangers. Thomas Schelling won the Nobel Prize in Economics for this particular insight. He was examining housing discrimination in the United States and created a simple stylized model (see Figure 6 in the photo insert). A two-dimensional grid was populated with households, with each one corresponding to a single square. There were two different types, which we can call red and green for the moment. Initially, they were randomly intermingled and scattered all over the square, so that there were no clear areas that were dominated by households of a single color. A few squares were also left deliberately empty to represent available unoccupied housing that people could move to.

A simple rule was introduced: If more than one-third of the squares in your immediate vicinity were the same color—your "kin"—you were happy and would choose to stay. However, if a third or less of the squares were kin, you were unhappy and would move to a random unoccupied square.

The result is a cascade. The people in the game make individual decisions to move to locations where they are "happier." As they begin to do so, the colors begin to congregate together in different areas of the board. As they move, others in their vicinity find themselves becoming happy or unhappy, triggering further moves. Taken to its final state, you end up with a board that now has stark red and green patches all over, reminiscent more of a psychedelic Andy Warhol cow than a chessboard.

These individual preferences are not necessarily racist and can be very mild on an individual level. They could be just a slight preference to be near people of your ethnicity, influenced perhaps by family or friends, for example—often an influence seen in many immigrant communities. However, that slight bias soon turns into a distinct neighborhood, be it upscale or downmarket, dominated by one type. A complexity has emerged from our simple individual actions.

The evolution of investor or speculator concentration in certain sectors or investment themes follows a similar cascade effect, both on the way up and on the way down. There are naturally more factors at play, notably the different biases we talked about earlier as well as the role of money and credit in extending the reach of networks and the rate of change. However, the principles remain the same. From simple human actions emerges a complexity of communal behavior.

An example may be seen in the prisoner's dilemma, a famous example of economic game theory, which shows that people are likely to destructively prioritize their own self-interest. Two robbers are arrested on suspicion of burglary and placed in separate rooms for questioning. If neither confesses, they will both be sentenced to one year in prison on some lesser charge. If one betrays the other, he will go free while his accomplice will get five years. If both confess, both will receive a punishment of two years. The logical outcome is to keep quiet, but in practice, self-interest dominates and both parties end up worse off.

Expand this to a cast of thousands, and it becomes easy to see how a few individuals selling at the height of a bubble can rapidly reverberate throughout the system. A general panic emerges as everyone seeks to preserve what wealth they have. The result is that a bubble always bursts dramatically, rather than deflating gradually.

THE COMPLEX WEB OF CAPITALISM

By marrying money to human emotion and interaction, we create powerful networks. Unlike the simple models discussed above, these have far more agents with more extensive connections. Moreover, the individual nodes vary in size, which affects their influence on others and the network as a whole. For example, stock pundits, wealthier individuals, journalists, policy makers, and others of their ilk have more influence and therefore tend to impart direction to a crowd—a trait that in good times we often denote as leadership. Similarly, institutions have a much larger influence through their typical hierarchical structures, which codify groupthink, and their significantly larger balance sheets.

The cell structure of capitalism is akin conceptually to the Internet. Some websites and bloggers have far more influence than others, and vast conglomerates such as Facebook or Google have enormous social reach. Popular sites tend to become ever more connected and can act rapidly to disseminate trends throughout the web (see Figure 7 in the photo insert). This cascading behavior is how videos can suddenly go viral and tweets can be heard around the world.[6]

Thus, during the Boston Marathon bombings in 2013, Twitter proved to be a far better mechanism for communicating unfolding events rather than media outlets, as the individual 140-character messages of bystanders and friends quickly spread through their network of connections and conveyed far more information. Equally, it also demonstrated how that connectivity could propagate error, as rumors in the aftermath of the bombings spread rapidly as to who the culprits or causes might be.

Returning to our world of markets and money, it is worth noting that such interconnectivity supports and rewards innovation. New products, services, and technologies have natural mechanisms for spreading outward, as initially a few influencers adopt them, followed later by many others. There is a feedback component to this also. The potential for profitable adoption by others ensures that people will always look to invest or speculate on interesting opportunities, which then encourages further innovation. The aim always is the same—to be a larger cog in that complex economic machine.

All this connectivity also naturally leads to business cycles—the arc of economic expansion and contraction seen in individual companies as well as industries. Stylistically, mainstream economists have often considered the business cycle to be driven by the interplay of supply and demand. As demand rises, so do prices, and people rush to provide goods or services in response to the profit of scarcity. However, as supply rises, prices fall and those same people now scale down or withdraw as profit margins shrink. The results are the reassuringly regular graphs seen in endless economic textbooks that bear little relation to the outside world.

The inclusion of money, credit, and more people changes this dynamic to one of boom and bust. Others can now bring money to the table to accelerate growth and earn their own rewards for this facilitation. Simplistically, as demand appears and suppliers respond, the provision of money and availability of credit allow them to scale up far more quickly. If demand appears stable, such as for tulips, our bias toward extrapolating the recent past means that we are willing to invest more and more money in return for those reward of speculation. A few investors can soon become a crowd, thanks to the miracle of our networks. A boom is born.

The provision of money and credit allows the economy—the sum of all these transactions—to grow more rapidly than it might otherwise. It yokes together the savings and efforts of many people to efficiently allocate capital to where innovation and growth might be emerging. The lure of profit ensures that people are willing to speculate not just on foreseeable demands in the present but also on future hypothetical demands, which may or may not arise. This fuels further innovation by encouraging people to give rein to their imagination. The electric bulb, the car, and the plane, to name a few, were all born of this confluence of entrepreneurs and their moneyed backers, speculating on markets that might or might not exist in the future.

However, money and credit are a two-way street. One man's debt is another man's savings, though the dispersion of money through the complex web of an economy means that these truisms are soon forgotten. Money can be lent to both the customer and the supplier. The increase in personal wealth in times of growth coupled with easier credit can fuel further demand, which in turn ensures that more investment is needed.

As the boom expands, suppliers are willing to borrow money for longer periods as they grow confident that demand is persistent. More secondary speculators are attracted to the opportunity in question as they see sustainable avenues for growing their own wealth. The network deepens. A financialization inevitably follows suit that allows credit to build further and draws in the savings of even more people, multiplying them in the process as demand and growth march forward. This is where a boom can turn into a bubble.

However, demand is dynamic. New innovation leads to competition and the destruction of any transient stability. For example, the demand for horses at the end of the nineteenth century was replaced by one for bicycles and then cars. Landline telephones have found themselves losing out to mobile phones in recent decades. Equally, a demand can also simply be saturated or stagnate for a host of other reasons. Regardless, as profits shrink, a few individuals and then more and more disperse in search of returns elsewhere.

However, the links formed of money and credit cannot be so quickly removed. The supplier finds himself owing money to the bank or investors that must be repaid, regardless of cash flow. People look to exit en masse, perhaps resulting in sharp falls in prices. The complexity of the network is such that suddenly, the provision of credit to unrelated areas of the economy is curtailed as money begins to move. Growth suddenly stagnates. Bankruptcies rise and the social mood turns pessimistic. A new phase of complexity cascades through the system. We are now in a recession. The boom has become a bust.

This is natural. The flip side of fueling innovation and accelerating growth is that an economy will also periodically take time out to reallocate resources and money as it changes form. Above the interplay of business supply and demand, there is the supply and demand of money and credit. The two are not perfectly aligned, ensuring that booms and busts will always be with us.

Joseph Schumpeter typified this process as creative destruction, where markets will periodically clear out the old and replace the new, always with a view to nurturing innovation. Capitalism is at best transiently stable. Its dynamism ensures that it is always changing, and that the complexity of its behavior is beyond the ability of most to fathom or predict.

THE GROWTH OF COMPLEXITY

Individual economic actors make simple, myopic decisions that are influenced by their environment. But as we have seen, in the aggregate and on larger scales, these decisions soon evolve a complexity that is far more than the sum of its constituents. The problem is that the more complex a system becomes, the harder it becomes to fathom the unintended consequences of our actions and the more damaging our myopic horizon.

With the introduction of money, every recession is a financial crisis. However, these financial crises vary hugely in their aftermath. Tulipmania left little perceptible economic impact on the wider Dutch society, and the Wall Street crash of 1987 turned into a great buying opportunity within months, despite the legends that arose after the fact. Others, however, have more lasting effects, whether it is the political ramifications of the 1772 credit crunch in Britain or the psychological scars of the Great Depression. They linger in cultural memory and can influence attitudes for generations thereafter.

The South Sea bubble in eighteenth-century England and the Mississippi bubble overseen by John Law in eighteenth-century France were painful episodes for both countries. The two countries evolved down very different economic, social, and political paths thereafter. As a result, one embraced mercantilism and began to establish a trading empire that would later turn into a colonial one. The other found itself growing increasingly disenchanted and was torn apart by social tensions, culminating in the French Revolution of 1789, as the system failed to move on from its paroxysm, and an entire population sought new answers to a never-ending parade of financial crises.

What differentiates a depression from a mere recession? We can point to several factors. The amount of money and debt in the system is critical. The deleveraging is inevitably proportional to the leveraging prior to the crisis. An exponential panic sweeps away the once pervasive and exponential extrapolation of sempiternal prosperity. It may take years or decades to pay down old debts if growth suddenly disappears and trust falters, hampering a speedy recovery and the servicing of all those loans. In this sense, a depression is just an extreme form of the financial instability inherent in our system of credit.

Complexity also plays a role. The same complexity that powered growth also accelerates contraction. Complex linkages ensure that more money and credit will inevitably translate into greater numbers of people able to give expression to their biases, and a more densely interconnected web that can transmit shocks as efficiently as it did gains previously. The greater the complexity, the greater the impact.

The United States was the great emerging market of the nineteenth century and had tremendous economic growth. However, this growth was not just organic. It was fueled by large flows of investment capital from Europe and Latin America into areas such as agriculture and railroads. As recessions inevitably occurred, money also flowed out quickly, accentuating the impact of recessions and creating a set of financial crises that left their mark on U.S. history. Some recessions were triggered not by the internal dynamics of investment running ahead of reality but rather by the fact that money was flowing out in response to other competing opportunities elsewhere. Economies had formed linkages that crossed national boundaries, creating new levels of complexity.

But money and incentive also go hand in hand, feeding off each other. Therefore, a depression also results from a distortion of incentive, such that increasingly large numbers of individuals find their environment shepherding them down the same path. This weakens the ability of the system to sustain shocks because there is little diversity of thought. These incentives come from historical experience, institutions, laws, politics, and so on—in short, from anything that has the ability to affect a society and its outlook. As we noted previously, the past creates these incentives, and each crisis inevitably creates new incentives, sowing the seeds of future ones. That is why crises occur in cycles, building on one another in a crescendo until the system enforces destructive change.

Through it all, there is the myopia of those in charge. There is a tendency to forget that institutions are actually run by people and that these people have the same cognitive biases as the rest of us. Long-term planning and management of society sit in an uneasy alliance with human frailties. In times of transient stability, all is well. Extrapolation is a useful tool. Ideological dogma and mathematical models are invaluable, reliable guides. If all else fails, to do nothing and make small incremental decisions

born of electoral or bureaucratic cycles is an efficient strategy to maintain
a successful status quo.

But these caretaker actions always have a horizon far shorter than
the complexity of the system. The foundations of extrapolation—whether
we call them experience, intuition, or carefully crafted models—change
over time. Little decisions one day play out in big ways the next as the
network of actors in the economy respond individually to them and the
incentives they procreate. New permutations of group behavior and,
thereby, complexity are born. As these feed back through the economy,
the outcomes are always path dependent.

Some will inevitably reinforce existing bubbles or create new ones.
However, like any phase transition, these bubbles have a critical point they
will reach at some point in the future when emotions tip over and confidence turns to growing concern. As we approach these critical points and
pass through them, there is a disconnect between the time scale over
which the whole system evolves and the time scales over which we view
and judge decisions.

At these moments, we prioritize the urgent today over the important
tomorrow. And though the system may be precarious and later still, begin
to unravel, few are willing to change this mode of thought. Institutions are
powerful repositories of trust, which grants them enormous influence and
allows them to make binding decisions on behalf of the collective. In particular, the ability to exert some control on the perception and flow of
money—the medium whereby we accumulate status and glue together the
disparate threads of a society—is a powerful tool with which to shape future
behavior and outcomes. However, that same influence means that they
hold in their hands the power to exacerbate the magnitude of the inevitable
paradigm shifts that occur within a society. At these turning points, when
the disequilibrium beneath the surface comes to the fore, failing to appreciate the complexity of what you are dealing with can cause far more harm
despite all the best intentions. The small decisions can accumulate, allowing the herd to grow far larger than it might do otherwise and always too
little to right the structural weaknesses when the cycle turns. In time, they
crescendo and an otherwise recession becomes something far more scarring that can threaten the sustainability of an economy and way of living.

As noted earlier, a depression is fundamentally a tragedy of small decisions. Bubbles are born in the minds of individuals, nurtured by the incentives of their environment and grow to adulthood in the complexity of economies. Their aftermath is dictated by these same as well. And the Great Depression is the archetypal example of what can happen if these influences are not understood.

CHAPTER 14

A Tragedy of Small Decisions:
The Great Depression

No one was responsible for the great Wall Street crash. No one engineered the speculation that preceded it. Both were the product of free choice and decision of hundreds of thousands of individuals.

—J. K. GALBRAITH (1908–2006)

The first panacea for a mismanaged nation is inflation of the currency; the second is war. Both bring a temporary prosperity; both bring a permanent ruin. But both are the refuge of political and economic opportunists.

—ERNEST HEMINGWAY (1899–1961)

T HE Great Depression of the 1930s is seared into cultural memory, particularly in the United States. It has influenced entire generations of policy makers as well as economists, and continues to appear regularly in popular culture. It has also become another heuristic where everyone believes he or she knows what went wrong but few are actually aware of the actual events, their causes, or their aftermath. For most, their perspective is jaundiced by their ideological leanings.

There is a tendency to see the great crash of the Dow Jones Industrial Average in 1929 and the Great Depression as being the same. This is wrong. The first was a very public demonstration of fear and evaporating trust. The second was the painful deleveraging of a complex global economic system that had far too much bad debt sitting beneath the surface. The events of late 1929 may have woken the wider world to a deep-rooted problem, but it was a symptom, not the cause. Like many financial crises, the seeds of the Great Depression had been sown many years earlier. Behind the façade, the economy was under strain, and the great crash was the chance event that huffed and puffed and blew a flimsy house down. Even in its absence, some other event would inevitably have come along and become synonymous with the Great Depression in popular myth.

But that is getting ahead of ourselves. One of the problems of path dependency is that you could go back a very long way to identify when the first little flutters began that became so resounding in the end. It is akin to the tracing of what precise sequence of childhood events produced a criminal or a genius. *Reductio ad absurdum*, one could go back to the interplay between parental stability, discipline, and affection in those first two or three years; breast-feeding or bottle-feeding in those early months; the playing of classical music and the staging of banal conversations while the child is in the mother's belly; and the selfish genes that randomly spliced together in coitus to create said individual.

Therefore, we have to draw a line somewhere.

MOLDING THE INDIVIDUAL AND CREATING THE CROWD: THE FIRST GREAT DEPRESSION

Our story begins with individual actors and the incentives created in the aftermath of another Great Depression, that of 1873. Since renamed the Long Depression to avoid confusion, and erased from cultural memory by its later namesake, this was a grinding sixty-five-month recession from October 1873 to March 1879—the longest GDP trough on record even today. Triggered by the bursting of an international bubble of railroad speculation in the United States and the United Kingdom, the panic had followed the classic debt-deflation spiral as the vast amounts of debt proved too large for the system to deal with. The disorderly liquidation led to large numbers of banks and companies closing down, and falling asset prices punishing those that remained open. Unemployment surged to previously unknown heights. Though few detailed records survive, anecdotal evidence talks of one-third of Pennsylvania's workers being unemployed for an extended period, while another estimate had a quarter of New York's laborers being unemployed in the winter of 1873. Prices settled into a deflationary grind and nominal wages fell alongside them, dropping in the United States by more than a quarter over the decade.

Even when recovery came in 1879, respite was fleeting. Another recession in 1882 proved to be the third-longest on record, at thirty-eight months—hard times exemplified in urban legend by stories of Kansas farmers burning their own corn in 1885 for fuel, finding it cheaper than coal or wood.[1] There were recurrent international bank crises around railroads afterward till 1896. In its aftermath, many academics viewed the whole period from 1873 to 1896 as one long depression.

Paradoxically, it was also an era of enormous prosperity. From 1870 to the early twentieth century, the world at large went through an unprecedented surge in growth and wealth. Global trade and colonial empires expanded greatly. Millions migrated across borders, largely to the shores of the United States where the phenomenon of the American dream was being born. The modern corporation took shape and a middle class sprang into existence with sizable purchasing power. Some businessmen made unprecedented fortunes and went down in legend collectively as the "robber barons" of the nineteenth century: Andrew Carnegie, John D. Rockefeller, J. P. Morgan and Cornelius Vanderbilt. The United States as a country went from being a promising emerging market to an upstart nation on the cusp of toppling Great Britain from its perch as the dominant industrialized nation in the world.

Behind this paradox lay the double-edged nature of change. The latter half of the nineteenth century also saw the Second Industrial Revolution, when technology again took a giant leap forward. The scientific advances of the early nineteenth century—electricity, magnetism, and thermodynamics—were finding commercial expression in diverse ventures such as commercial telegraphs, steam engines, and the telephone. The stock ticker appeared in 1867 and Thomas Edison unveiled the first commercially viable light bulb in 1870. Within a few years, telegraph lines connected cities and later countries, while power stations began to pop up all over the developed world. Automation became a reality and the first mass-production factories began to appear.

All of this was helped along by the new transport infrastructure of railroads, which enabled the cost of transportation to fall to less than a cent per ton-mile. In the background stood a network of other key landmarks, such as the invention of dynamite by Alfred Nobel in 1857, the invention of the Bessemer process in 1855 that allowed durable steel to be mass-produced, and the drilling of the first commercial oil well in 1859. The world was convinced that, barring a few minor loose ends, science as a discipline had answered all questions. In 1897, the patent office in Zurich prematurely closed its doors on the grounds that there simply wasn't likely to be enough demand for its services in the future.

All this change fueled tremendous growth in productivity and wealth. Indeed, in real terms, the U.S. economy grew by some 6.8 percent per annum over the decade from 1869 to 1879 and an equally impressive amount the following decade. However, this growth also fueled large spec-ulative flows of money into the system. These drove numerous booms and busts as they ebbed and flowed in response to the perceived growth pros-pects of the United States, the United Kingdom, and other countries. They also increasingly became correlated as the world underwent its first major bout of globalization and the financial system grew in complexity.

Rapid growth was also highly disruptive for the established business order, which suddenly found itself being overtaken by this new technologi-cal economy. This was creative destruction in all its glory. The rises in productivity meant that many businesses were suddenly far more expen-sive and, therefore, an anachronism. Many workers suddenly found that previously labor-intensive tasks could be done much more cheaply by machines and that their jobs were no longer needed. Prices began to fall rapidly and wages followed suit, sinking to new levels that were acceptable to the market. The sharp rise in immigration in the latter half of the nine-teenth century only ensured that the economic adjustment was faster and that the GDP per capita shrank, even as growth took off in real terms across the whole economy.

There are two forms of deflation: good and bad. When increases in productivity lead to goods becoming cheaper, no one complains. Indeed, one could argue that in recent decades, the vast pools of cheap labor supplied by the Chinese economy exported a highly beneficial form of deflation around the world that ensured inflation was contained and perpetuated the boom of the 1980s and 1990s. This form of deflation is highly beneficial for an economy, as it means that people are able to purchase more with their money, even in the absence of wage growth. In other words, they become richer in real terms. They have more disposable income, which allows them to save more, spend more, and drive the metrics of growth to new heights.

However, when deflation strikes the assets that we use as collateral for our debts or hold as stores of our wealth, it is instinctively seen as bad. In the first case, it makes debt servicing that much more difficult, as the value of the debt grows in real terms. In widespread cases, it can trigger the dreaded debt-deflation spiral as entire bodies of companies, people, and banks are taken down. The fear attached is understandable. But in the second case, when deflation strikes our net worth in the absence of debt, the horror is more a product of our human bias. We are focused on nominal values, and even though we may be getting richer in real terms, we psychologically feel poorer as the digits and decimals shrink. Our loss aversion kicks in and we find ourselves despondent. That makes our response to such deflation just as powerful and explains why the mass fear of deflation always dominates, even if the individual memories fade with time.

When Mark Twain coined the phrase "Gilded Age" to describe the last quarter of the nineteenth century, he was satirizing this explosion of wealth for a perceived privileged few against the social trauma that he saw about him. Certainly, the period of the Long Depression was one typified by social tension and obsessions about the value of money. Periodic surges in unemployment and falling nominal wages were blamed on immigration and foreign competition, and concerned bodies sprang up to lobby for restrictions. Bills were passed such as the 1882 Chinese Exclusion Act that effectively barred China's first attempt to export its labor globally and led to the ubiquitous Chinatowns seen in so many cities. Native Americans and blacks were further disenfranchised, as economic priorities became an additional divisive issue. Various countries passed protectionist measures to control capital flows and protect domestic industries.

The growth and soundness of money became an international obsession. The United States, for example, in 1878 passed the Sherman Silver Act, which effectively allowed the government to inflate the money supply by purchasing large amounts of silver with paper money and reissue it as coinage. A wave of colonization in Africa took place as countries unconsciously took a page out of the Roman handbook from nearly two millennia ago and sought to grow their economies and wealth through conquering and acquisition. The British fought a series of wars against Afrikaner colonists—the Boer Wars—for control of the gold and diamond mines of South Africa in the closing years of the nineteenth century. The gold standard emerged as a global system as countries agreed to fix their currencies to gold in an effort to bring about monetary stability. In time, as growth returned in nominal terms, the above actions were lauded for rescuing economies alongside innovation and entrepreneurship. In fact, the Long Depression ended as the adjustment to a new, more industrialized economy ran its course and jobs eventually followed growth.

This was the environment that influenced society in the dawning years of the twentieth century. A new complexity of economy and society had emerged. It brought growth and prosperity, but it also contained within it psychological influences, economic incentives, innovations, and new permutations of money that would lay the foundations of the second Great Depression.

As the painful adjustments of the first Long Depression receded into hazy memory and the last century, the world was prosperous and growth continual. People felt richer every year and had more disposable income. Automation was reaching new heights—the car, the radio, the moving picture—and these products were no longer simply the preserve of the rich but were available to a far greater emergent middle class. Businesses had an ever-growing pool of customers alongside an ever-decreasing cost of production.

For all the difficulties of recent decades, economies had demonstrated continued and sustained growth, which encouraged investor confidence. The financialization of the markets had engineered a revolution in entrepreneurship and allowed fortunes to be made (and lost) by speculating on future growth and sentiment. Debt was fast becoming a structural part of the corporate landscape and was even beginning to leach over into the personal space. But in people's eyes it was not to be feared as in the past. Rather, it was to be embraced as an engine of further growth.

The rapid rise of the middle class and the fortunes minted by a few meant that the American dream was well entrenched in the popular psyche. Anyone could make a fortune with the proper graft, greasing, and luck. Money was becoming an all-important signal of status, far more than family heritage and titles.

The world entered the twentieth century in a blaze of economic glory, with large numbers of middle-class citizens, all with increasingly large amounts of disposable income. The recurrent stock market crashes associated with this new capitalism continued at periodic intervals, but increasingly the public began to put its faith in the ability of lawmakers and bankers, who understood this new complex world of international money and had nurtured such an explosion of growth out of the horrors of the Long Depression. Societies and economies had become bound closer to one another, ushering in the first era of globalization.

In 1913, following yet another set of stock market crises and recessions, Congress passed the Federal Reserve Act, creating the Federal Reserve to provide a stabilizing influence on the U.S. economy. Trust passed henceforth into this institution to steer the country through future storms. It soon formed close links with other central banks and across the banking industry to ensure that global growth would continue unabated. Lawmakers were pleased as well. They now had their experts and could focus on the dearer task at hand of continuing prosperity for their new voters and popularity for themselves.

But in the background, a loss aversion also lingered from the days of the Long Depression. Conflict between nations simmered beneath the surface, buried for now by an avalanche of growth, but ready to reappear when needed to protect each one's share of the rich economic pie. Additionally, social tensions were never far, particularly as the working classes became more urbanized and powerful as an influence within society. The international financialization of society and the accompanying rise of large institutions (both sovereign entities such as central banks and private ones such as banks and investment houses) meant that a dense, complex web of relationships yoked everyone together. If financial turmoil hit, contagion stood waiting in the wings to spread the pain further than ever.

This new complexity was agnostic, like every other complex system. It imparted a nuanced dynamic to propagate human action and its consequences throughout a growing society. But as is the nature of systems of money and trust, this dynamic was also fragile and evolved down a better or worse path with every decision taken by individuals and sovereigns. Its features were not understood. In the absence of any appreciation of the law of unintended consequences, small decisions could reverberate across time in unwanted ways and accentuate the fragility of the economic system. With poor judgment, a boon could easily turn into a burden, rapidly transmuting prosperity to penury. The ramifications of the First World War were to provide the catalyst to effect this particular phase transition.

CREDIT AND MONEY: THE FIRST WORLD WAR AND ITS AFTERMATH

The First World War is a complicated story and we cannot do it justice in a few lines. However, it is important to note both the role economic tension played in its birth and the continuing impact in its aftermath. By the end of the nineteenth century, the world had become smaller, not just in terms of trade and technology but also in terms of land. Africa had been divided up; China had become the latest colonial frontier, albeit with nominal independence; the Wild West had been domesticated.

A smaller world was richer but also more claustrophobic. Growth could no longer be gained by simply expanding territory. The Roman problem of how to sustain forward momentum now reemerged. The result was a growing set of political and military skirmishes as countries began to step on each other's toes in an attempt to gain power and a larger piece of the economic pie. This was particularly true in Europe, which had evolved over the centuries into a dense political patchwork of nations and interlocking alliances. While the alliances were meant to mitigate geopolitical risk, they also provided a transmission mechanism that could cascade a small skirmish or diplomatic spat into a far wider conflict. On June 28, 1914, the assassination of the Archduke Franz Ferdinand by a young Serbian nationalist named Gavrilo Princip provided the spark that would radiate through this network, emerging at the other end as the conflagration known as the First World War.

When war came, it was perversely an enormous boon to global growth. The advances in metallurgy, technology, and automation were put to deadlier uses. The warring nations all abandoned any pretence of sticking to the gold standard and began to print increasing amounts of money to fund their war efforts. As the death toll grew, aggregate demand surged and manufacturing found a new engine of growth. The result was a boom in economic prosperity for the colonies that exported food and resources, and for American companies that were supplying all the accouterments of war. At the same time, the inability of European countries to finance all of this distemper meant that there was good money to be made in extending loans to warring nations. Banks both in Europe and across the Atlantic profited handsomely from this in the war years.

Arguably, economic considerations were as much behind the American decision to enter World War I as humanitarian ones, particularly as the Allied nations in Europe (Britain, France, and their acolytes) were the primary recipients of all of this. The U.S. government also lent heavily to the Allies, and in the closing years of the war it even mobilized the growing pool of wealth and savings within the country. A government debt ceiling was established and Liberty bonds were issued to help the government meet its new obligations.

The latter innovation was to have an enduring impact on the financial development of the United States. Five Liberty Loans were issued from April 1917 through to April 1919, totaling a combined $21.5 billion. The inability of the U.S. government to repay these and the subsequent decision to refinance instead was a key driver behind the advent of the government bond market. The Liberty Loans also legitimized and introduced financial instruments to many Americans, millions of whom purchased these bonds. Their government backing lent them an air of security and provided another home for the money that this new economy was throwing off. The interest was also largely tax free, resulting in the creation of tax incentives that attracted even more people.

The debt ceiling was progressively raised and new loans issued until by the end of 1919, the U.S. government had some $25 billion of government debt on its books. In comparison, its expenditures at the start of the war had been under \$1 billion. This enormous aggregation created a common purpose and a herdlike mentality that was to drive U.S. foreign policy for the next two decades.

Our hedonic bias ensures that we only ever want to move forward, while our loss aversion hates seeing any reduction in wealth. For the United States, the prosperity produced by all this unexpected aggregate demand had to be sustained as a political imperative. Alongside, the savings glut born of growth had found a home in government debt and corporate expansion. It would not tolerate losses on what was real money in their eyes but just layers of fragile debt in reality.

However, as the First World War drew to a close, the surplus of aggregate demand across the world was replaced by a sudden deficit. In the aftermath, Europe faced two crippling problems. First, the conflict ravaged infrastructure and capital. Thousands of bridges, factories, roads, and mines had been destroyed. Entire industries were crippled. Some ten million military personnel and six million civilians had been killed on both sides. An additional twenty million soldiers were wounded, and many of them now depended on the state. The second major problem was financial: there were no creditors left in Europe. All the countries were heavily in debt, the natural consequence of such a punitive war. Colonial wealth had been taxed and liquidated. Money had been borrowed from domestic markets, from other European countries, and finally, in the case of the victorious Allied Powers, from the United States. Britain's national debt, for example, surged from 33 percent of GDP in 1913 to 144 percent of GDP by 1920, while all other European countries saw similar debt explosions.

Not only did Europe face huge rebuilding costs but it also suffered a massive loss of competitiveness, especially compared to the United States. Recurring bouts of inflation and persistently high unemployment were also common.

The world economy had also fundamentally changed. Before the war, Britain had been the dominant economic power. Many of the world's credit flows ran through its colonies. These holdings were large exporters of food and commodities, running substantial trade surpluses with other nations. These in turn ran surpluses with Britain, which funded its deficits by harvesting the surpluses generated by its colonies, selling goods back to them, and collecting the interest on the loans made to help them develop their industries.[2]

After the war, the model was broken. European countries were running large deficits and had crippling debts to repay. The colonies found the boom fueled by the wartime years turning to bust. Trade declined as prices fell steeply in the postwar years. The United States had grown its trade surplus significantly and was keen to protect its nascent powerhouse status.

A sharp recession occurred in 1920 and 1921 across the United States and Europe as their economies tried to find a new equilibrium in peacetime. Large numbers of soldiers now were back in the workforce looking for jobs. Meanwhile, governments and central banks had begun the task of controlling spiraling inflation by raising interest rates. Money became a more expensive and precious commodity.

The result was a protectionist orgy in the 1920s as first, Britain, then the United States, and finally Europe all began to enact tariff barriers to protect and grow their precious few revenue streams to the exclusion of others. It was a reaction born of past experience as noted earlier, but all these efforts to right individual imbalances were in vain.

At the end of World War I, the Treaty of Versailles began to examine the thorny issues of detailing the peace, unpicking this complex web of debt, and repairing sovereign balance sheets. At the outset, U.S. president Woodrow Wilson outlined his (in)famous Fourteen Points, espousing themes of reconciliation, free trade, disarmament, the rollback of colonialism, and self-determination. The Nobel Committee had no hesitation in awarding him the Nobel Peace Prize that year for his honorable intentions. Unfortunately, intentions and outcomes are not the same thing.

Though the Fourteen Points brought everyone to the table with grand humanist ambitions, there was little camaraderie. The alliances born of war soon fell apart as each country rushed to pursue its own self-interests. The United States demanded repayment of the $12 billion the Allies owed it. The Allies demanded in turn the billions lent to each other, chiefly by Britain to the Continent. Germany as the main aggressor was asked to provide reparations to cover both the damages suffered during the war as well as the sums owed to the United States. The French had the most austere demands, driven by a potent national-ist cocktail reflecting their long enmity and desire to see Germany permanently weakened.

There was anger that the United States, which had ended the war with enhanced prosperity and established itself as the new global super-power, demanded repayment in full and would not countenance any form of debt forgiveness. The British were loath to pay the Americans till they got money from France, Germany, and others. The French wouldn't pay the British or the Americans until the Germans paid them for the war damages and the wounds inflicted on their national pride. The Germans claimed they couldn't afford to pay the amounts demanded without bankrupting their nation. Over all of this hung the specter of the October Revolution of 1917 in Russia, where the incoming Bolsheviks had defaulted on all of Russia's foreign debts, wiping out billions owed to the British and French.

Bitterness, suspicion, and hostility were soon commonplace. John Maynard Keynes—then part of the British delegation—resigned in frus-tration and published his famous polemic *The Economic Consequences of the Peace*. In it, he argued that the punitive damages being sought and the inflexible attitudes toward war debts on all sides would destabilize European economies and eventually culminate in another war. It was a prescient statement.

A CRISIS OF MONEY

Negotiations dragged on into 1920 and then 1921. The American govern-ment tired of the bickering, and the American public, weary also of the ongoing recession, began to clamor for an isolationist policy. Without U.S. support, Wilson's grand international forum, the League of Nations, which had been designed to handle all future disputes, foundered and eventually became ineffectual and ceremonial. The French seized control of proceed-ings and pushed forward their own agenda of neutralizing any future German threat.

Despite these troubles, reparations initially got off to a good start. The Germans had accepted the principle of reparations as the necessary price for peace. They also agreed that this extra burden on the public finances would require deep structural reforms. Accordingly, they over-hauled their archaic tax code and replaced it with a central regime in an attempt to raise revenues. Together with a postwar bout of inflation, this gradually helped to rebuild the government's balance sheet.

In 1921, the Inter-Allied Reparations Commission (charged with overseeing negotiations and ensuring compliance) finally agreed to a repa-rations bill for Germany of 269 billion goldmarks, some $800 billion in today's terms. After further negotiation, this was revised down to 132 billion goldmarks later that year. The reparations consisted of three tranches: "A" bonds totaling 12 billion goldmarks, to compensate for direct war damage to the Allies; "B" bonds totaling 38 billion goldmarks, earmarked for repayment of the inter-Allied war debt owed by Britain and France to the United States; and "C" bonds totaling 82 billion goldmarks, aimed at neutering Germany economically.

The denomination in goldmarks was significant. Like the rest of Europe, Germany had effectively suspended the gold standard during the war and resorted to credit and currency debasement to fund its war effort. The resulting inflation had been a boon, eroding the value of its debt in real terms. By 1920, the paper mark was worth only 10 percent of its prewar value and public debt had actually fallen as a share of GDP. Because the Allies didn't want the Germans to inflate away the repara-tions debt, now they fixed its value to the historically stable prewar gold standard. At the same time, a strong consensus of economists and politi-cians also believed the international gold standard should be restored at prewar parities.

All combined, the reparations were equivalent to around 260 percent of Germany's prewar GDP. When these reparations were coupled with the existing public debt, Germany faced a total debt burden of over 300 percent of GDP. It is important to point out that the "C" bonds were purely punitive. In practice, creditors focused only on the payment of the "A" and "B" bonds, though these were still 99 percent of German GDP on their own. The repayments were critical for relieving the pressures on the British and French economies. Though it is debatable whether the Allies really intended to collect on the "C" bonds, the headline numbers made for grim reading and added to the growing sense of resentment and anger in Germany.

The reparations sowed the seeds of a series of German economic disasters that signposted the road to the Great Depression. They played a pivotal role in Germany's hyperinflation episode of 1923. When the Allies attempted to make reparations more palatable under the 1924 Dawes Plan, growth returned but accompanied by a huge credit bubble thanks to unsustainable foreign capital inflows. With the introduction of the Young Plan in 1929, the bubble burst and the economy collapsed—even before the U.S. stock market crash later that year, which is often seen as the start of the Great Depression.

Once the reality of reparations became clear, the mood in Germany soured. Tax revenues began to fall, strike action became more common, and populist parties emerged, either advocating mass socialism or fanning the flames of nationalism. The government was denounced as a traitor for signing the Treaty of Versailles. In August 1921, Matthias Erzberger—the former finance minister who signed the treaty and authored the resulting tax reforms—was assassinated by the Organization Consul, an ultranationalist group. A few months later, Walther Rathenau, the foreign minister, was also murdered.

This climate of hostility toward the Allies also encouraged a greater tolerance of inflation. Printing money soon became a natural way for the government to try to plug the hole in its public finances. Officials also hoped that by pushing down the exchange rate, they could boost exports and growth. While higher inflation helped German businesses and reduced the real value of domestic debts, it did nothing to alleviate the real burden of reparations because these had to be paid in either gold or foreign currencies.

Alongside, the new dynamics of the global economy meant that every European country was trying to repair an ailing sovereign balance sheet. Germany was particularly vulnerable: reparations were critical to restoring fiscal order for the Allies, but those same countries also impeded German recovery through protectionist barriers.

This quickly became an inflationary spiral. In the absence of rapidly growing exports, Germany printed marks to buy the foreign currency it required. As the money supply expanded, the paper mark fell in value, which required further increases in the money supply to maintain the same level of payments. The same vicious spiral also inflamed geopolitical tensions both within Germany and between Germany and its creditors. The Treaty of Versailles allowed part of the reparations to be paid in kind, particularly raw materials that would help the Allies rebuild their shattered industries. France took the largest share of these because the war had hit its industry particularly hard. But German apathy, coupled with an economic incentive to divert production toward exports that generated foreign currency reserves, meant shipments of these goods were often delayed, smaller than promised, or cancelled.

The growing tensions and Germany's inflationary efforts came to a head in early 1923. The previous December, the Germans had failed to deliver a shipment of lumber to the Allies. In January, they defaulted again—this time on a coal delivery.[3] France began to argue for direct military pressure, while Britain suggested that perhaps reparation payments should be reduced. Battle lines were drawn between those who saw the Germans as unwilling to pay versus those who saw the Germans as unable to pay.

The French view prevailed. In early January, the Reparations Commission declared Germany in default and on January 11, 1923, France and Belgium invaded and occupied the Ruhr valley, the heartland of German industry, accounting for 80 percent of German production of coal, iron, and steel. The aim was to force the Germans to keep their side of the reparations treaty. It backfired. The Germans undertook a policy of passive resistance that increasingly acquired shades of a self-righteous war. During this *Ruhrkampf*, the government supported the population in its protest through an expansive program of benefits and industry bailouts. Production stalled—falling to a third of its previous level within a year—and the costs for both sides rapidly mounted. The result was more money printing. Inflation, already high, now rapidly spiraled out of control, and a population psychologically surrendered to fears about an uncertain future, stoking monetary velocity. The results were forever

seared in cultural memory as the Weimar hyperinflation episode. A toler-
able exchange rate of 6.7 marks to the U.S. dollar at the end of 1919 had
given way just four years later to one where it cost 4.2 trillion marks to
purchase a single dollar.[4]

The impasse was resolved only in November 1923, when the
Germans introduced a new currency, the rentenmark, which was backed
by physical assets and indexed to gold. Replaced by the reichmark a year
later, it signaled the end of hyperinflation and a return to the gold standard—albeit a slightly modified one—that existed before the war.

Germany was not the only nation wedded to the gold standard. For
most of the other European countries, notably Britain, there was a rose-
tinted melancholy associated with gold and its perceived stability. They
saw a return to the gold standard at prewar exchange rates as a precursor
to restoring their economic health. This was ill-advised.

The system had evolved in complexity since 1913. Wages and prices
had become a lot less flexible after the war, thanks to the growth of trade
unions, the advent of the middle class, and their increasing political clout.
At the same time, debt and prices had exploded in the interim. Any return
to the prewar gold standard meant engineering a deep recession. But forcing change by hammering those further down the social pyramid was no
longer going to work. The interplay of deflation and debt was also not fully
appreciated. The obstinate refusal to let go of this obsession with the gold
standard meant that these countries were condemned to deflationary
forces and lackluster growth for most of the 1920s. This was to have a
terrible toll on national psyches and lead to a renewed focus on resolving
the debt burdens across Europe.

THE SOOTHING EMBRACE OF DEBT

Across the Atlantic, none of this underlying tension was particularly visible
to the American public. In the United States, real wages stagnated since
the end of the war, a consequence of an excess of labor coupled with
increases in productivity. The 1920–21 recession was a sharp and painful
Schumpeterian adjustment. Farmland prices collapsed and manufacturers
suddenly found orders falling. Bankruptcies inevitably followed. All this

was exacerbated by the raising of interest rates by the Federal Reserve in an effort to control inflation. Warren Harding, Wilson's successor as president, responded with a mixture of tax cuts, spending cuts, and reallocations toward public spending. By 1921, growth had resumed and the recession soon faded into obscurity.

However, the recession also raised issues of how to perpetuate growth in the longer term. Tariffs became a popular political mainstay. Firms began to focus more on domestic demand and the banks stepped in to provide the necessary tools to fuel this. The miracle of credit began to ripple outward in society, through innovations such as paying on credit— where you could choose to buy now and pay back in installments. A virtuous circle was created whereby credit gave physical expression to demand today leading to more transactions, rising growth, a growing confidence in the future, and the extension of further credit. Corporate profits grew thanks to a potent cocktail of stagnating real wages, productivity gains from automation, tax incentives, trade barriers to foreign competition, and the resumption of lending. Alongside, money flowed in as first, gold fled the uncertainty of Europe for the growth reappearing on American shores, and second, the vast pools of wealth generated domestically in recent decades sought new opportunities to buttress their status. Meanwhile, the Federal Reserve had now become sensitized in the aftermath of the 1920–21 recession to the political ramifications of raising interest rates too quickly. In later years, this was bound to come back to haunt them as they ummed and ahhed over interest rates in the late 1920s.

Meanwhile, weak global growth and continued sovereign strains in Europe meant that debt renegotiations remained high on the international policy agenda. The Harding administration established the World War Foreign Debt Commission in February 1922 to negotiate repayments of inter-Allied war loans. No debts were to be written off and strict limits were put on the maturity and interest rates of any loans renegotiated. In practice, maturities were continually extended and interest rates steadily reduced in negotiation after negotiation, as it became clear that the Allies were unable or unwilling to pay.

In an effort to preserve its economic strength in the face of repeated European debt crises, the United States gave Charles Dawes, a former director of the U.S. Bureau of the Budget, the task of finding a solution to the European impasse. His proposal saw the United States become the lender of last resort and a direct financier of European government deficits.

The Dawes Plan of 1924 cut annual German reparations significantly to 1 billion marks, rising gradually to 2.5 billion marks after five years. France and Belgium withdrew their military forces from the Ruhr and the Germans introduced new taxes as well as restrictions on the Reichsbank. The Americans provided a loan of $100 million to Germany to help stabilize and rehabilitate the economy.

Most important, the Dawes Plan introduced a clause whereby the Reichsbank agreed to satisfy all foreign commercial claims before dealing with reparation payments. This made Germany a more attractive target for commercial loans because these would effectively rank above the reparation bonds. Germany's perceived credit risk declined and a huge wave of U.S. bank lending flooded the country. A new web of war debt emerged, where U.S. loans to Germany effectively funded reparations to other European nations, allowing them to pay off their own war debts to each other and finally back to the United States.

This ignited a powerful boom within Germany, so much so that by 1929, the country was the second-largest economy in the world. From 1924 to 1929, Germany borrowed some 18.6 billion marks from abroad, with only 10.5 billion marks being paid out in reparations. The country went on a spending binge, pouring money into public infrastructure such as subways, public housing, and transport. The spending quickly translated into rapid economic growth.[5]

The Dawes Plan ushered in a period of apparent prosperity. Policy makers hoped the calm in markets would reassert political stability and translate into sustainable growth by a process some would have called "positive contagion."[6] The more troubling question of whether the war debts were sustainable in the long term remained unanswered.[7]

Within the United States, consumption and financial speculation were firmly entrenched as engines of growth. Financialization followed all this money coming in, providing supply to meet the demand. Loans were made first to good credits and later to more and more speculative ones as the excess of money flowing in drove yields steadily downward. Latin American loans, the harbinger of many a financial crisis, found themselves back in fashion. The stock market became a visible barometer—mistakenly—of economic growth and public confidence. The rapid gains and fortunes that could be made here excited a new generation of investors, who found the process of compounding steady gains too long and tedious. Money was lent to invest in stocks. Brokerages sprang up rapidly offering to facilitate investments and allow people to invest on margin.[8] This was leverage pure and simple.

As incentives evolved, an arbitrage of emotion followed as people increasingly focused on the immediacy of generating profits. The emphasis changed from generating profits in real terms to financial wizardry. Companies developed sophisticated capital structures with multiple layers of debt that allowed them to leverage small rises in earnings into far larger rises in profitability at the top level. Investment companies were set up whose only purpose was to take clients' monies and invest them in all these new exciting opportunities. Sustainability increasingly became an afterthought as strong growth perpetuated.

The system was interconnected as never before. But this new complexity evaded those charged with its oversight. The Federal Reserve was more worried about global stability and events in Europe. Interest rates were lowered in 1925 and again in 1927 in an attempt to prevent too much gold flowing outward to U.S. shores. The knock-on effect was to allow money and credit to grow exponentially as the cost of borrowing dwindled and the returns of speculation remained enticingly high.

The well-trodden fallacy of justification became prevalent. The passing of the Nineteenth Amendment to the U.S. Constitution in 1920 gave women the vote. The familiar refrain of the bicycle boom years at the turn of the century was resurrected. As all these fiercely independent women joined the workforce and began to invest their savings, both demand and the stock market surely only had one future direction. Others pointed to the continuing rapid pace of technological progress and the resulting increases in productivity. Then, there was the consumptive boom driven by an exuberant economy—cars, radios, and cinemas were the new paradigms for a growing pool of consumers, who would earn even more in years to come. Even Prohibition became an engine of growth in the eyes of some, who argued that the ban on alcohol would result in higher productivity and increased demand for other goods.

The property market boomed as well. Mortgages became a widespread phenomenon for the first time as people could now borrow half the money to buy homes. This represented a huge leap forward in affordability for the emerging middle class. Developers began to build ambitious new projects to take advantage of the growing demand for offices, houses, hotels, and the like. In Florida, for example, the value of a building permit in Miami rose from $89,000 in 1919 to a staggering $7,993,500 in 1925—a rise of nearly 9,000 percent during a short-lived land boom.

Nationally, home prices quadrupled in value. By the middle of the 1920s, the big metropolises such as New York and Chicago went on an orgy of building that would remain unmatched for another eighty years. Between 1921 and 1932, New York alone built 235 skyscrapers, including icons such as the MetLife Building and the Empire State Building. Most were financed through the stock market and bonds issued to a wide spectrum of sophisticated and public investors.

Participants like to believe that a boom can be perpetual. But debt is only ever a tool, not an answer. The vast volume of savings and the web of debt that they represented were money borrowed against future growth. As they grew, it became all the more imperative that the rosy growth they projected came true. However, the complex network of an economy is inherently dynamic and fragile with every added layer. There will inevitably be shocks to the system; often they will be small, but sometimes they will be large. If the system lacks the structural flexibility to accommodate change and failure—often when people and institutions are similarly myopic and euphoric—the adjustment and ramifications caused by these inescapable shocks can spread rapidly and cause severe damage.

THE PRESSURES OF COMPLEXITY

Beneath the surface, the economic and trade imbalances across the global economy continued to widen. Protectionism remained the de facto domestic economic policy of choice. Europe collectively found itself growing its debt burden but without new markets to expand into.

Most countries—especially the United States—were not willing to embrace free trade. Large-scale debt forgiveness of war loans, reparations, and so on looked impossible. The global financial system was also becoming increasingly fragile—the duration of reparations, war loans, commercial and personal debt, and deficits increased while the loans that financed them were much shorter-term. This left the large economies increasingly susceptible to shifts in sentiment in the financial markets.

An additional problem, for Germany in particular, was that most of this debt was foreign, not domestic. This reduced policy makers' ability to effectively manage any economic downturn. The stabilization of currencies and the return of the gold standard meant that countries were yoked together once again through fixed exchange rates. But this time, they were all dependent on credit from the United States. As leverage in the system grew, the underlying problems became more acute.

In 1928, the first worries among investors about the creditworthiness of German debt emerged. The debt burden had grown thanks to Germany's vigorous use of the financial markets and reparation payments had also risen in line with the Dawes Plan. It was unclear if there was sufficient appetite in the financial markets to refinance reparations past the "A" bonds, particularly given the growing size and short-term nature of the commercial debt burden.

At the same time, U.S. banks and corporations saw better opportunities on the domestic front, where private investment was still booming. Although the Federal Reserve had begun to raise interest rates, speculation remained intense given the potential returns on offer. Margin lending rose rapidly over 1928 as the stock market continued to boom. That year saw the launch of more than two hundred investment trusts, which were soon adding to both the speculative frenzy of buying and selling shares as well as lending their surplus cash out to others.

In December 1928, a new trust was launched by Goldman Sachs, one of the new breed of investment banks born of the financialization of the American economy in the late nineteenth century. Named the Goldman Sachs Trading Corporation, it soon spawned a number of new entities such as the Shenandoah Corporation and the Blue Ridge Trust over the next few months. As Goldman and its subsidiaries borrowed more and more money against the ever-growing value of their assets—the collateral mistakenly convincing their lenders that they had ample security—leverage grew. The various trusts began to speculate in each other's shares. The biased view of investors meant that this was seen as a wonderful innovation. Goldman Sachs stood to make vast profits for itself and its investors thanks to all this implicit leverage. But leverage goes both ways, and the firm also faced large losses if any of these firms fell into difficulty.

Beneath this financial gloss of success, the economy was under strain. The combination of low rates and easy credit had led to an unparalleled boom. However, stagnating wages and the growing reliance on credit also meant that debt servicing was a fact of life for many businesses and families in the real world. It is never the quantum of debt that matters. Rather, it is the monthly and annual cost of the payments that are made on that debt. As more and more debt is taken on, the margin for error and misfortune shrinks. A lost job, a bad harvest, an unexpected rise in interest rates, or a fall in sales or margins can now take an individual or business down. The foundations of prosperity have become fragile and the field of dreams contains numerous hidden landmines.

The Federal Reserve's raising of interest rates in 1928 may not have done much to dampen speculation, but it did make it harder for those with real loans to pay them back. The Federal Reserve had failed to realize that control of interest rates did not translate into control of money and credit. Innovation means that money takes many different forms when there is an excess of demand for it, as we have seen numerous times. Central bankers were learning firsthand that like Pandora's box, the forces of debt were impossible to corral once unleashed. They had been so focused on the growth of speculative credit that they had become oblivious to the results of their actions on the real economy that underpinned these layers of speculative leverage.

There had been earlier opportunities to prick the euphoria. The 1925 land boom and bust in Florida in 1925, for example, had led to a natural downturn in the stock markets. But nothing was done, thanks to political sensibilities and an inability to appreciate the complex ramifications of laissez-faire when it came to the debt building up within the system. Indeed, the subsequent cuts in interest rates had only served to spur more frantic rounds of speculation as the mind-set took hold that the stock market was sacrosanct to the authorities.

The overhang of real estate debt was problematic now, as many of these skyscrapers proved to be an economic ambition too far. The troubles in Europe meant that American exports faced renewed weakness in key markets. The booming market in lending to sovereign nations—Germany and Latin America chief among them—was finding out that there was such a concept as sovereign risk (and default). The population was reaching a saturation point when it came to debt, and the rise in interest rates only added to the pressure on them.

All this escaped the notice of European money heading to American shores. Europe was preoccupied with its own obsessions. The Allies had stabilized their currencies and were seeing growth again. The United States had concluded its long series of bilateral debt renegotiations with them and didn't want to concede further write-downs. Political pressure was growing to reach a final settlement on the reparations to be paid by Germany and, by implication, on the certainty of the Allied payments to the United States.

As 1929 began, Germany found itself trapped once again in the nightmare of 1922. Loans were drying up and the economy was suffering. Meanwhile, reparations had moved up the agenda precisely when German policy makers felt unable to afford them. The gold exchange standard created an additional complication. In 1928, as the Federal Reserve raised interest rates, gold reserves left the vaults of central banks in Europe and rushed across the Atlantic. The deflationary actions of the United States rapidly transmitted globally as central banks elsewhere were forced to raise interest rates to mitigate these gold outflows.[9] Germany was particularly badly hit, given its dependence on foreign inflows of credit. The deleveraging and downturn gathered momentum.

The German population was accustomed to growth and a returning sense of status. Admission into the League of Nations had signaled an end to international isolation. But beneath the surface, reparations were still an unresolved emotive issue. The terrible uncertain years of the Weimar hyperinflation were still fresh in memory.

Concerns over Germany's credit worthiness now led to another official "solution" to the reparations issue—the Young Plan. Reparations were reduced slightly to 112 billion goldmarks while annual payments now stretched out to 1988. The larger part could be postponed for up to two years if needed. Germany could also avail itself of new "stabilization loans" from the Allies. All this would be overseen by a new body—the Bank for International Settlements—run by the world's central banks.

In the sterile world of policy making, the Young Plan represented a modest improvement for the German people. But in the real world, it was far less pleasing. The revised reparations bill was still set far in excess of what the Germans had been expecting, creating further resentment within the country. In addition, the Plan removed the "transfer protection" clause that had made private loans to Germany senior to reparations. This intensified the market's emerging concerns about Germany's credit rating—its ability to repay debt going forward, as assessed by independent ratings agencies. In particular, these ratings captured both economic and political risks.

As details of the deal leaked out, markets reacted poorly. A German government bond issuance failed; there was a run on the Reichsbank; and capital began to flow out more rapidly. As public confidence evaporated and unemployment rose, strikes resumed. Unlike in 1922–23, German policy makers and the Reichsbank did not respond by printing money because they didn't want to destroy their new hard-won credibility. They hoped the Young Plan—though stricter than anticipated—was a final step to restoring full German sovereignty, especially as the Plan included the withdrawal of the remaining French troops from German territory.

THE POINT OF CRITICALITY

The Young plan emphasized adherence to the gold exchange standard. This immediately presented major difficulties as Germany needed to run a trade surplus with the United States and France if it was to avoid a repeat of the early 1920s. Yet, unlike those early years, there was no currency to devalue to regain competitiveness. Rather, with the exchange rates fixed under the gold standard, austerity and deflation were the only way to try to rebuild export markets. Germany started cutting costs and wages to restore competitiveness.

While many Germans initially supported austerity, the experience of it turned out to be very different from what they expected. The aftermath of the Weimar hyperinflation had wiped out the savings of many ordinary Germans, making wage stability and growth paramount in their eyes. Widening inequality was also creating rising social tensions. The benefits of subsequent growth were perceived to have gone to just a small elite of industrialists, financiers, and insiders. A comprehensive program of social benefits had created a cordon sanitaire to prevent these tensions from boiling over. But that was now at risk.

The raw emotions beneath the surface began to reemerge. In 1929, demands by extremist parties for an end to reparations, a repudiation of war guilt, and the denouncement of the "traitors" who had signed these agreements led to a national referendum on a "Law against the Enslavement of the German People."[10] The turnout was poor—a mere 14.9 percent, which meant it was not legally binding. But of these, 94.5 percent voted to approve the law. It was a warning sign of the depth of feeling waiting to be tapped.

Meanwhile, across the Atlantic, the U.S. economy had begun a downturn in mid-1929. The market didn't immediately wake up to this fact. But as the network assimilated little bits of information, the social knowledge that Hayek had hypothesized began to emerge as growing tremors in the stock market.

On September 3, 1929, the Dow Jones closed at 381.17—a new record high. It would be 1954 before that milestone would be surpassed. The record was an unusual upsurge in an increasingly weak market. A series of particularly strong wheat harvests around the world in the summer had caused wheat prices to crash. Agriculture was still a significant part of the American economy, and the glut of wheat threatened to derail both farmers and their lenders. Capitol Hill had begun to debate the Smoot-Hawley Tariff Act—the most sweeping protectionist legislation yet, which raised tariffs on over twenty thousand categories of goods. Dozens of international trading partners had lodged protests and threatened retaliatory measures. The market was perturbed.

A few days later, Clarence Hatry—a prominent British tycoon with the only rooftop pool in London—was refused an emergency loan by the Bank of England, and trading in the shares of Hatry Group was suspended on September 20. The London Stock Exchange crashed in response, which sent jitters through U.S. markets. Rumors began to spread about weaknesses elsewhere and sentiment grew distinctly more cautious as the market trended slightly downward.

October began with frenzied activity. On October 4—thereafter known in popular parlance as Black Thursday—the Dow opened down 11 percent as investors began to sell positions. A series of audacious purchases by a consortium of leading bankers meant that the day closed only slightly down—less than 2 percent. But the market was rapidly assessing and transmitting panicked knowledge. As papers began to cover the events in enormous detail, even more investors rushed to sell their stocks.

On October 28, Black Monday, the Dow lost 13 percent of its value. Black Tuesday saw another 12 percent effortlessly vanish from tickers. The Wall Street crash was under way.

The spectacular downturn in the United States accelerated the flight of gold and capital back to the United States as the crowd headed for the nearest exit. U.S. investors called in their foreign loans, sought liquidity from their overseas holdings to meet their losses, and hoarded perceived safe assets such as gold in an effort to preserve their shrinking wealth. In 1929, U.S. financial institutions stopped all new lending and began to exit existing loans. Global economic depression was now setting in.

Across in Germany, industrial output began to fall and businesses were failing at an alarming rate. A debt deflation spiral took hold. Reserves fell and the money supply contracted. In response, the government pursued yet more austerity, cutting its spending in the face of dwindling revenues. Over the next three years, revenues would drop by 27 percent while spending would fall by nearly 31 percent. As the self-defeating mathematics of austerity bit, the debt to GDP ratio rose from 75 percent to over 100 percent. Unemployment soared to over 30 percent by 1932.

The Young stabilization loan represented the only capital inflows into Germany at this time. Driven by demands from the Allies for continued austerity, a minority government ushered in increasingly unpopular policies through emergency decrees rather than parliamentary votes. New elections took place in September 1930 that starkly illustrated the frustration of the German populace and their growing disenchantment with the international community. Parties at the extreme ends of the political spectrum saw significant gains. The Nazi Party increased its seats from just 12 to 107 to become the second-largest party in the Reichstag, with the bulk of its growth coming from lower-middle-class voters worried about unemployment and future hardship. Alongside, the Communists gained 23 seats to become the third largest party with 77 seats. This further inflamed investor concern about the stability of the German economy.

Meanwhile, the U.S. downturn had caused a major global credit crunch. The situation was exacerbated by poor policy making. U.S. president Herbert Hoover tried to let the markets sort their own mess out by encouraging them to set up their own stabilization vehicles—a complete misreading of the psychological state after the confidence-shaking events of 1929 and thereafter. The Federal Reserve rushed to stabilize the economy in light of all the gold flowing in and raised interest rates, accelerating the pain. Between the government and central bankers, there was suddenly an absence of leadership. No one seemed to take any responsibility for stemming the collapse in the economy that was becoming apparent. Four thousand banks went under between 1929 and 1932 in a series of runs that destroyed much of the economic infrastructure and transmission mechanisms of the complex American economic network. Given their role as lenders to the wider world—through exports and directly—this was a severe and destructive unwinding of complexity at the global level. When Hoover finally did set up a rescue vehicle—the Reconstruction Finance Corporation—in 1932, it was given only $2 billion—a wholly inadequate amount and far too late.

The money stock in the first half of 1931 began to shrink at an annualized rate of more than 6 percent. Countries began to pursue policies they felt to be in their own interest but which only intensified the collective failure. The Smoot-Hawley Tariff was passed in 1920 and the threatened retaliations became facts. U.S. exports suddenly found themselves shut out of key markets at a time when the engines of growth desperately needed fuel. Successive nations introduced a series of protectionist measures, intensifying the hoarding of precious capital into perceived safe havens and causing a collapse in world trade from $2.9 billion in 1929 to just $1.1 billion in 1932.

In May 1931, the Creditanstalt Bank collapsed. It was the largest bank in Austria and in its aftermath, a series of bank runs forced the Austrian authorities to abandon the gold standard. The contagion spread to Germany as investors worried about the future value and safety of their German deposits and loans. In the absence of any coordinated action from central banks, companies and banks began to go under. A wave of nationalizations took place as the banking system collapsed. But Germany still stubbornly refused to give up on the gold standard.

The crisis came to a head in June 1931, with Germany claiming it was in danger of defaulting on its payments of both commercial loans and reparations. Hoover quickly negotiated a one-year moratorium on all sovereign debts in an effort to stem the crisis. It was a popular move with the financial markets—the German stock market jumped more than 25 percent in a single day. However, it was less popular with the French, who believed the German threat was just another attempt to wriggle out of reparations. The resulting wrangles ensured it was some months before everyone returned to the negotiating table.

European representatives organized a conference in Lausanne in 1932. They concluded that both inter-Allied war loans and reparations should be written off, almost completely. German reparations were to be eliminated by the issuance of 3 billion reichsmarks' worth of bonds to the Bank for International Settlements. These would then be sold on over the next fifteen years to private investors. At the same time, they hoped the United States would write off all the inter-Allied war loans.

The deal didn't hold. Despite support from banks and businesses, the U.S. Congress rejected the proposal in December 1932, insisting that war loans were separate from reparations. The moratorium expired with no deal in place. For Germany, it was already too late. The year 1932 had been one of complete economic and social paralysis. Three chancellors had come and gone. Unemployment had risen to over 30 percent. Deflation was entrenched. The population had grown tired of never-ending austerity and the politicians and bankers who were responsible for the crisis.

Extremist political parties had become mainstream. With every uptick in unemployment, the Nazis and other extremist parties had increased their share of the vote and their seats in parliament over successive elections. Over half of the Reichstag was now composed of communist and Nazi parliamentarians, and the elections of 1932 had established the Nazis as the largest party in the Reichstag. In January 1933, the aging president of the German Republic, Paul von Hindenburg invited Adolf Hitler, the leader of the Nazi Party, to form the next government. Economic conditions had begun to ease but socially and psychologically, it was too late. New elections in March 1933 gave Hitler 288 seats, 43 percent of the popular vote and growing power.

Shortly after, Germany defaulted on all its reparation debts. Commercial loans were renegotiated and a policy of autarky (economic self-sufficiency) replaced an export-led economy. Other countries followed suit and the whole web of reparations and inter-Allied war debts collapsed amid widespread defaults. In response, the U.S. Congress angrily passed the Johnson Debt Default Act in 1934—a law prohibiting future loans to nations that had defaulted on previous loans from the United States. But it was an impotent nod to a domestic audience under economic and psychological stress.

Eventually, even the mighty United States defaulted in April 1934 on the final Liberty Loan. It was a stealth default—rather than paying in gold as the terms required, the United States chose instead to pay in paper dollars, resulting in bondholders receiving back less than 60 cents on the dollar in real terms.

Over the rest of the decade, as growth slowly resumed, the United States pursued a series of increasingly interventionist policies that concentrated ever greater power in the hands of the state. The welfare state began to take shape in the form of the New Deal. Fannie Mae and Freddie Mac ensured that the government would effectively underwrite the lowest common denominator of status—housing—going forward. The government would now stand firmly behind the economy, ready to support it with fiscal and monetary stimulus in the future. Regulation would provide the fortress against future financial crises. Central bankers would be the new soothsayers, reading the tea leaves of uncertainty to warn against future danger. The lenders of last resort had come of age.

All of this was welcomed by a population scarred by the last few years. The Great Depression became part of its cultural memory and a staple in literature and the movies. A more cautious approach to the world appeared as people began to save more and obsess about the perils of debt. Savings began to rise, ready to fuel the next cycle when it emerged. Most important, trust grew in policy makers and their promises, making institutions more powerful and influential in this new paradigm.

American reforms were not alone. Europe and other countries took similar paths. A new complexity had emerged from the ashes of the old. It introduced new variables, created new incentives, and despite its best intentions would birth more bubbles in the future. The intrinsic nature of our moneyed networks went unappreciated once more.

By the latter half of the 1930s, almost all economies had recovered strongly, buoyed by a massive Keynesian stimulus. Unfortunately, much of that stimulus had gone on building tanks, battleships, and fighter planes. In the following years, the stimulus would rise even more as all these were brought into use and a renewed appetite for commodities and industrial supplies led to booming economies once again.

And the rest, as they say, is history.

Part V
Lifting the Veil

CHAPTER 15

Greeks Bearing Gifts:
A Tragicomedy

The human species, according to the best theory I can form of it,
is composed of two distinct races, the men who borrow, and the
men who lend.

—CHARLES LAMB (1775–1834)

In an avalanche, no single snowflake feels itself responsible.

—VOLTAIRE (1694–1778)

IN the fourth century B.C., thirteen Greek city-states took out large loans
from the Temple of Apollo at Delos to help meet their ongoing expenses.
They were collectively known as the Delian League and were the vestiges
of a once grander empire led by Athens.

Athens had become the dominant city-state in Greece following
victory against the Greeks' hated enemies, the Persians, in 479 B.C. As a
military and economic powerhouse, trade, slaves, and money all flowed to
Athens in the subsequent few decades. Athens's network of trade links,
states and individuals grew more complex. The money supply and demand
for currency to facilitate trade, tribute, and the demonstration of status
grew in tandem, each feeding off the other.

Inevitably, human innovation ensured that a secondary industry of
finance sprang up to enable this growth in complexity. It offered to take
deposits and preserve wealth on one hand, while greasing the wheels of
this new economy with maritime, agrarian, and other necessary loans. By
modern standards, ancient Greek finance was limited. The state was all
dominant and wealth was concentrated in far fewer hands. Credit was
extended to only the most secure—sovereigns, businesses, and wealthy
individuals—and the most desperate, who would pay anything to gain
precious money immediately. But it was enough to help yoke together

human actors and their dealings into a complex whole that none truly understood. As prosperity and a feeling of confidence diffused across society, memories grew short. An illusion of control over an uncertain world took hold. As incentives shifted, the nature of society began to change as well.

Cities grew larger and more urbanized thanks to all this trade. Wars ensured that one-third of the population was now slaves—a deep pool of cheap labor. The wealth of Athens and its vassals meant that the local harsh agricultural terrain was no longer a limiting factor for growth. Grain could be imported and the population soon swelled well beyond its Malthusian limits. A new middle class of urban residents sprang up above the vast underclass of subsistence seen in so many other ancient societies. Many were capable of buying houses and having surplus monies to spend or save.

Out of these simple individual actions and their complex aggregate emerged a golden age under the leadership of Pericles that led to ancient Greece's pervasive influence on the course of human history. This was the stage for many of the ancient Greek philosophers and writers we now know so well: Socrates, Plato, Sophocles, Herodotus, and so on. The first scientists, such as Democritus and Anaxagoras, sprang up to ponder what the atom and the universe might look like. The father of medicine, Hippocrates (whose name is still invoked by doctors to this day in the Hippocratic Oath) was born. The Acropolis—the pinnacle of Greek architecture—and many other beautiful temples throughout the country were constructed. The foundations of democracy and the proto–welfare state began to take shape as Athens and its followers harbored grander political and social ambitions.

This was the upside of complexity. Innovation may be viewed as a positive shock to a system. A man's thoughts, ambitions, and dreams could be shared, discussed, and refined with others till society benefited from this exchange. Money was a key ingredient. The surplus of money allowed Athenians time for leisure and encouraged closer interaction. Whether they chose to use that to watch Greek plays, build grand buildings, or impress their contemporaries with their quick-wittedness, money was a constant thread in that tapestry.

On the downside, a complex network was also capable of transmitting negative shocks. The collection of so many bodies in close quarters meant that epidemics were common, with Pericles himself dying in a plague outbreak in 429 B.C. The intricate network of political and trade alliances ensured tensions and wars were never far away. By 440 B.C., Athens was fighting an extended war with Sparta, its main rival, for Greek hegemony. Successive wars dragged on for decades and eventually led to the collapse of the Athenian empire.

There was also the question of debt. Complexity is expensive. The grand ambitions of Athens and its vassal states meant enormous costs for the state. Trade and repeated warfare were also expensive affairs. In 378 B.C., the Delian League reformed under the auspices of Athens to challenge Sparta. The members agreed to take on significant costs by providing the League with ships, weapons, and men. With empty treasuries at home, the city-states approached the temple of Apollo at Delos for loans. As repositories of public confidence coupled with an aura of divine protection, temples were the proto-depositories and primeval banks of the ancient world.

The following year, the Spartans launched a surprise attack on Athens and imposed a naval blockade to prevent food coming in. It was an old tactic, successfully deployed in the last war to break Athens's spirit. Panic set in and a run on the banks ensued. Several major banks went under. As revenues collapsed, the members of the Delian League found themselves exposed. Even the prospect of divine retribution bowed to the realities of finance, as the ability to repay the loans diminished and sovereign insolvency beckoned. Eventually, two of the thirteen states in the Delian League defaulted completely. Another eight likely apologized profusely to Apollo and his earthly representatives as they defaulted on part of the loans.

We have few other details but this was the first recorded financial crisis in history. Today, twenty-four hundred years on, we have seen another financial crisis play out in modern Greece—once again brought on by the ramifications of a complex web of debt coupled with naivety and myopia.

There are two lessons to be drawn.

First, for all of the intervening years of progress, knowledge, politics, social evolution, and so on, not much has really changed when it comes to our fundamental nature. Our human biases remain unchanged—a few millennia being but an instant on the grand time scales of human evolution. The world is still too complex for us to fathom or control most of the time.

Second, complexity is a double-edged sword. The golden age of ancient Greece and the first financial crisis were products of the same evolving complexity. Short of disowning progress and returning to small isolated communities, one cannot remove systemic crises. Even then, we cannot excise the ebb and flow of human emotion that arise from the biases within us all.

CHAPTER 16

Alpha and Omega:
Two Millennia of Crises

If all else fails, immortality can always be assured by colossal failure.

—J. K. GALBRAITH (1908–2006)

Money is a dangerous subject. Polite conversation avoids it. You may talk about economics, but not raw money.

—MAX PLOWMAN (1883–1941)

H UMANS are gregarious creatures. We interact all the time and continually seek out the company and approval of others. Our interactions are familial, coital, pugilistic, social, and aspirational, to name but a few flavors. Hidden within these interactions are a host of cognitive biases that stem from our nature and environment.

They are not failings but rather shortcuts we use to navigate an uncertain world. Rather than analyzing everything meticulously, we instinctively leverage off experience to find quick answers and make quick decisions. At their core, all our biases revolve around nurturing our ego and promoting an optimistic view of the world. That is hardly surprising. The fact is that we are an insignificant race inhabiting an insignificant planet orbiting an insignificant star in an insignificant part of the universe at some insignificant time in its history. Our existence may be a cosmological quirk or a biological chance accident. Everything we do today will pass into obscurity. Even those acts or achievements that endure only do so for a while, before the whimsical tides of posterity wash them away beyond all memory and record.

None of this is conducive to ambition or progress. Indeed, it even begs the question of human survival: why even bother?

But we do. We create identities and purposes for ourselves out of nothing. We create gods and philosophies to give us and the uncertain world around us meaning. We choose to examine everything through rose-tinted glasses that exhort focus and progress. Speculation comes naturally, as it represents a way forward of thought, order, status, money, and whatever else we may hold dear.

Forward movement is all-important. A bias emerges within us that is happy only when we are deemed to progress. We become unhappy in the event of stagnation or loss. At a personal level, gifts, salary raises, and the love of others are welcomed initially but soon become an accepted part of the environment and our focus moves onto the next frontier. Even at the level of societies, we have always obsessed about growth, to the extent where any growth—military or economic, no matter how fueled or what the cost—is better than none. The fetish of GDP is a case in point.

But the world around us is always shifting in unpredictable ways. And so, we learn that others are important to counter this uncertainty. We can find purpose, whether it is in the arms of one or in the words of another. We can band together, form communities, and leverage off each other. We can collect our biases and move forward to achieve mutual goals that make us feel happier. We can tame the uncertain outside world and carve out psychological oases that give us certainty.

Trust becomes an essential shortcut. Once freed of the burden of understanding and analyzing everything, we can outsource aspects of our lives and our thoughts. Rules emerge, lending an order we crave. Rationality becomes an intent. The crowd is deemed to assimilate knowledge much faster, and we benefit from the efficiencies of production, allocation, protection, and so on. Our general well-being is raised, and often we are better off than if we had remained alone.

At the same time, ego also ensures that we still compete with one another to pursue our own self-interest and demonstrate our relative superior status. Hierarchies naturally emerge, influenced by our circumstances and environment, such as the Japanese psyche born of their feudal past. There are power structures within families. There are chains of command within armies and companies. There are political or religious structures within societies. These allow us to find new purpose and also ensure an efficiency of decision making. Leaders of different types emerge that can influence crowds and shape future events.[1]

In short, simple motivations have created a complex emergent society. Few would argue that the evolution of society was a bad thing and we have alluded to some of the benefits above. The complexity of what we create is a direct result of our search for belonging and control. Within this dense network, we are all nodes—some more influential than others depending on where we are within the hierarchy. Institutions and other collective bodies represent particularly large nodes that disproportionately influence those around them, creating new incentives. As the world around us shifts and our actions change, the complexity evolves in response. Our links with others allow us to benefit and for most of the time, we can carry on with our lives uninterrupted as a result.

However, the forming of relationships brings new risks. Falling in love with someone can bring fulfillment. It can also bring heartache, though this is deemed an acceptable risk, particularly with our optimistic views of the world. Similarly, within the complexity of a society, we accept tacitly that the links we have formed can also be harmful at times. Jobs can be lost. Companies can go bankrupt. Institutions can turn repressive. Conflicts can erupt as different parts of a network clash, propagating and drawing in many others once on the periphery.

However, the benefits of complexity mean that we usually try to find solutions to these more adverse side effects of complexity. And if the complexity turns out to be dysfunctional, then we simply withdraw inward and it unravels under its own tensions till a new status quo is reached. The fall of the Roman Empire as noted earlier is a case in point, where the punitive costs of an overextended empire eventually drove many small nations to secede and tiny feudal estates to emerge.

However, this is just the complexity born of our collective psychology. In the absence of all else, it is likely we would never evolve past a tribal society. The catalysts for further development are money and credit—both natural extensions of the interactions we have. Examples can be seen in the ancient tablets of Hammurabi, the humble wooden tally of England, and more lately, the Linden dollar of Second Life. Societies produce goods and services. Often, these become specialized thanks to the influence of hierarchies and institutions, whose goals create incentives for some to focus on more than just pure subsistence. From here, trade

evolves naturally both within societies and between different communities. This strengthens existing links and forms new ones, increasing the
complexity of the system.

Alongside, we all have debts. These may be of affection or of loyalty
on a personal level, but at a societal level, they soon evolve into wider
debts to relative strangers to help facilitate trade, for example, or to institutions and governments to help maintain themselves as well as social
cohesion. While these may have been in kind in the past—jury duty being
a rare modern example—the need to denominate and account for these
led to the advent of money.

Once created, money becomes a powerful glue. It introduces a
common medium of exchange and thanks to its national patronage, a
standardized metric of wealth across a wide swath of people, including
complete strangers. Importantly, it now adds a dimension of time to the
fruits of human labor. You can produce and sell your goods or services
today but your payment no longer needs to be decided or consumed in a
timely manner. Instead, you can store the money you have received in
lieu for your output to spend on whatever it might purchase at some
future date.

The value of exchange is thus depersonalized and commoditized.
Money becomes a synonym for human interaction. The knock-on impacts
on the complexity of a society are tremendous. An economy develops as
people begin to buy and sell in a common medium. Specialization becomes
easier as your output needs to appeal to only a small group willing to pay
for it, rather than being something to barter with or subsist on. National
hegemonies such as the Roman Empire two millennia ago expand as their
influence through the money they print extends beyond just the reach of
their armies. Additionally, the bonds between state and individual deepen.
Trust is engendered more strongly in the system as people increasingly put
their human capital in the form of money that has been lent authority by
some nation or powerful institution.

Progress and status can be measured on some level. Whether it is a
piece of gold or a scrap of paper, money is equally worthless unless it is
moving around the economy. The greater the volume of transactions, the
more growth we perceive and the richer we get, as we total up the sum of

our interactions. As long as these interactions are put to productive use, we are better off in reality.

From here, it is a simple step for people to realize that money can itself be traded, rather than merely being a temporal substitute. There is no even distribution of wealth in the world and people have varying needs. Therefore, money may be lent, invested, or speculated with to make more money. As more money equals more status, this seems eminently sensible to us. In our self-interest, we find ourselves becoming rentiers, charging others economic rents to borrow our wealth for a while to facilitate their needs, for example, buying a house or financing a shipping convoy.

We have created a sophisticated economy of debtors and creditors. There are intermediaries, such as banks, to facilitate their exchange and to allow the many to borrow against their future output from the few—an economic version of Jesus's feeding of the five thousand. This is leverage and it accelerates growth. There are also policy makers and institutions, who are concerned with on one hand, using some part of all the money flowing around the economy to pursue their own sociopolitical agendas; and on the other hand, with ensuring that the status quo is not destabilized.

The complexity is tremendous. The money we have and that we earn typically represents debt claims on the future output of others. Sometimes, it is implicit such as the money deposited in a bank or in money market funds, which is then lent out repeatedly. At other times, it is explicit such as the instruments of government debt we may own that are deemed safe enough to count as near-money in our eyes, through to riskier instruments such as loans to companies and other individuals. There are also more speculative investments which represent small pools of optionality and where our returns may be greatly magnified, such as equities. In turn, we typically also have debts of our own. These may be debts of necessity or aspiration, such as a house or a business loan. They may be opportunistic, such as credit cards for consumption and money borrowed to invest elsewhere. Regardless, the fact remains overall that our perceptions of wealth and the stability of our balance sheet rest in the hands of others.

In times of prosperity, this pooling of resources and sharing of risks can ensure that innovation quickly finds the funds it needs to grow and that demand is met. The Industrial Revolution, for example, was funded almost entirely by private enterprise that saw in its promises of greater productivity the path to significantly greater fortune. It can help society as a whole to grow faster by accelerating change, enhancing trade, and raising the quality of our lives faster than they might otherwise do organically. After all, GDP itself is little more than an approximate quantification of the growth of complexity—the inference from our pursuit of GDP growth being that more interconnectivity is better for society and for each of us as a whole.

Booms and busts are a natural consequence of this complexity. As money flows around our complex network, it rapidly transmits to where we see opportunities for gain and where there is demand for a good or service. As these opportunities fade, it quickly moves on elsewhere. This efficiency of allocation is one of the chief benefits of our complex network. As Hayek noted, the economy assimilates individual bits of information from us all and in return, gives an aggregate understanding to everyone through the prices we see changing around us. These flows of capital, however, are not instantaneous. They are driven by the mechanisms of human bias and crowd behavior. By unconsciously following the incentives laid out before us as well as the advice and actions of others more explicitly, we create a herd that moves money to where it is wanted. As more money comes in, a boom is created.

However, as the demand for a good or service is saturated, the returns on investment fall. Our bounded rationality soon turns elsewhere but there is first a time lag. The increasing flows of capital inward continue for longer than needed thanks to our propensity for extrapolation. More money flows in than needed as people are willing to pay more for expected future profits. Then, there are losses as the opportunity runs its course. And first one, then more, and eventually a whole herd rushes for the exit. This is a bust.

The money moves on elsewhere in search of new opportunities and the cycle repeats anew. The size of these booms and busts is directly correlated to two things.

First, there is the size of the crowd that gets drawn in. This is related to the rewards on offer; the influence of the nodes in our complex network which propagate this information or affect the relevant environment; and the level of trust we place in them. For example, the United States and Britain in the nineteenth century had repeated railroad booms. The technological changes, the promised increases in productivity, the ability to dramatically increase the reach of trade, and so on all promised huge future benefits to society and, therefore, rewards to entrepreneurs and investors. At the same time, the railroads benefited from government monopolies and support. The fascination of the media with new technology and the grand visions outlined meant that a wide swath of moneyed society was drawn into the web. Clever promoters expertly leveraged off this coverage and employed a host of tools from grandiose self-promotion to stock manipulation to outright fraud to distort pricing signals and create the illusion of strong returns. The result was a self-fulfilling prophecy that led to enormous amounts of capital flowing in.

A succession of dramatic booms and busts followed as the supply of rail track occasionally became a glut before new demand spurred another round of building. Many fortunes were made. At the same time, many of the companies went bankrupt and many people lost their savings. But at the end of all this, the countries were left with an infrastructure that fueled tremendous growth for decades thereafter. The broken fortunes of the few were the price paid for an increased prosperity for society as a whole.

Second and strongly intertwined, there is the quantum of money at play within the system. Money is always in demand and we all want more of it. However, an excess of money can result in the value of things being bid up too far and too fast as too much money tries to enter the same opportunity at once. The Roman Depression of A.D. 33 was one example. The Japanese bubble of the 1980s was another. We see the same pattern in every financial crisis, where the bust is always preceded by an increase in the money supply or a boom in credit. Additionally, it may result in the allocation of our pools of capital to more and more speculative ventures that have little to no productive use. The apogee of speculative idiocy may be the South Sea bubble of 1720–21 when the demand for South Sea Company shares was so high that it launched a new venture with the description "For carrying on an undertaking of great advantage but no one to know what it is."

Similarly albeit to a lesser extent, the railroad boom was also fed by the fact that the Industrial Revolution had created significant fortunes and led to the ascendancy of a growing middle class that was eager to grow its status further. At the same time, the growth of colonial empires was driving a new round of enforced globalization and ensured that there was a lot of wealth hitting European shores looking for new homes.

One may typify these booms and busts as financial crises. Certainly they cause significant financial pain for some, and in extremis they can lead to a loss of public confidence that will show up as a reduction in growth in the near term—the dreaded recession. They are a natural emergence of the flows of money around the complex economy that we have created. By pooling our emotions, we create crowds that leverage human bias. By adding in money, we leverage yet further and extend the crowd even more. There is no way to remove them without removing the network that binds us. As some have argued, this creative destruction is fundamental to the success of capitalism.

The real danger comes when complexity creates deeper systemic linkages within the system that we do not fully understand. As financial intermediaries become increasingly structural to our fabric, their leverage echoes throughout the economy. Their alchemy of money facilitates growth by allowing others to borrow the same pool multiple times. Implicit within this multiplication of debt is a belief that the money lent will be repaid out of future growth when the time comes. However, there are limits to how much debt a system can sustain. Debt must be serviced and therefore, the more debt one takes on, the more of one's income is consumed. At some point, repayment becomes difficult or the financial position too precarious to the shifting winds of change.

Concomitantly, the institutions at the center of this leverage become key nodes in the network, whose influence extends across a wide swath of society. As their size increases, they become concentrations of risk, whose unraveling can severely weaken the fabric of an economy. Losses in one part of their book can ramify throughout the rest as leverage moves in the opposite direction. When this problem is coupled with the vagaries of human behavior, notably our aversion to loss, we can have bank runs that force money out of the system by imposing punishing losses across the board.

Suddenly, debts are called in elsewhere, companies are unable to refinance, savings are revealed to be mere accounting entries and so on. This is a credit crunch, where the system starts to deleverage as money is destroyed.

This is a far more serious type of financial crisis. As key nodes or institutions vanish, they leave a void in the network. The loss of money weakens links between different parties. And the loss of trust that accompanies this fuels further rounds of contraction as people begin to take back their precious stores of wealth from others and weaken the system further. It becomes a vicious circle, which we have described elsewhere as the debt deflation spiral. Through this hoarding, the system is starved of its life-giving medium and starts to shrink. Transactions fall and complexity unwinds. Growth shrinks and we are all left poorer, not just in our minds and wallets but also in our future potential.

Schumpeter always feared that capitalism was ultimately doomed to die because the conflagrations of creative destruction caused might become too large and destroy the entirety of the system. Certainly, in extremis, we have seen that threaten to happen in history as with the Roman Empire, the origins of the French Revolution, and the Great Depression.

But history also tells that these crises of complexity are linked to their evolution. Institutions have a common influential voice that is still all too human in its myopia and biases. A failure to understand the law of unintended consequences and the complexity of what is being dealt with means that as in the Great Depression, small decisions can compound into systemic flaws. These will inevitably lead to decline as in the absence of lasting solutions, a series of successive crises can build up to a punishing crescendo.

But money is only one aspect of society. The links we form are also social and political. With the growing complexity of our economic networks, these acquire growing importance also as more and more people are exposed. The search for status (and therefore, money) creates natural divisions. In normal times, these are maintained in modern society through the medium of social mobility. We all believe we can reach the top of the tree.

However, one of the dangers of too much debt is that it results in the transfer and concentration of wealth into fewer hands over time. The growing financialization that accompanies this also creates a divide between the real economy and the speculative arena where money changes hands. This creates further barriers of inequality and stokes social tensions. People grow poorer even as they are more interconnected into the fabric of the economy. This strains the social and political ties we share. Most revolutions have their origins in either the cost of living or in the battles between debtors and creditors. The feeling of disenfranchisement by the many, as in interwar Germany, is a powerful thread in human history.

Complexity will always resurface in time, being the natural product of our interactions. However, the challenge for us is how to manage the economic networks we create. Regulation and central banks are often held up as the answer. Indeed, their evolution in history may be seen as an attempt to swap the sharp pain of correction for the less painful, if longer, therapy of stagnation.

However, crises are still endemic and as the complexity of our systems have grown, so has the fallout from them. The lesson to be learned is simple.

You cannot fight complexity with complexity.

THE WORLD TODAY

Today, we live in a truly globalized economy that has reached a new pinnacle of complexity. This book has deliberately refused to consider the most recent financial crisis that began in 2007, other than in passing. This is because the facts have been covered in copious detail by others and our purpose here was to understand what led us to these recurrent bouts of fragility. Complexity is also detailed and the events of today are still unfolding. Another book beckons for the full analysis.

But we can understand some things about how we got here. The steepening rate of growth of complexity has meant that global growth has outstripped expectations consistently, notwithstanding the disruptions caused by periodic reallocations of money. As a result, debt has transformed from what used to be a negative phrase in ancient times to a virtue today. We have consistently borrowed more and more, because borrowing more is associated with growing more as an economy. Today, debt in some form or the other is part of the structural landscape for everyone.

Alongside, the stock of money and our perceived wealth have boomed as well. Debt and wealth are often just two perspectives on the same thing. One man's liabilities are another man's assets. Coupled with this has been the growing role of financial innovation and transformation to manage this alchemy.

Consequently, our search for security over the last half century has led to a rapid growth for two innovations that are little commented on: insurance and pensions. Through these, financial networks have attempted to facilitate the aggregation, transfer, and management of unwanted risks. In turn, these allow people and companies to mitigate uncertainty, formulate long-term plans, and invest accordingly. At the same time, this aggregation of savings and, therefore, resources also allows more efficient allocation of capital throughout the economy.

These savings can be channeled into sectors needing large dependable amounts of investment, often in return for set cash flows to meet future claims. In particular, it is unlikely the corporate bond market and other fixed income sectors could have developed to the extent they have without the presence of savings aggregators such as insurance companies and pension schemes to act as keen providers of longer-term capital to the economy. The importance of both sectors can be seen in their sheer size today—about $10 trillion each. By comparison, global GDP today is about $60 trillion.

However, this growth in savings has also created enormous global imbalances, as all this money also underpins an even larger amount of debt. That debt extends across all of society. Successive generations have participated in the growth to date and our whole standard of living has grown as a result. The extrapolation of that means that homeownership is far higher today. Consumption is far higher today. Investment is far higher today. Collectively, debt is much higher as a result as these advances in our quality of life are financed by borrowing more against future earnings.

Incentives have also evolved significantly. Governments have become increasingly dominant within society and trust has come to reside more and more with regulators and central bankers to manage the complexities of the system. Therefore, the perception of risk has lessened as uncertainty recedes behind these pillars. The belief has grown that they can manage the economy through the inevitable storms ahead safely, with the result that our extrapolations acquire a growing certainty in our mind.

The excess of money coupled with the dampening of our risk perception has fueled enormous speculation. Governments have utilized the prosperity of recent decades to push forward social and political agendas, such as homeownership for everyone and an increased commitment to providing a base quality of life for everyone. The rapidity of innovation has meant that capital flows move ever faster through the world in search of the next fleeting opportunity. And to facilitate all of these sociopolitical objectives and flows of money, there has been a huge growth in the financialization of our society.

The result has been a saturation of debt in society and a complex web that extends across both countries and individuals. Cheap finance combined with pent-up demand created rapid growth globally in recent years. Particularly in the developed world, a focus on consumption as a driver of growth and a surge in imports led to a spectacular deterioration in their balance of trade with the world. With policy makers expecting the boom times to continue indefinitely, they rapidly increased government spending. The plan was to strengthen social safety nets and raise living standards for everyone. However, the failure to develop new industries meant that deficits became a part of the status quo. The system hollowed out from within, particularly as these deficits could only be financed by accumulated debt. Total debt, government and private, especially in the developed world boomed until it became totally unsustainable.

The amount of debt is not important. It is merely the ability to service it that matters. In 2007, the world reached a tipping point, from which we are still trying to find a way out today.

The impact of the 2007 crash has been tremendous. Economic losses have been compounded by social ones. Millions of people now find a previously safe future endangered by lost savings and growing uncertainty. Unemployment—the first casualty of a downturn—has risen dramatically from pre-crisis levels. However, the impact is not just a financial hit. It is also a psychological blow. Families are put under financial strain; the social and welfare fabric of the state is tested; the feelings of confidence in the good days are replaced by fears over an uncertain future.

Contagion has now spread onto the social and psychological arenas, with policy makers so focused on dealing with the short-term financial traumas that they have failed utterly to understand the longer-term social tensions and psychological traumas being unleashed by their current policies. Trust and cooperation—the lifeblood of our economy—are evaporating, making countries and whole blocs such as the European Union increasingly unstable. Once purely economic tensions are spilling out in political upheaval such as the Arab Spring and the rise of populist parties globally.

There are many proposed explanations for the recent crisis: securitization; derivatives and other exotic instruments; lack of regulation; the provision of easy money from central banks; irrationality; greedy bankers; savings gluts in the emerging markets; and a desensitization to risk-taking. All have some merit but they are also reminiscent of the Indian parable of the blind men and the elephant.

Six blind men stumble across an elephant one day. Finding their path impeded, they all begin to feel the creature to find out what it is.

"It's a pillar," says the first touching the elephant's leg.

"No, it's a rope," says the second as he grabs its tail.

"You're both wrong—it's the thick branch of a tree," says a third man, feeling the trunk of the elephant.

"I think it's a fan," exclaims the fourth, as his hand brushes against the ear of the elephant.

"A wall!" shouts out the fifth man, walking into the belly.

"I know—it's a pipe," proclaims the last blind man, gently prodding the tusk.

They all begin to argue about the elephant, with each one insistent that he is right. The fight grows more and more heated. A wise man passing by sees this and asks them why they are quarrelling.

They all explain their opinions and he laughs. "All of you are right. The only reason every one of you has a different story is because each of you touched a different part of the elephant. The elephant is all of those."

Truth comes in many flavors. The explanations for the crisis all have grains of truth. This is because they are all expressions of the complexity of what we created. As the system comes under strain, our myopic views focus in on one facet or the other and blame it for the crisis. Our biases also reinforce this as we are loath to blame ourselves. Our inability to see and understand the linkages and incentives we have created means that our anger and outrage at others is reinforced.

The recent financial crisis, like so many others, was a creature of our own making. Our current inability to resolve it comes from a failure of understanding. Like other crises, we will survive. No country ever went bankrupt forever. We will evolve further. But it is up to us to choose whether we come through this easily or painfully. It is up to us to learn the lessons of how to manage the inevitable crises that will assert themselves in the future. Otherwise, the complexity we crave will dissipate and we will all be poorer for it.

CHAPTER 17

In the Land of the Blind:
Searching for Answers

Forgive us out debts, as we forgive our debtors.

—MATTHEW 6:12, NEW TESTAMENT

Fools ignore complexity. Pragmatists suffer it. Some can avoid it. Geniuses remove it.

—ALAN PERLIS (1922–1990)

THE answers we crave come in two flavors. There is the issue of dealing with the crisis once it has arrived on our doorstep and the system is in stress. And then there is the wider issue of how to proactively minimize reaching the point of maximum stress ever again.

TODAY . . .

For the first, the prescription is simple. The accumulation of so much debt means the old economic model is broken. No creditor is willing to write down what's owed to him and share the pain, particularly as he believes the debt accrued is the sole responsibility of the debtor. However, if debtors seriously attempt to repay these debts in full—as current prescriptions demand—they will impose an unbearable burden on the global economy for years to come. They will create a scarring, extended stagnation that will compound dire economic conditions, right up to the point where the status quo becomes politically and socially unworkable.

The capacity to repay today's debt—as in so many other crises—is limited, both in terms of hard economics and in terms of what is socially as well as politically acceptable. The option of borrowing more to repay is suspect and only postpones the structural issue to another day. Unfortunately, that is the primary route currently being taken.

We could try to grow our way out of this mess by fueling even more interaction and trade. But history—notably the backdrop to the Great Depression—has taught us that in times of stress, our focus turns inward and we rush to preserve our economic share by beggaring our neighbors. In truth, we beggar only ourselves.

We could cut spending and thereby meet our debt servicing needs. In the absence of growth, we consume less and we invest less. Unfortunately, this triggers the debt-deflation spiral, where the ramifications of our actions rebound. The system now becomes starved of money and starts to unravel slowly. Our debts increase in real terms and our ability to meet them falls daily.

That leaves only two options: default or debt forgiveness.

Default comes in many forms. Inflation has always been the preserve of governments as it erodes debts, though it also has a rich history of social upheaval attached to it. It has also proved stubbornly hard to trigger. Inflation, as Milton Friedman noted, is everywhere a monetary phenomenon. But it only works if money moves through an economy, In the absence of velocity, what we find is that the money being put in ends up in assets and in more speculation. Old bubbles reinflate and new bubbles form. Meanwhile, the real economy remains abandoned and the gulf between the financial markets and economic reality continues to grow.

Outright default is also not to be recommended. It removes the debt and also destroys someone's precious pool of savings. The resulting loss of trust can ramify through a system exponentially in the short term, particularly when it is disorderly.

But debt forgiveness can also come in the form of restructuring debt. This is preferable. It reduces the total amount owed and restores capacity to the system so it can regrow. It also is kinder to the cognitive biases we have that will not countenance a total loss. Debt reduction can occur without cutting the nominal amount of the loans. Instead, the current value (and total burden) of the loans can be written down by issuing longer-dated debt with lower fixed interest rates. In real terms, as steady inflation chips away over years, we have reduced the debt but our fixation on nominal values ensures that for most, their capital is still deemed secure. This also has the added advantage of reducing the overreliance we have currently on refinancing shorter-term debt in the financial markets. Some of the debt could be converted to perpetual loans (similar to the British restructuring of World War I debt into a perpetual War Loan that is still traded today). This is a conversion of a promise to an aspiration. The United States, for example, still has more than $1 million of debt outstanding from before 1917, including some $55,000 from its first bond issue in the aftermath of the Revolutionary War in 1790. The United Kingdom has £2 billion (about $3 billion) of World War I debt that is still traded today as the aforementioned perpetual loan. It is unlikely that these loans will ever be paid off, given that little effort has been made in more than two hundred years to do so. However, the trust remains, and so people trade these notional numbers, viewing them as a store of wealth. The promise that binds together a society endures.

Coupled with reforms that reinforce global trade and remove barriers, debt restructuring can restore stability and lead to the resumption of complex growth. Our memories are short and our biases strong. When Iceland defaulted on its external debts in 2008, it became a pariah in international financial markets. Three years later, it returned to the same financial markets and issued $1 billion of five-year government bonds with a coupon of less than 5 percent—hardly what one might charge an untrustworthy borrower. It was the brevity of financial memory in action. However, the rationale for investors was simple: once Iceland defaulted, there were no other creditors with a claim on the country's revenues. In their absence, investors felt they had far more certainty about being paid back in the future, despite past behavior.

Debt restructuring shifts the focus decisively from self-defeating survival in the near term to collective growth in the long run. The costs are far less than those we might all incur in the event of a spiraling debt-depression trap and the ensuing collapse in trade.

. . . AND TOMORROW

The above measures only rescue us in the aftermath of our most recent crisis. They restore stability and the conditions for growth to resume. However, the economy is dynamic and with growth, it will only become more complex. Our future decisions will lead to future crises. That is the Faustian pact we all signed up to. But we can choose whether these future crises are transient and bearable, or punishing and threatening to our way of life. That requires us to address the question of how to manage the consequences of complexity, else we will find ourselves reliving recent events again.

The answer is simple if paradoxical. Don't fight crises, work with them instead.

Our situation today is the result of a systemic crisis, where participants were responding to the incentives of the complex system they inhabited without appreciating the wider unintended consequences of their actions. On an individual level, this was born of human bias and too much money. On a collective level, it was an error of assumptions.

Our understanding of how an economy works needs to be rebuilt. The new foundations need to reflect the diversity and complexity of what an economy and its players are. These are tenets such as:

- Man is not a perfectly rational creature. We are motivated by self-interest and influenced by our cognitive biases, social interactions, and environment. At best, our rationality is bounded and in a complex system, much of that is further replaced by blind process.
- Our simple actions do not aggregate simply like addition at the level of an economy. Instead, they cascade exponentially and the simple rules we use to navigate the world emerge as complex behaviors when passed through a crowd. The whole is much more than the sum of its parts.
- Economies are not isolated entities in a static equilibrium. They are dynamic pools of exchange interwoven with political as well as social dimensions. This continually destabilizes them from within, thanks to the inconsistent behaviors of their human constituents. The dynamism they exhibit is part of a continual process of adjustment, much as an acrobat might walk a tight-rope. Practice and an imperfect understanding create the illusion of steady progression. A closer look reveals the intricacy of movement.

- Linked to the above, economies are not everlasting in the absence of external events. Notwithstanding the banality of denying the external shocks of chance, the inherent instability and unpredictability at the heart of an economy—driven largely by the inconsistent behaviors of its human constituents—mean that its endogenous dynamics will always lead to shifts. These may be good (innovation and booms) or these may be bad (overextension and busts).
- Efficient markets do not exist. Information is contextual, subjective, and sometimes, plain wrong. There are asymmetries of information that exist and unless we all become automatons, the market cannot aggregate all knowledge perfectly. There is also the paradox that if markets were truly efficient and the sum of all information, we would all give up trying to make the effort to find information ourselves. In doing so, we would cease to share information, becoming a tribe of mutes, and the market would find it hard to detect any coherence in that silence.
- Free markets are a limiting idealistic case. In practice, there are pervasive influences on markets that limit the truly free exchange of trade and money. These may be nations, cartels, regulators, and other institutions. Therefore, we are at best quasi-free. The market may still be the best mechanism of aggregating and transmitting our collective knowledge quickly, but we cannot ignore its other dimensions or our own biases. Our urge to control our environment will always lead to barriers on truly free exchange. Nations like to control the printing and legitimizing of money. Businesses, once they have become big, have the same aversion to losing market share that we have to losing money and seek to create trade barriers and cartels. Our attempts to control our environment lead us to create institutions that will distort the landscape and bias the flows of money that occur within it.
- We live in a complex network of interlinked people and institutions. Our actions have unforeseen consequences and small perturbations can lead to unexpectedly large outcomes, as we

have seen with the fall of the Roman Empire and the echoes of
the 1772 crisis, for example.

We cannot understand all the intricacies of the system we have created.
Complexity by its nature sits beyond our understanding. We cannot aggregate and analyze information better than the entirety of society at all times.
To do so is to ape complexity, and you cannot fight complexity with
complexity. Whatever regulation and institutions we create, they will prove
inadequate and indeed, may cause more harm than good.

As a simple example, we have aggregated all of our financial institutions today into larger and larger entities. To manage them requires more
and more metrics, more and more information, more and more oversight.
All of this has a cost associated with it. Meeting this cost is a diversion of
productive resources toward unproductive ones and though all the people
hired will add to the GDP of our system, they will not contribute anything
to the sustainability of our economy.

Banks such as Citigroup now sit across some 150 regulatory bodies
globally. People talk hopefully of cross-border agreements and international initiatives. But in practice, these are doomed to founder on the rocks
of human behavior.

I am reminded of a dinner I had with a central banker in December
2012. He explained to me the "living wills" they had created for large
banks and the resolution regimes to ensure that if Citigroup or Deutsche
Bank or HSBC got into trouble, it could be shut down in an orderly way
with minimal damage to the global economy.

"It works perfectly," he said to me. "I've run it through the scenarios
and I know it can be done." He paused. "The only problem, however, is
that if HSBC ever threatened to go to the wall, I don't know which government would ever stand back and say, 'Well, let's see if this works.'"

Human behavior trumps analysis at every point. No government will
ever take the electoral risk of bank failure. Governments throw money at
the problem, even if it is in vain, because their incentives are based on
perpetuating their political hegemony.

That is not to say we cannot understand the generality of the
system. By understanding the nature of the beast, we can use its

strengths to better handle the vagaries of the future. Part of it requires going against the grain of our psyche and embracing the uncertainty of future outcomes.

The strands to tease out are simple.

- Complex systems are made up of individual nodes of varying sizes and influences.
- These interact with one another, both changing and adapting to their environment, that is, creating as well as responding to incentives and the influences of their peers.
- The nodes are dynamic, adjusting their interactions in response to changing conditions, that is, flows of money, trust, and sentiment.
- They spontaneously self-organize to develop unexpected aggregate behaviors, which continually change as the system evolves—for better and for worse.
- The key instabilities that can cause harm from our perspective are the destruction of key nodes (i.e., large institutions or nations) and systemic risks that can cascade through the system.

From these, answers naturally evolve.

No One Is Too Big to Fail

First, the players in a network have varying levels of influence. Particularly with regard to institutions, this can become too large and their influence, therefore, too destabilizing. It becomes vital to ensure that no institution is too big to fail. If the vanishing of an institution will destroy the network of our economy, it is too large to survive. Citigroup will one day go bust. Probability and evolution tell us that. Therefore, we can either keep trying to postpone the inevitable or remove the anomaly. This can be done over time by shrinking the institution through incentive or breaking up the institution. The same also applies to states and their apparati. A state that becomes too large also creates distortions that weaken an economy and society.

We Need to Restore Failure as an Option at All Levels

Economies spontaneously organize themselves and will reestablish new connections when old ones vanish. We already accept failure as an option for individuals and firms. There are bankruptcy codes to deal with the fallout and ensure that disruption is minimal. The same needs to apply to financial institutions and sovereigns.

My early career was in hedge funds, as noted previously. Sometimes typified as the Wild West, a hedge fund is also a place where you live and die by the sword. Good performance brings high reward. Bad performance inevitably leads to the death knell of your fund. However, the failure of almost no hedge fund has threatened to destabilize the system.[1] It is because, first, hedge funds know there are no rescuers waiting in the wings, and second, they are too small to impact the system in more than a localized way.

In late 2010, former Federal Reserve chair and special White House advisor Paul Volcker met with leading hedge fund and private equity bosses to get their feedback on the proposed Volcker rule in the aftermath of the credit crunch. It was the latest iteration of regulation and sought to prevent banks from engaging in unduly speculative activities. One of my acquaintances was in attendance. As he tells it, Volcker—a very tall man—walked in and looked around the room.

"I don't know any of you guys," he finally said after an imperious slow sweep of the audience. "And for you, that's a good thing."

It was a crushing blow to their egos, but it reminded them that for all the hype, they were not masters of the universe. They were not even large enough to matter in the question of whether the system—then creaking under so much strain—would survive in its current form.

We Need to Create the Right Incentives

We all respond to incentives. Therefore, we need to ensure that the incentives of a system encourage behavior that strengthens the links among different nodes, reduces destabilizing influences, and perpetuates a network. For example, capital and tax incentives can make it disadvantageous for entities to grow beyond a certain optimal size. Compensation can be aligned to longer-term behavior. Bank compensation, for example, can be tied to metrics such as return on assets rather than return on equity, reducing the incentive for leverage.

Institutions and Systems Should Be Designed to Counterbalance Our Natural Cognitive Biases

We need to counterbalance our natural biases in a way that doesn't limit the benefits they also confer. This may be done by creating a longer-term memory for the network that remembers the lessons of the past. One of the great tragedies in economics occurred two decades ago, when many university departments either closed down their economic history groups or hived them off to sit with the history department. The loss of knowledge was vast. The study of history may not be as quantitative, but the qualitative analysis of human behavior and network failure it brings to the table is a vital input into the decisions we make on an ongoing basis to sustain an economy. These groups also house within them a memory that is far longer than our human bias. Indeed, I would argue that every central bank and every treasury function needs a repository of institutional memory.

Our Understanding of the Role of Money and Credit Within an Economy Needs to Be Reassessed

Crises are linked to the saturation of debt and their resolution to the creating of new capacity to allow growth to resume. Policy makers—for all their best intentions and hopes—only control the smallest modicum of what can be construed as money. The innovation and leverage we apply on top are out of their hands. Additionally, the composition of debt cannot be controlled. People will borrow to invest in productive assets and they will borrow to speculate in unproductive assets. Short of dictating human behavior, you cannot tell people what to borrow for. And arguably, speculative borrowing and financial wizardry have their role to play in fostering innovation and managing risk.

What matters is the quantum of debt. Too much debt equals too much money sloshing around the system unproductively. It fuels bubbles far beyond the size that the system might otherwise allow them to attain. However, there are levers policy makers can pull to limit leverage permeating through the system. For example, banks can have maximum leverage ratios. Entities such as money market funds that can serve as quasi banks can automatically be judged to come under stricter supervision should their assets grow beyond a certain size.

Institutions Need to Encourage Heterogeneity and Diversity Across the Entire Economic Ecosystem

Central banks, regulators, and governments should have people with backgrounds not just in mainstream economics but from other areas that can help make sense of our complex world, for example, behavioral finance, information science, network analysis, political economy, economic history, and so on. These perspectives add differences of opinion and, therefore, create a richer, more complete understanding. Financial institutions should have a diversity of models and approaches to investment. The crowd will always be with us, but by promoting countervailing views, we encourage multiple foci. The exchange of opinions has historically been good for innovation. There is no reason why it should not be as useful in helping address the likelihood of negative shocks.

The Role of Regulatory Oversight Needs to Change

As we have said before, complexity cannot be fought with complexity. Regulation should aim for simplicity and transparency. There will always be an asymmetry of information between two parties in the real world. This is because, notwithstanding the most rigorous of processes and attendant paperwork, there are fundamental uncertainties about the future. Historical evidence and statistical models can only yield a fuzzy range of potential outcomes at best and therefore, a limited range of potential future stress points. Future unknowns such as wars, productivity shocks, bankruptcies, fraud, and the like can result in unexpected and potentially critical turning points. Therefore, trying to aggregate all known information seems fool-hardy, especially in a world as today, where information grows exponentially over time. Regulation should focus on mitigating the adverse effect of these information asymmetries. To regulate a complex economy, we need to understand its essential characteristics, not every last bit of information. Doing the latter only pulls us back into the cognitive trap of substituting process and models for critical reasoning.

Further, the widespread reach of banking, insurance, and other financial intermediaries in an economy is predicated on the assurance that they are "safe." In this sense, they are all subject to the same dependence on public confidence for their viability and survival in the long term. However, the distinction between strong and weak financial institutions is inconsistent over time. The best differentiator is the market, which can aggregate and disseminate information far faster than regulators. Therefore, transparency is paramount. More disclosure means more information to the market and a clearer idea of whether institutions are likely to honor their obligations.

Create Flexibility and Countercyclical Mechanisms

We need to introduce adaptive mechanisms into the economic network to stop shocks propagating. Panics are self-organizing as well and, in an inter-linked economy, can spread exponentially fast. To stop them, sometimes you have to counter them. Counterbalancing can be through pumping money into a system during periods of extreme stress—the fabled lender of last resort—to stabilize it. It can also be the suspension of links for short periods, circuit breakers that stop a wave becoming socially destructive, such as temporary capital controls when money is running out of a country or banks and businesses are trapped in a debt-deflation spiral.

Lose the Fetish for GDP

GDP is an imperfect metric that treats all growth and investment as equal. In practice, the structure and stability of demand matters. If it is artificially inflated rapidly through too much money or debt before the promised glorious future has come to pass, its deflation is punishing and given our hedonic bias, socially distressing. The aim of whatever metrics we choose should be to judge sustainable, valuable growth. As before, a diversity of metrics and opinions is always better than one.

Inequality Matters

Crises accentuate inequality in the system, adding a social dimension that is far more destabilizing. It is also harmful to the long-term sustainability of our desired economic trajectory. Today, the focus on consumption above all else also drives inequality. For example, the rich grow richer every year not through earnings but through the investment income on their savings. However, people in lower quartiles are encouraged to consume more and more. If they do not save, their wealth remains unchanged because they have no money for investment and future growth. The rich, however, may consume all their income but still benefit from their existing savings. Over time, this comes through in increasing inequality, not because of malicious intent but because of the nature of the growth we have chosen for ourselves. As savings-fueled debt propagates through the system, it heightens this inequality. We have a continual transfer from the many to a few as money is borrowed and debt is repaid. Eventually, as history has shown us repeatedly, these economic rents grow divisive and society tears itself apart.

*   *   *

We talk constantly of flows: the flow of ideas, the flow of emotions, the flow of people, the flow of money, the flow of life. It is an unconscious acceptance of the fact that we live in a dynamic world and that all life is movement. It is time that epiphany broke through to the conscious surface.

As humans, we innovate. This is the foundation of the complexity we have created. It is time we reasserted that tenet.

Acknowledgments

No book is written in isolation. Every story carries within it echoes of other voices—the myriad environments that influence the author and imbue the words with more meaning than an individual can ever hope for. We—and more personally, I—are richer for that crowd.

First, my thanks to my wife, Radhika, who nurtured this book, read innumerable iterations, and patiently put up with me through the whole journey as I repapered our home; my son, Maanas, who refused to arrive until I had submitted its précis; and to my daughter, Anaia, who deigned to grace me with her smile only once I had submitted the manuscript.

Second, to my wider family. My grandfather, Ashoke Sen, gave me curiosity, self-belief, and an enduring love for history. My parents, Shailendra and Krishna Swarup, gave me every opportunity to explore my imagination. My sister, Aparajita, was a thoughtful friend and source of strength. My father-in-law, Rajiv Dogra, took on the role of master worrier through the whole proceedings of this book and diligently read every page with a care far surpassing mine. My mother-in-law, Meenakshi Dogra, flew seven thousand miles west to mother and babysit in the final days of the writing. And my brother-in-law, Ram, provided incisive comments and never took me too seriously.

Third, my gratitude to all those who saw something in my initial halting thoughts. Conrad Gardner at Bloomsbury took a proposed essay title for a collection we were working on and encouraged me to do something more, championing the book throughout. Anuj Bahri at Red Ink took an early proposal and persuaded me to let him run with it. Don Fehr and Claire Roberts at Trident Media Group took those rough outlines, threw in a generous helping of advice, and helped create a book. Peter Ginna at Bloomsbury took a chance and has ably shepherded me down a difficult path. And Pete Beatty (who repeatedly chided me for the "and" at the start of so many sentences) did a magnificent job of editing my prose into something far more polished and concise.

Fourth, my appreciation to all those who shared conversations, thoughts, theories, and stories with me. We live in a world with an excess of information and they all helped me to filter sense from among all that glorious noise. Ryan Kloster debated many of my earlier thoughts vigorously and gave invaluable feedback. Peter Allen and I set the world to rights over many a long lunch, and he gave me the opportunity to chance some of my analysis on the Great Depression in the public amphitheater of Lombard Street Research. Dario Perkins collaborated with me, sharing insights and making me into a far better economist, as we wrote *Till Debt Us Do Part* and examined the parallels between Europe in the 1920s and today. Then there was Philip Booth, who provided another invaluable sounding board and a heterodox perspective; Jim Chanos, who gave me a reading list of books to get me started; Bruno Prior, who shared his library with me; Adrian Phillips, who told me all about the Birmingham bicycle boom; Bucky Isaacson and Frank Pusateri, who volunteered their time and their conference audiences as willing guinea pigs to road-test my ideas; and Charlie Hambro, who shared his experiences over the years and of the Swedish banking crisis in particular. There are innumerable other chance conversations and invaluable inputs with friends, colleagues, and random strangers—their influence is evident in these pages. Lastly, there are all the thinkers, writers, economists, financiers, and bloggers, whose clashing arguments and theories form the backdrop to my professional life.

This is a book about people, our unbidden influences, and the complexity we create. Its creation is also a small testament to the same.

Notes

CHAPTER 1: OF MEN, MONEY, AND MANIA

1   For those with a keener knowledge of the intricacies of finance, it was a structured note that returned two times the excess return over government bonds on a basket of senior bonds issued by twenty-five global banks. Inevitably, it was marketed heavily. The instruments had become perennially popular thanks to the layers of fees that could be hidden within their folds.

2   It had seemed like a very good idea at the time. In mid-2007 before it all went belly up, the senior financial bonds index had traded at a yield of 0.07 percent over the risk-free rate. This ridiculously low risk premium arose as people thought these to be as solid and guaranteed an investment as you could hope to get. In the months after the first wobbles, this spread blew out fourfold to 0.30 percent, and suddenly it seemed like an amazing buying opportunity that many investors— including my aforementioned friend—ran to take advantage of. But the spread continued to only go in one direction, ever wider, and by March 2009, the quoted spread was north of 4.00 percent. My friend sold out at the end of 2011 for a 10 percent loss. He considered himself lucky. His employer thought him uniquely talented.

3   In a July 2007 interview with the *Financial Times*.

4   This was later rechristened the Long Depression to differentiate it from the antics of its successor and what we now know as the Great Depression.

5   Gresham's law states that bad money drives out good money. This is based on two facts: first, that money is often viewed as a store of value; and second, multiple currencies co-exist at any given point. If governments indulge in tactics that reduce the future value of money for a particular ilk, such as printing lots more banknotes today or in older times, reducing the precious metal content in coins, it impacts human behavior. People begin to hoard whatever currency is perceived to retain its value better (i.e., good money) and will rapidly try to spend the affected currency today before it devalues further (i.e., bad money). The result is that bad

money begins to dominate transactions while good money disappears from circulation. Sellers typically respond to the falling value of money by demanding higher prices, often sowing the seeds of an inflationary spiral.

CHAPTER 2: DECONSTRUCTING THE GRUFFALO

1 Amphorae were clay vessels used for storing and transporting goods such as olive oil and wine in Roman times.

2 As discussed in chapter 1, the first-ever documented sovereign default was in the fourth century B.C. in ancient Greece when ten states defaulted on their debt to the temple of Apollo at Delos. Economic recessions were not uncommon either and were often accompanied by banking crises, which did little to endear the profession to the populace.

3 Though the term *bank deposit* has muddied the waters and conferred a false modicum of security on the money we believe we have entrusted to our banks.

4 A derivative is an instrument whose value and profit are linked to the future behavior of a financial market, entity, or commodity. These days, the ability to speculate on virtually any aspect of our environment (e.g., weather derivatives) means that the descriptor "financial" in the definition above may no longer be required.

5 Public companies that bid for government contracts.

6 The historian Suetonius laments in his chronicle of Vespasian's life that he continued "quite openly carrying on traffic which would be shameful even for a man in private life."

7 For example, the Roman senator Cato the Elder is recorded having to deal with a debt crisis in Sardinia in 198 B.C. by Livy, who also mentions other crises in the Greek provinces some twenty-five years later.

8 Catiline himself escaped, only to be killed in battle shortly afterward and vilified in Roman lore.

9 Some critics uncharitably sneered that Keynes's approach implied that in extremis, the government should pay people to dig up countless holes and fill them in again, all to keep employment high.

10 Example taxes included a 1 percent tax on auction sales, a 4 percent tax on the sale of slaves, a 5 percent tax on the freeing of slaves, a wealth tax of 1 percent for the provinces, and a poll tax.

11 As noted earlier, the continual influx of plentiful slave labor from Roman conquests meant that ordinary Romans could not compete for most jobs. By Augustus's time, the sight of Roman plebeians congregating in the Forum to sell themselves and their families into slavery was a common one. Thus, the burden of sustenance was removed. If you discharged yourself well and your master was rich, you might even be freed and given money of your own as a reward—the beginnings of fortune for many freedmen.

12 The praetor was one of the senior magistrates of Rome charged with maintaining the rule of law and adjudicating over trials involving Roman citizens.

13 Suetonius caustically noted that this was but one of the two instances where Tiberius showed generosity to the public, evidencing perhaps more the importance of money to public perception rather than Tiberius's own character.

14 Along the way, Nero also earned the eternal enmity of future generations of Christians as the architect of the first Great Persecution of this new religion in the aftermath of the Great Fire. The Bible is particularly caustic on the perceived economic corruption of Rome. Revelations 18:12 says that "when the Romans are destroyed, there will no longer be a market for all manners of luxuries and the bodies and souls of men."

15 This is equivalent to an annualized inflation rate of 10–12 percent per annum, which may seem modest by hyperinflationary standards. However, it is worth noting that changes would have occurred in sharp concentrated bursts that we would have termed hyperinflation today. For example, the silver content of Roman coins fell from 40 percent to the abovementioned 0.02 percent—a reduction in value by a factor of 2,000—over just eighteen years from A.D. 250 to 268.

16 The echoes of this cultural memory are to be found in the name Europe gave its semi-servile acquisitions around the world from the sixteenth century onward—colonies.

CHAPTER 3: ALL THINGS BEING UNEQUAL

1 I should note that readers should apply the same advice to this book if they enjoy it.

2 First hypothesized by the ubiquitous John Maynard Keynes.

3 Devised by Gauti Eggertsson, an economist at the New York Fed.

4 The interaction of supply and demand is one of the fundamental tenets of conventional economics. As demand for a good increases, its price follows suit until supply has increased to match this new excess demand. The converse holds true also. Prices and quantities move around until an equilibrium between the twin poles of supply and demand is found. Any change thereafter is driven by some external event that impacts either supply or demand.

5 For a more detailed exposition of the many contradictions inherent within mainstream economics, *Debunking Economics* by Steve Keen and *The Death of Economics* by Paul Ormerod are an excellent starting point. For financial markets, I refer the reader to *The (Mis)Behavior of Markets* by Benoit Mandelbrot, one of the pioneers of chaos theory, and Richard Hudson.

6 Some now term it the "Great Recession" of 2007, while others talk of the credit crunch. However, given that we are still working our way through the consequences—sovereign panic in Europe being its latest phase—there is still plenty of time for us to reinterpret this as a depression in due course.

CHAPTER 4: EGO AND EUPHORIA

1 There is certainly good historical evidence for the Japanese monarchy from the sixth century A.D. onward.

2 In 1989, the car manufacturer Toyota made $2.9 billion from cars and $1.2 billion from financial deals. Many other Japanese corporations such as Hitachi, Sony, and Mitsubishi also rapidly transformed into the hulking conglomerates that we know today.

3 Nippon Telegraph and Telephone.

4 Depending on your preference, NTT was more valuable than the French, Swiss, German, or Hong Kong stock markets. At several points, it was even more valuable than varying combinations of the above.

5 As mentioned, Japan has historically been a nation of savers. Both insolvency and failure carried strong social stigmas, which would have encouraged the rapid reversal from spending to increased saving.

6 A measure of the extent of the previous bubble is that even now, these are considered to be among the most expensive real estate in the world.

7 In turn, Flöttl found himself another forced seller of his assets a few years later in the aftermath of another financial fiasco—the Russian default crisis of 1998.

8 The bank is UFJ-Mitsubishi and its position there is only thanks to the fact that it is a merger of two previous stalwarts.

9 Their conservative nature and aversion to loss is reflected in an ambitious return target of 1 percent per annum.

10 Arguably, the Asian currency crisis of 1997 was the result of a deluge of capital exiting Japan and rushing into the Asian tigers that ring-fenced the country. The not unexpected result was a rapid rise in asset prices, a faster rise in loans against those assets, and a painful lingering aftermath.

CHAPTER 5: THE ROAD TO NEWNHAM

1 See his excellent book *Thinking Fast and Slow* for a fuller exposition of behavioral finance. Kahneman won the Nobel Prize in 2002 for his work on intuitive judgment and decision making.

CHAPTER 6: THE TEMPLE OF JANUS

1 According to a famous 1981 study that found 93 percent of U.S. citizens rated themselves as above average for driving skill and 88 percent rated themselves above average for safety.

2 As a sociopolitical aside, a stunning example of this was seen in the countries of the former Soviet bloc following their disorderly exits. In many places, the communists were swept from power only to be returned in various guises in subsequent elections as people romanticized the benefits of strong central authorities.

3 Noted in the previous chapter and not an invented name à la Maecenas.

4   http://www.youtube.com/watch?v=vJG698U2Mvo&noredirect=1 (retrieved August 2, 2012).

5   According to Simmons and Chabris, a Cambridge academic tried something similar in the 1930s by dressing up in a sheet as a ghost to see how many people would notice. A few curious cows notwithstanding, he was perturbed to find that no one seemed to have seen him, even when he leisurely walked across the screen at a movie theater.

6   Best known for inventing the terms *black hole* and *wormhole*, thereby enriching the lives and vocabularies of science fiction fans forevermore.

7   As an analogous example, I live in central London. When I travel, the difference between going to Cambridge and to Oxford in terms of distance and time is material to me, even though they are less than five miles and a few minutes apart. However, deciding between San Francisco or Los Angeles feels more immaterial. They seem instinctively to be about the same distance away and to take about the same amount of time to reach. But if you live on the West Coast of the United States, you almost certainly will disagree with me.

8   http://www.youtube.com/watch?v=6EjJsPylEOY#t=0m12s (retrieved September 5, 2012).

9   In particular, the general perception that house prices tend to rise over the long run plays a large role in this conclusion.

10 In countries such as China or India, where traditionally the ability to borrow was severely limited and punitive, the levels of debt are far lower. In recent years, the debt levels have risen rapidly, buoyed by a virtuous cocktail of rising incomes, a growing banking sector, an increasing supply of credit, and an expanding middle class with aspirations.

11 This bias is in itself a rational response to the career risk of taking a longer-term perspective.

12 The oil services and shipping industries are classic examples.

13 This is hardly surprising as property prices are a significant contributor to GDP, given the sums involved.

14 So-called value-at-risk models, commonly used in almost all financial institutions. What is perhaps most remarkable is that no one seems to have found it troubling that they all relied on somewhere between a mere five and twenty-five years' worth of data to make predictions.

15 This is not surprising. Currencies have a wealth of data to analyze and find spurious patterns in, which has drawn many quantitatively minded funds to the space.

CHAPTER 7: THE GREATER FOOLS

1   Doubly so when you examined the salaries for qualified researchers and their lifetime trajectories.

2   The erroneous assumption I made—following a long tradition—was that this was an industry based on careful analysis and informed judgments. That is the exception, not the rule.

3 For those of you unversed in the genius of Douglas Adams, the Babelfish is a strange creature that lives off brainwave energy and when inserted in your ear, functions as a universal translator. As Adams noted in his novel *The Hitchhiker's Guide to the Galaxy*: "Now it is such a bizarrely improbable coincidence that anything so mind-bogglingly useful could evolve purely by chance that some thinkers have chosen to see it as a final and clinching proof of the nonexistence of God."

4 An expression for traders and investment bankers popularized by Michael Lewis in *Liar's Poker*. The name reflected their testosterone-fueled and overconfident approach to life and is a badge of honor in the industry. The cognitive bias to frame the last of these three words in a positive rather than negative light is telling.

5 Not his real name.

6 The smaller fall in dollar terms was because from 2008 onward, as the Fed unveiled multiple rounds of aggressive stimulus, the U.S. dollar fell sharply against the Swiss franc.

CHAPTER 8: THE MADDING CROWD

1 Einstein's theory of general and special relativity had made a deep impression on society's perception of time and the cosmos. The spaceflight program was under way and the first manmade satellite would launch only three years later. And science fiction—both in printed and cinematic forms—had begun its golden age.

2 Arguably, procrastination has part of its origins at least in the inability to distill information into clear choices and the propensity to overanalyze to the point of fault.

3 Returning to Rome momentarily, the crime of parricide—the murder of an elder family member—was the most heinous crime.

4 As it happens, these simple filters help limit his choice to the same pool of managers in most cases and represent an institutionalization of his unconsciously imposed bounds.

5 In later years, hedge funds began to appear here as well though their intake of graduates was always very limited. As I learned, few funds had the patience to go through the training regime of two to three years to produce a decent analyst.

CHAPTER 9: MAN, MEET MONEY

1 It should be noted that even this is tied up with the notion of influence. For example, you may be in politics or the media, someone with past achievements of note in your field, or you may simply be someone who represents a key bottleneck, for example, a trustee or human resource.

CHAPTER 10: LIFE AFTER DEBT

1   A point most famously articulated by the economist Hyman Minsky, who saw fragility and financial instability as intrinsic to any economy that contained banks and debt. His protégé Charles Kindleberger wrote the definitive book on manias and panics, as noted earlier.

2   One minute for every year of his life and one minute on top for good measure. It is an amazing and powerful example of how the threat of social exclusion and disapproval really terrifies us all, even from a very young age. As a parent, it is heartrending—even for those few minutes—and an equally powerful example of how hard it is to divorce emotion from principles and actions.

CHAPTER 11: ALL THAT GLITTERS

1   A word that was popularized by the Austrian School of economics, best typified by Friedrich Hayek and Ludwig von Mises. Now a heterodox branch of economics, it is often associated with free markets and libertarian ideologies.

2   De Busbecq was the ambassador of the Holy Roman Emperor Ferdinand I of Germany to the Ottoman imperial court at Constantinople. Among other things, he is also credited with introducing the lilac to Europe.

3   The Fuggers were a powerful banking family, who made their fortune through a monopoly on the sale of papal indulgences and the ownership of major mines and trading interests throughout Europe and the New World. By the sixteenth century, they were also the largest lenders to European sovereigns—a trade that made them the richest and most powerful family in all of Europe. Unfortunately, that was also to prove their undoing and the family lost a large part of their wealth in the repeated Spanish defaults of the late sixteenth century.

4   The sixteenth century was defined by the rise of Protestantism and the increasingly violent confrontations between the Protestant north and Catholic south of Europe.

5   Another example of Gresham's law that created a vicious spiral. In the end, Spain—despite all its wealth—managed to default seven times over the course of the sixteenth and early seventeenth centuries.

6   A portrait of the aforementioned Carolus Clusius.

7   This in itself only meant a temporal supply bottleneck. Once a bulb had been grown, the cultivation of offsets meant that clones could be produced that flowered within a year or so. Indeed, by the early seventeenth century, the common tulip varieties were regularly sold in markets all over Holland and prices had fallen, reflecting the mass consumer product they had become.

8   Indeed, the fortunes of many entrepreneurs and speculators have been made by being among the first to a new party. And a key reason why they are then hailed as visionaries is because to them, the "fundamentals" are attractive when so many others are woefully pessimistic.

9 It should be noted that the English, motivated by similar concerns, had set up the English East India Company in 1600.

CHAPTER 12: A UNIVERSAL TRUTH

1 A far simpler example is the little cracks within or the small bubbles of trapped air inside an ice cube when it is formed.

2 In cosmological terms, they exhibited a stronger gravitational force and curved the fabric of space-time.

CHAPTER 13: BIRDS OF A FEATHER

1 A chromatic motif that continues to this day.

2 No, not a typo, rather proof that the cosmos has a sense of humor.

3 Possibly one of the first examples of dumping—the international equivalent of supermarket loss leaders, where goods are sold excessively cheaply in order to gain trading advantages.

4 Ironically, the mantra of efficient markets castigated earlier has its origins in this insight, with its chief flaw resting on the twin assumptions that people were wholly rational everywhere and that prices conveyed all the available information.

5 London now officially has the sixth-largest French population of any city in the world and elects a member to the French National Assembly.

6 The stunning visual is testament to how a lack of structure (in this case, of information) at the individual level can morph into a complexity of structure at much larger scales. Its similarity to the structure of the universe seen earlier or the human brain is not coincidental because mathematically, the same cascading dynamics are at play.

CHAPTER 14: A TRAGEDY OF SMALL DECISIONS

1 The two were separated only by the Great Depression of the 1930s, which lasted for forty-three months.

2 Arguably, this was a key factor in the growing discontent and eventually, the rise of independence movements in many of Britain's colonies. For example, Britain used to import raw cotton from India and sell manufactured cotton goods back to the Indians, all through a tightly controlled process to ensure a British monopoly. The Swadeshi movement begun by Gandhi directly challenged this and advocated the purchase of locally produced goods.

3 It has been noted that this was the thirty-fourth coal default in three years, which says more about the German desire to pay reparations than any underlying economic inability.

4 Some historians and many policy makers still view this period with trepidation and associate it with the rise of Nazism. But that is not strictly true. Yes, unemployment

rose rapidly, which created more misery, and there was widespread anger from the perceived injustice of reparations. This naturally led to a fillip for extremist parties—Hitler most famously attempted his abortive Munich putsch in a beer hall in 1923—but, critically, the popular support needed for them to gain any lasting traction was not there. As hyperinflation died, their brief increase in popularity rapidly faded away.

5   Privately, German officials were delighted as these capital inflows also created an army of creditors in the United States, aligning American interests with those of Germany. The Americans were more likely to help find a solution to the reparations problem. European creditors were not exactly adverse to this credit merry-go-round either—it made it more likely their debts would be written down as well.

6   Though there was little in the way of concrete ideas for where growth might actually come from.

7   The U.S. World War Foreign Debt Commission concluded some fourteen debt restructuring agreements over the next few years as it became clear that debtors couldn't make repayments. However, these were timid steps that successively extended the duration of the debt and reduced interest rates. In total, a final principal amount of $11.5 billion was accepted, to be paid off over sixty-two years with interest rates averaging slightly above two percent.

8   In other words, investors only had to put down a fraction of the money up front and thereafter simply put additional money in if there were losses.

9   France also benefited from inflows of gold. Its recent economic strength meant that the French became perceived as a safe haven.

10 This referendum was also notable for giving the fringe National Socialist Party—the Nazi Party for short—a veneer of respectability and communicating its message for the first time to the population at large, as it took the lead in the campaign for a Yes vote.

CHAPTER 16: ALPHA AND OMEGA

1   It should be noted that once little groups form with distinct viewpoints, they generally try to perpetuate their distinct ordered view of the world. This may be through assimilating others, weakening them, or simply pursuing a policy of isolationism. Given that they are not unique in this, tensions and conflicts often follow. One can see this dynamic at different levels with office cliques, cults, religions, political parties and nations. Arguably, once any collective is formed, it becomes extremely hard for an individual to stay as such.

CHAPTER 17: IN THE LAND OF THE BLIND

1   With perhaps the exception of Long-Term Capital Management in 1998.

Bibliography

Adams, D. 1979. *The Hitchhiker's Guide to the Galaxy*. London: Pan Books.

Aglietta, M. 2002. "Money: A Matter of Credit and Trust." *Les Journées Internationales d'Economie Monétaire et Bancaire*. http://www.univ-orleans.fr/deg/GDRecomofi/ Activ/doclyon/aglietta.pdf.

Ahamed, L. 2009. *Lords of Finance: The Bankers Who Broke the World*. New York: Penguin Press.

Akerlof, G. A. 2001. Prize Lecture: Behavioral Macroeconomics and Macroeconomic Behavior. Nobelprize.org. Nobel Media AB 2013. http://www.nobelprize.org/ nobel_prizes/economic-sciences/laureates/2001/akerlof-lecture.html.

Akerlof, G. A. and W. T. Dickens. 1982. "The Economic Consequences of Cognitive Dissonance." *American Economic Review* 72: 307–319.

Allen, F. and E. Carletti, 2007. "Banks, Markets and Liquidity." In *The Structure and Resilience of the Financial System*, edited by C. Kent and J. Lawson, 201–218. Sydney: Reserve Bank of Australia.

Almunia, M., A. Benetrix, B. Eichengreen, K. H. O'Rourke, and G. Rua. 2009. "From Great Depression to Great Credit Crisis: Similarities, Differences and Lessons." *CEPR Discussion Papers* 7564, C.E.P.R. Discussion Papers.

Alphaville Herald. 2007. "Ginko Financial's End-Game." August 6. http://alphaville herald.com/2007/08/ginko-financial-2.html.

Andreau, J. 1999. *Banking and Business in the Roman World*. Translated by J. Lloyd. Cambridge: Cambridge University Press.

Andrews, A. 1949. "The Roman Craze for Surmullets." *Classical Weekly* 42(12): 186–188. http://penelope.uchicago.edu/Thayer/E/Journals/CW/42/12/Roman_Craze_for_ Surmullets*.html.

Arthur, W. B. 1994. "Inductive Reasoning and Bounded Rationality." *American Economic Review* 84(2): 406–411.

Asch, S. E. 1952. *Social Psychology*. Upper Saddle River, NJ: Prentice-Hall, Inc.

Atchity, K. J. and R. McKenna, eds. 1998. *The Classical Roman Reader: New Encounters with Ancient Rome*. Oxford: Oxford University Press.

Augustus. c. A.D. 14. *Res Gestae Divi Augusti*. Translated by F. W. Shipley. In Loeb Classical Library, Harvard University Press, 1913–1914. Also available at http://penelope.uchicago.edu/Thayer/E/Roman/Texts/Augustus/Res_Gestae/home.html.

Bagehot, W. 1873. *Lombard Street: A Description of the Money Market*. London: Henry S. King and Co.

Balke, N. S. and R. J. Gordon. 1989. "The Estimation of Prewar Gross National Product: Methodology and New Evidence." *Journal of Political Economy* 97: 38–92.

Barberis, N. and R. H. Thaler. 2003. "A Survey of Behavioral Finance." In *Handbook of the Economics of Finance*, edited by G. M. Constantinides, M. Harris and R. M. Stulz, Volume 1, 1053–1128. The Netherlands: Elsevier.

Barga, M. 2013. "The Long Depression (1873–1878)." http://www.socialwelfarehistory.com/eras/the-long-depression/.

Barlow, C. T. 1980. "The Roman Government and the Roman Economy, 92–80 B.C." *American Journal of Philology* 101: 202–219.

Bartlett, B. 1994. "How Excessive Government Killed Ancient Rome." *Cato Journal* 14(2): 287–303.

Bear Stearns. 2007. Letter to Investors in *High-Grade Structured Credit Strategies and High-Grade Structured Credit Strategies Enhanced Leveraged Funds*. July 17. http://online.wsj.com/public/resources/documents/WSJ071707_Bear_Stearns_Co.pdf.

Bernanke, B. S. 2002. "Deflation: Making Sure 'It' Doesn't Happen Here." Remarks Before the National Economists Club, Washington, D.C., November 21. http://www.federalreserve.gov/boarddocs/speeches/2002/20021121/.

———. 2000. *Essays on the Great Depression*. Princeton, NJ: Princeton University Press.

———. 2009. "Financial Reform to Address Systemic Risk." Speech at the Council on Foreign Relations, Washington, D.C., March 10. http://www.federalreserve.gov/newsevents/speech/bernanke20090310a.htm.

———. 2005. "The Global Saving Glut and the U.S. Current Account Deficit." Remarks at the Sandridge Lecture, Virginia Association of Economics, Richmond, VA, March 10. http://www.federalreserve.gov/boarddocs/speeches/2005/200503102/.

———. 1995. "The Macroeconomics of the Great Depression: A Comparative Approach." *Journal of Money, Credit and Banking* 27(1):1–28.

———. 1983. "Nonmonetary Effects of the Financial Crisis in the Propagation of the Great Depression." *American Economic Review* 73(3): 257–276.

Bernanke, B. S. and H. James. 1991. "The Gold Standard, Deflation and Financial Crisis in the Great Depression: An International Comparison." In *Financial Markets and Financial Crisis*, edited by R. G. Hubbard, 33–68. Chicago: University of Chicago Press.

Bernstein, S. 1956. "American Labor in the Long Depression, 1873–1878." *Science & Society* 20(1): 59–83.

Bikhchandani, S. and S. Sharma. 2000. "Herd Behavior in Financial Markets: A Review." *IMF Working Paper* No. 00/48. IMF Institute. http://dx.doi.org/10.2139/ssrn.228343.

Birley, A. R. 1976. "The Third Century Crisis in the Roman Empire." *Bulletin of the John Rylands Library* 58(2): 253–281.

Blume, L. E. and D. Easley. 2008. "Rationality." In *The New Palgrave Dictionary of Economics*. 2nd ed., edited by S. N. Durlauf and L. E. Blume. Palgrave Macmillan. doi:10.1057/9780230226203.1390.

Bordo, M. 1986. "Financial Crises, Banking Crises, Stock Market Crashes and the Money Supply: Some International Evidence, 1870–1933." In *Financial Crises and the World Banking System*, edited by F. Capie and G. E. Wood, 190–248. New York: St. Martin's Press.

Bordo, M., B. Eichengreen, D. Klingebiel and M. S. Martinez-Peria. 2001. "Is the Crisis Problem Growing More Severe?" *Economic Policy* 16(32): 51–82.

Bowles, S. 1998. "Endogenous Preferences: The Cultural Consequences of Markets and Other Economic Institutions." *Journal of Economic Literature* 36: 75–111.

Brackey, H. J. and G. Bulfin. 2009. "Former Madoff Ally Breaks His Silence." *South Florida Sun-Sentinel*, March 8. http://articles.sun-sentinel.com/2009-03-08/news/0903070146_1_ponzi-scheme-bernard-madoff-scandal-doubt-bernie-madoff.

Caesar, Julius. *The Civil Wars*. Translated by W. A. McDevitte and W. S. Bohn. http://classics.mit.edu/Caesar/civil.html.

Capie, F. and G. E. Wood. 1997. "Great Depression of 1873–1896." In *Business Cycles and Depressions: An Encyclopedia*, edited by D. Glasner et al. New York: Garland Publishing.

Cecchetti, S. G., M. Mohanty, and F. Zampolli. 2011. "The Real Effects for Debt." Working Papers No. 352, Bank for International Settlements. http://www.bis.org/publ/work352.htm.

Chabris, C. and D. Simons. 2010. *The Invisible Gorilla*. New York: Harmony.

Chancellor, E. 2000. *Devil Take the Hindmost*. New York: Plume.

Clapham, Sir J. 1944. *The Bank of England: A History* (2 Vols.). Cambridge: Cambridge University Press.

The Code of Hammurabi. Translated by L. W. King. 2004. Whitefish, MT: Kessinger Publishing. Available also at the Avalon Project, Lillian Goldman Law Library, Yale Law School., http://avalon.law.yale.edu/subject_menus/hammenu.asp.

Comazzi, G. B. 1729. *The Morals of Princes, Or An Abstract of the Most Remarkable Passages Contain'd in the History of All the Emperors Who Reign'd in Rome: With a Moral Reflection Drawn from Each Quotation*. London: T. Worrall. books.google.co.uk/books?id=GnQ2AAAAMAAJ.

Congdon, T. 2011. *Money in a Free Society: Keynes, Friedman, and the New Crisis in Capitalism*. New York: Encounter.

Connelley, W. E. 1918. *A Standard History of Kansas and Kansans*. Chicago: Lewis. Transcribed by students and staff from USD 508, Baxter Springs Middle School, Baxter Springs, Kansas. http://skyways.lib.ks.us/genweb/archives/1918ks/toc.html.

Constantinides, G. M., M. Harris, and R. M. Stulz. 2003. *Handbook of the Economics of Finance*. The Netherlands: Elsevier.

Crafts, N. 2012. "Returning to Growth: Policy Lessons from History." Royal Economic Society Policy Lecture, October 17. http://www.res.org.uk/SpringboardWebApp/userfiles/res/file/res_policy_slides.pdf.

Crawford, M. 1975. "Finance, Coinage and Money from the Severans to Constantine." *ANRW* 2(2): 560–593.

Crévier, J. B. L. and J. Mills. 1761. *The History of the Roman Emperors from Augustus to Constantine*. J. and P. Knapton. http://archive.org/details/historyromanemp 05millgoog.

Damasio, A. R. 1994. *Descartes' Error: Emotion, Reason, and the Human Brain*. New York: Grosset/Putnam.

Damasio, A. R., D. Tranel, and H. Damasio. 1990. "Individuals with Sociopathic Behavior Caused by Frontal Damage Fail to Respond Autonomically to Social Stimuli." *Behavioural Brain Research* 41: 81–94.

Davies, G. 2002. *A History of Money from Ancient Times to the Present Day*. 3rd ed. Cardiff: University of Wales Press.

Davis, W. S. 1910. *The Influence of Wealth in Imperial Rome*. New York: Macmillan.

DeLong, J. B. 2012. "This Time, It Is Not Different: The Persistent Concerns of Financial Macroeconomics." Available at http://delong.typepad.com/20120411-russell-sage-delong-paper.pdf.

The Dialogue Concerning the Exchequer. c. 1180. Translated by E. F. Henderson. In *Select Historical Documents of the Middle Ages*. London: George Bell and Sons. 1896. Available also at the Avalon Project, Lillian Goldman Law Library, Yale Law School. http://avalon.law.yale.edu/medieval/excheq.asp.

Dickens, Charles. 1855. *Speech to the Administrative Reform Association, Theatre Royal, Drury Lane, Wednesday, June 27, 1855*. In *The Speeches of Charles Dickens*, edited by K. J. Fielding, 213–222. Oxford: The Clarendon Press, 1960. Reprint, Newcastle-upon-Tyne: Cambridge Scholars Publishing.

Dimand, R. W. 1993. "The Dance of the Dollar: Irving Fisher's Monetary Theory of Economic Fluctuations." *History of Economics Review* 20:161–172.

———. 1994. "Irving Fisher's Debt-Deflation Theory of Great Depressions." *Review of Social Economy* 52: 92–107.

———. 2003. "Irving Fisher on the International Transmission of Booms and Depressions Through Monetary Standards." *Journal of Money, Credit and Banking*. Vol 35(1): 49–90.

Dio, Cassius. *Roman History*. Translated by E. Cary. In *Loeb Classical Library* (9 Vols). Harvard University Press, 1914–1927. Also available at http://penelope.uchicago.edu/Thayer/E/Roman/Texts/Cassius_Dio/home.html.

Donaldson, J. (author) and A. Scheffler (illustrator). *The Gruffalo*. 7th ed. New York: Macmillan Children's Books.

Duncan-Jones, R. 1994. *Money and Government in the Roman Empire*. Cambridge: Cambridge University Press.

———. R. 1990. *Structure and Scale in the Roman Economy*. Cambridge: Cambridge University Press.

Duranske, B. 2012. *Virtually Blind* blog. Posts on Ginko Financial http://virtuallyblind
.com/category/virtually-blind-series/ginko-financial/.

Durlauf, S. N. and L. E. Blume, eds. 2008. *The New Palgrave Dictionary of Economics*.
2nd ed. New York: Palgrave Macmillan.

The Economist. 2007. *Trouble in Paradise* (August 16, 2007). The Economist
Newspaper Limited.

Eggertsson, G. B. 2010. "The Paradox of Toil." Federal Reserve Bank of New York
Staff Report, No. 433.

Eggertsson, G. B. and P. Krugman. 2012. "Debt, Deleveraging, and the Liquidity Trap:
A Fisher-Minsky-Koo Approach." *Quarterly Journal of Economics* 127(3):
1469–1513.

Eichengreen, B. 2004. "The British Economy Between the Wars." In *The Cambridge
Economic History of Modern Britain*. 1st ed. Vol. 2. Edited by R. Floud and P.
Johnson, 314–343. Cambridge: Cambridge University Press. Also available at
Cambridge Histories Online. doi.org/10.1017/CHOL9780521820370.013.

———. 1992. *Golden Fetters. The Gold Standard and the Great Depression 1919–
1939*. Oxford: Oxford University Press.

———. 2002. "Still Fettered After All These Years." NBER Working Paper No. 9276.
http://www.nber.org/papers/w9276.pdf.

Eichengreen, B. and P. Temin. 2010. "Fetters of Gold and Paper." *Oxford Review of
Economic Policy* 26(3): 370–384.

Emerson, R. W. 1841. *Essays: First Series*. http://www.emersoncentral.com/essays1
.htm.

Eslinger, P. J. and A. R. Damasio. 1985. "Severe Disturbance of Higher Cognition
After Bilateral Frontal Lobe Ablation: Patient EVR." *Neurology* 35: 1731–1741.

European Central Bank. 2012. *Virtual Currency Schemes*. http://www.ecb.int/pub/pdf/
other/virtualcurrencyschemes201210en.pdf.

Fackler, M. 2005. "Take It from Japan: Bubbles Hurt." *New York Times*, December 25.
http://www.nytimes.com/2005/12/25/business/yourmoney/25japan.html.

Fama, E. F. 1965. "The Behavior of Stock Market Prices." *Journal of Business* 38(1):
31–105.

———. 1998. "Market Efficiency, Long-term Returns, and Behavioral Finance."
Journal of Financial Economics 49(3): 283–306. http://dx.doi.org/10.1016/
S0304-405X(98)00026-9.

Feinstein, C. P. Temin and G. Toniolo. 1997. *The European Economy Between the
Wars*. Oxford: Oxford University Press.

Feldman, G. 1993. *The Great Disorder. Politics, Economics, and Society in the German
Inflation, 1914–1924*. Oxford: Oxford University Press.

Fels, R. 1949. "The Long-Wave Depression, 1873–97." *Review of Economics and
Statistics* 31(1): 69–73.

Ferguson, N. 1996. "Constraints and Room for Manoeuvre in the German Inflation of
the 1920s." *Economic History Review* 49: 635–666.

———. 1998. *The Pity of War*. London: Penguin Press.

Ferguson, T. and P. Temin. 2003. "Made in Germany: the Currency Crisis of 1931." *Research in Economic History* 31: 1–53.

Finley, M. I. 1985. *The Ancient Economy*. 2nd ed. London: Hogarth.

Fischer, D. H. 1996. *The Great Wave*. Oxford: Oxford University Press.

Fishback, P. 2010. "US Monetary and Fiscal Policy in the 1930s." *Oxford Review of Economic Policy* 26(3): 385–413.

Fisher, I. 1933. "The Debt-Deflation Theory of Great Depressions." *Econometrica* 1(4): 337–357.

———. 1911. *The Purchasing Power of Money: Its Determination and Relation to Credit, Interest and Crises*. 2nd ed. New York: Macmillan.

Fitzgerald, F. Scott. 1925. *The Great Gatsby*. New York: Scribner (reprinted 2004).

Fogel, R. W. 1964. *Railroads and American Economic Growth: Essays in Econometric History*. Baltimore and London: John Hopkins Press.

Forbes, Sir W., 6th Baronet. 1860. *Memoirs of a Banking-House*. 2nd ed. London and Edinburgh: William and Robert Chambers. http://www.archive.org/stream/memoirsofbankhouse00forb/memoirsofbankhouse00forb_djvu.txt.

Forster, C. T. and F. H. B. Daniell. 1881. *The Life and Letters of Ogier Ghiselin De Busbecq*. Vol. 1. London: C. Kegan Paul & Co. http://www.archive.org/stream/lifelettbusbecq01forsuoft/lifelettbusbecq01forsuoft_djvu.txt.

Frank, T. 1927. *An Economic History of Rome*. 2nd ed, 2004. Ontario, CA: Batoche Books.

———. 1935. "The Financial Crisis of 33 A.D." *American Journal of Philology* 56(4): 336–41.

Frankel, S. H. 1977. *Money: Two Philosophies. The Conflict of Trust and Authority*. England: Basil Blackwell.

French, D. 2006. "The Dutch Monetary Environment during Tulipmania." *Quarterly Journal of Austrian Economics* 9(1): 12–13.

Friedman, M. 1992. "Franklin D. Roosevelt, Silver, and China." *Journal of Political Economy* 100(1): 62–83.

———. 1969. *The Optimum Quantity of Money and Other Essays*. Chicago: Aldine.

Friedman, M. and A. J. Schwartz. 1963. *A Monetary History of the United States, 1867–1960*. Princeton, NJ: Princeton University Press.

Galbraith, J. K. 1954. *The Great Crash 1929*. New York: Houghton Mifflin.

———. 1990. *A Short History of Financial Euphoria*. New York: Penguin Books.

Gibbons, E. 1782. *The History of the Decline and Fall of the Roman Empire*. London: John Murray (1845). Available on Project Gutenberg, http://www.gutenberg.org/files/25717/25717-h/25717-h.htm.

Gilbert, P. 1925–1930. *Report of the Agent General for Reparation Payments*. Berlin: Agent General.

Gilovich, T., D. Griffin, and D. Kahneman, eds. 2002. *Heuristics and Biases: The Psychology of Intuitive Judgment*. Cambridge: Cambridge University Press.

Glasner. D. et al., eds. 1997. *Business Cycles and Depressions: An Encyclopedia*. New York: Garland Publishing.

Goldgar, A. 2007. *Tulipmania: Money, Honor, and Knowledge in the Dutch Golden Age*. Chicago: University of Chicago Press.

Goodman, G. J. W. 1981. *Paper Money*. New York: Summit.

Graber, P. 1989. "Tulipmania." *Journal of Political Economy* 97(3): 535–560.

Graham, F. 1930. *Exchange, Prices and Production in Hyper-inflation: Germany, 1920–23*. Princeton, NJ: Princeton University Press.

Grossman, S. J. and J. E. Stiglitz. 1980. "On the Impossibility of Informationally Efficient Markets." *American Economic Review* 70(3): 393–408.

Haldane, A. G. and R. May. 2011. "Systemic Risk in Banking Ecosystems." *Nature* 469: 351–355.

Haley, E. W. 2003. *Baetica Felix: People and Prosperity in Southern Spain from Caesar to Septimius Severus*. Austin: University of Texas Press.

Hamilton, H. 1956. "The Failure of the Ayr Bank, 1772." *Economic History Review* New Series 8(3): 405–417. http://www.jstor.org/stable/2598492.

Haskell, H. J. 1947. *The New Deal in Old Rome*. New York: Alfred A. Knopf.

Hayek, F. A. 1988. *The Collected Works of F. A. Hayek*. Ed. W. W. Bartley et al. Chicago: University of Chicago Press.

———. 1996. *Individualism and Economic Order*. Chicago: University of Chicago Press.

———. 1945. "The Use of Knowledge in Society." *American Economic Review* 35(4): 519–530.

Herlihy, D. V. 2004. *Bicycle: The History*. New Haven, CT: Yale University Press.

Hetzel, R. L. 2002. "German Monetary History in the First Half of the Twentieth Century." *Economic Quarterly* 88 (Winter). Federal Reserve Bank of Richmond.

Higgs, R. 2006. *Depression, War and Cold War: Studies in Political Economy*. Oxford: Oxford University Press.

———. 1971. *The Transformation of the American Economy, 1865–1914: An Essay in Interpretation*. New York: John Wiley & Sons.

Hixson, W. F. 1993. *Triumph of the Bankers: Money and Banking in the Eighteenth and Nineteenth Centuries*. London: Praeger.

Hobsbawm, E. 1989. *The Age of Empire (1875–1914)*. New York: Vintage Books.

———. 1999. *Industry and Empire: From 1750 to the Present Day*. 2nd ed. New York: New Press.

Hoffman, N. and J. Gant. 2012. "Bicycling in the 19th century." Recollection WI, October 12. http://recollectionwisconsin.org/bicycling.

Hopkins, K. 1995–1996. "Rome, Taxes, Rents, and Trade." *Kodai: Journal of Ancient History* 6/7: 41–71.

———.1980. "Taxes and Trade in the Roman Empire (200 B.C.–A.D. 400)." *Journal of Roman Studies* 70: 101–25.

orace. c. 33 B.C. *Satires* 6, 65–92. In *The Works of Horace*, translated by C. Smart and T. A. Buckley, New York: Harper & Brothers (1863). http://data.perseus.org/citations/urn:cts:latinLit:phi0893.phi004.perseus-eng1:1.6.65.

Hudson, M. 2003. "The Creditary/Monetarist Debate in Historical Perspective." In *The State, the Market, and the Euro: Chartalism Versus Metallism in the Theory of Money*, edited by S. A. Bell and E. J. Nell. Northampton, MA: Edward Elgar.

Ingham, G. 1996. "Money Is a Social Relation," *Review of Social Economy* 54(4): 507–529.

International Monetary Fund. 2011. *The Multilateral Aspects of Policies Affecting Capital Flows*. IMF Policy Paper, October 13. http://www.imf.org/external/np/pp/eng/2011/101311.pdf.

International Monetary Fund. 2011. *The Multilateral Aspects of Policies Affecting Capital Flows—Background Paper*. IMF Policy Paper, October 21. http://www.imf.org/external/np/pp/eng/2011/102111.pdf.

James, H. 1986. *The German Slump: Politics and Economics 1924–36*. Oxford: Clarendon Press.

Jenner & Block. 2010. Lehman Brothers Holdings Inc. Chapter 11 Proceedings Examiner's Report. Available at: http://jenner.com/lehman/.

Johnson, H. 2009. "Former Madoff Associate Michael Bienes Breaks His Silence." South Florida Sun-Sentinel.com, March 9. http://www.sun-sentinel.com/business/sfl-flzmadoff0308pnmar08,0,5982371.story.

Jones, A. H. M. 1953. "Inflation under the Roman Empire." *Economic History Review*, 2nd series, 5(3): 293–318.

———. 1974. *The Roman Economy: Studies in Ancient Economic and Administrative History*. Edited by P. A. Brunt. Oxford: Blackwell.

Juvenal. *Satires X*. Translated by G. G. Ramsay. London: William Heinemann, 1918. Also available at http://www.tertullian.org/fathers/juvenal_satires_10.htm.

Kahneman, D. 2003. "Maps of Bounded Rationality: Psychology for Behavioral Economics." *American Economic Review* 93: 1449–1475.

———. 2011. *Thinking Fast and Slow*. London: Allen Lane.

Kahneman, D., J. L. Knetsch, and R. H. Thaler. 1991. "Anomalies: The Endowment Effect, Loss Aversion, and Status Quo Bias." *Journal of Economic Perspectives* 5: 193–206.

———. 1990. "Experimental Tests of the Endowment Effect and the Coase Theorem." *Journal of Political Economy* 98:1325–1348.

Kahneman, D. and A. Tversky. 1979. "Prospect Theory: An Analysis of Decision Under Risk." *Econometrica* 47: 263–291.

———. 1982. "The Psychology of Preferences." *Scientific American* 246: 160–173.

———. 1972. "Subjective Probability: A Judgment of Representativeness." *Cognitive Psychology* 3: 430–454.

Kahneman, D. and A. Tversky, eds. 2000. *Choices, Values and Frames*. Cambridge: Cambridge University Press and the Russell Sage Foundation.

Kallet-Marx, Robert. 1995. *Hegemony to Empire: The Development of the Roman Imperium in the East from 148 to 62 B.C.* Berkeley: University of California Press. http://ark.cdlib.org/ark:/13030/ft1x0nb0dk/.

Kang, S. W. and H. Rockoff. 2006. "Capitalizing Patriotism: The Liberty Loans of World War I." NBER Working Paper No. 11919.

Keen, S. 2001. *Debunking Economics: The Naked Emperor of the Social Sciences.* London: Pluto Press.

———. 2009. "The Global Financial Crisis, Credit Crunches and Deleveraging." *Journal of Australian Political Economy* 64: 22–36.

Kerr, A. W. 1908. *History of Banking in Scotland.* London: Black.

Kessler, A. 2010. "Cognitive Dissonance, the Global Financial Crisis and the Discipline of Economics." *Real-World Economics Review* 54: 2–18.

Kessler, D. and P. Temin. 2007. "The Organization of the Grain Trade in the Early Roman Empire." *Economic History Review* 60(2): 313–332.

Keynes, J. M. 1982. *The Collected Writings of John Maynard Keynes.* Cambridge: Cambridge University Press.

———. 1920. *The Economic Consequences of the Peace.* London: Macmillan.

———. 1963. *Essays in Persuasion.* New York: W. W. Norton & Co.

———. 1936. *The General Theory of Employment, Interest and Money.* Cambridge: Cambridge University Press.

Kidd, C., H. Palmeri, and R. N. Aslin. 2013. "Rational Snacking: Young Children's Decision-making on the Marshmallow Task Is Moderated by Beliefs About Environmental Reliability." *Cognition* 126(1): 109–114. doi.org/10.1016/j .cognition.2012.08.004.

Kindleberger, C. P. 1991. *A Financial History of Western Europe.* 2nd ed. New York: Oxford University Press.

———. 1986. *The World in Depression, 1929–1939.* 2nd ed. Berkeley: University of California Press.

Kindleberger, C. P. and R. Aliber. 2005. *Manias, Panics, and Crashes.* New York: Wiley.

King, G., O. Rosen, M. Tanner, and A. Wagner. 2008. "Ordinary Economic Voting Behaviour in the Extraordinary Election of Adolf Hitler." *Journal of Economic History* 68(4): 951–996.

Knight, F. H. 1921. *Risk, Uncertainty and Profit.* Boston: Houghton Mifflin Company. http://archive.org/details/riskuncertaintyp00knigrich.

Kodama, F. 1991. "Analyzing Japanese High Technologies: The Techno-Paradigm Shift." London: Pinter Publishers.

———. 1991. "Changing Global Perspective: Japan, the USA and the New Industrial Order." *Science and Public Policy* 18(6): 385–392.

Koo, R. 2008. *The Holy Grail of Macroeconomics: Lessons from Japan's Great Recession.* New York: Wiley.

Korte, G. 2011. "The U.S. Balance Sheet Includes Billions in Old Debt." *USA Today,* July 21.

Kosmetatos, P. 2013. "A Portrait of a Banking Calamity." March 14. http://www.cam .ac.uk/research/discussion/a-portrait-of-a-banking-calamity.

Krugman, P. 2009. "How Did Economists Get It So Wrong?" *New York Times Magazine,* September 2.

————. 1996. *The Self Organizing Economy*. Oxford: Wiley-Blackwell.

Krioukov, D., M. Kitsak, R. S. Sinkovits, D. Rideout, D. Meyer, and M. Boguñá. 2012. "Network Cosmology." *Scientific Reports* 2, article number 793. doi:10.1038/srep00793

Labaree, B. W. 1968. *The Boston Tea Party*. Oxford: Oxford University Press.

Landers, P. and D. Biers. 1997. "This Will Hurt." *Far Eastern Economic Review*, December 4: 74–78.

Landes, D. S. 1969. *The Unbound Prometheus: Technological Change and Industrial Development in Western Europe from 1750 to the Present*. Cambridge: Press Syndicate of the University of Cambridge.

Levick, B. 1999. *Tiberius the Politician*. New York: Routledge.

Life. 1954. "A New Look for Windshields." April 12, 34–35.

Linden Laboratories. 2009. "2009 End of Year Second Life Economy Wrap Up (including Q4 Economy in Detail)." http://community.secondlife.com/t5/Features/2009-End-of-Year-Second-Life-Economy-Wrap-up-including-Q4/ba-p/653078.

————. 2011. "The Second Life Economy in Q3 2011." http://community.secondlife.com/t5/Featured-News/The-Second-Life-Economy-in-Q3-2011/ba-p/1166705.

————. 2010. "Second Life Economy Stable in Q2 2010." http://community.secondlife.com/t5/Featured-News/Second-Life-Economy-Stable-in-Q2-2010/ba-p/664748.

Loewenstein, G. and R. H. Thaler. 1997. "Intertemporal Choice." In *Research on Judgment and Decision Making: Currents, Connections, and Controversies*, edited by W. M. Goldstein and R. M. Hogarth. Cambridge: Cambridge University Press.

Loftus, E. F. and J. C. Palmer. 1974. "Reconstruction of Auto-Mobile Destruction: An Example of the Interaction Between Language and Memory." *Journal of Verbal Learning and Verbal Behaviour* 13: 585–589.

Lunn, P. 2011. "The Role of Decision-Making Biases in Ireland's Banking Crisis." Economic and Social Research Institute (ESRI) Working Paper 389.

Mackay, C. 1852. *Extraordinary Popular Delusions and the Madness of Crowds*. Wordsworth Editions (1995).

Maddison, A. 2007. *Contours of the World Economy, 1–2030 A.D.: Essays in Macro-Economic History*. Oxford: Oxford University Press.

————. 2003. *The World Economy: A Millennial Perspective*. Paris: OECD. http://www.ggdc.net/MADDISON/oriindex.htm.

Mandlebrot, B. and R. L. Hudson. 2004. *The (Mis)Behaviour of Markets*. New York: Basic Books.

Mantoux, E. 1946. *The Carthaginian Peace, or the Economic Consequences of Mr. Keynes*. London: Oxford University Press.

Marks, S. 1978. "The Myths of Reparations." *Central European History* 11(3): 231–255.

Matyszak, P. 2008. *Ancient Rome on 5 Denarii a Day*. New York: W. W. Norton & Co.

McGinn, T. A. J. 2004. *The Economy of Prostitution in the Roman World*. Ann Arbor, MI: University of Michigan Press.

Meltzer, A. H. 2003. *A History of the Federal Reserve: Volume 1: 1913–1951*. Chicago: University of Chicago Press.

Menger, C. 1892. "On the Origins of Money." *Economic Journal* 2(6): 239–255.

Minsky, H. P. 1984. *Can "It" Happen Again?* Armonk, NY: M. E. Sharpe, Inc.

———. 1992. "The Financial Instability Hypothesis." Jerome Levy Economics Institute of Bard College, Working Paper 74 (May).

———. 1986. *Stabilizing an Unstable Economy*. New Haven, CT: Yale University Press.

———. 1977. "A Theory of Systemic Fragility." In *Financial Crises: Institutions and Markets*, edited by E. I. Altman and A. W. Sametz. New York: Wiley.

Mischel, W., E. B. Ebbesen, and A. R. Zeiss. 1972. "Cognitive and Attentional Mechanisms in Delay of Gratification." *Journal of Personality and Social Psychology* 21 (2): 204–218.

Mischel, W., Y. Shoda, and M. L. Rodriguez. 1989. "Delay of Gratification in Children." *Science* 244: 933–938.

Mises, L. von. 1953. *The Theory of Money and Credit*. New Haven, CT: Yale University Press.

Mishkin, F. S. 1991. "Asymmetric Information and Financial Crises: A Historical Perspective." In NBER book *Financial Markets and Financial Crises*, edited by R. G. Hubbard, 69–108. Chicago: University of Chicago Press.

Mitchell, B. R. 1988. *British Historical Statistics*. Cambridge: Cambridge University Press.

Mullainathan, S. and R. H. Thaler. 2000. "Behavioral Economics." NBER Working Paper Series No. 7948. http://www.nber.org/papers/W7948.

Musson, A. E. 1959. "The Great Depression in Britain, 1873–1896: A Reappraisal." *Journal of Economic History* 19 (2): 199–228.

Nakamoto, M. and D. Wighton. 2007. "Citigroup Chief Stays Bullish on Buy-Outs." *Financial Times*, July 9.

Nakamoto, S. 2008. Bitcoin: A Peer-to-Peer Electronic Cash System. http://bitcoin.org/bitcoin.pdf.

National Bureau of Economic Research. *Business Cycle Expansions and Contractions*. http://www.nber.org/cycles.html.

Neal, L., ed. 1993. *The Rise of Financial Capitalism: International Capital Markets in the Age of Reason*. Cambridge: Cambridge University Press.

Neal, L. and M. Weidenmier. 2002. "Crises in the Global Economy from Tulips to Today: Contagion and Consequences." NBER Working Paper No. 9147. http://www.nber.org/papers/w9147.

Oertel, F. 1939. "The Economic Life of the Empire." *Cambridge Ancient History* 12: 232–281.

Online Vintage Bicycle Museum. http://www.oldbike.eu/museum/. See also http://oldbike.wordpress.com/.

Ormerod, P. 1997. *The Death of Economics*. New York: John Wiley & Sons.

Parker, A. J. 1992. *Ancient Shipwrecks of the Mediterranean and the Roman Provinces*. British Archaeological Reports Int. Ser. DLXXX. Oxford: Tempus Reparatum.

Partnoy, F. 2008. *The Match King: Ivar Kreuger. The Financial Genius Behind a Century of Wall Street Scandals*. New York: Public Affairs.

Peden, J. R. 2009. "Inflation and the Fall of the Roman Empire," *Mises Daily*, September 7. mises.org/daily/3663.

Perseus Digital Library. 2013. Ed. Gregory R. Crane. Tufts University. http://www.perseus.tufts.edu.

Petronius Arbiter. *The Banquet of Trimalchio from the Satyricon*. From *Readings in Ancient History: Illustrative Extracts from the Sources*, Vol. 2, edited by W. S. Davis, 1912–1913. Boston: Allyn and Bacon.

Philo. 1st century A.D. *The Works of Philo*. Translated by C. D. Yonge, 1854. London: H. G. Bohn. Also available at: http://www.earlychristianwritings.com/yonge/.

Pliny the Elder. *Natural History*. 12.41. Translated by John Bostock. London: Taylor and Francis (1855). http://www.perseus.tufts.edu/hopper/text?doc=Perseus%3At ext%3A1999.02.0137%3Abook%3D12%3Achapter%3D41.

Price, J. M., ed. 1979. "Introduction." In *Joshua Johnson's Letterbook 1771–1774: Letters from a Merchant in London to His Partners in Maryland*, VII–XXVIII. http://www.british-history.ac.uk/report.aspx?compid=38786.

Rational Survivability blog. 2008. "Ginko Financial Collapse Ultimately Yields Real Virtual Risk (Huh?)" January 15. http://www.rationalsurvivability.com/blog/2008/01/ginko-financial-collapse-ultimately-yields-real-virtual-risk-huh/.

Reinhart, C. M and K. S. Rogoff. 2009. *This Time Is Different: Eight Centuries of Financial Folly*. Princeton, NJ: Princeton University Press.

Report of the Financial Crisis Inquiry Committee. 2011. http://www.fcic.gov/.

Reynolds, C. W. 1987. "Flocks, Herds, and Schools: A Distributed Behavioral Model." *Computer Graphics* 21(4) (SIGGRAPH '87 Conference Proceedings): 25–34. http://www.red3d.com/cwr/papers/1987/SIGGRAPH87.pdf.

Ritschl, A. 2012. "The German Transfer Problem, 1920–1933: A Sovereign Debt Perspective." CEP Discussion Paper No. 1155.

———. 2012. "Reparations, Deficits and Debt Default: The Great Depression in Germany." CEP Discussion Paper No. 1149.

Robertson, H. 2012. *Written Ministerial Statements, Culture, Media and Sport, Government Olympic Executive* (Quarterly Report). HC Hansard, October 23, col 45WS. http://www.publications.parliament.uk/pa/cm201213/cmhansrd/cm121023/wmstext/121023m0001.htm.

Rostovtzeff, M. 1926. "The Problem of the Origin of Serfdom in the Roman Empire." *Journal of Land and Public Utility Economics* 2(2): 198–207.

———. 1957. *The Social and Economic History of the Roman Empire*. 2nd ed., 2 vols. London: Oxford University Press.

Rothbard, M. N. 2002. *A History of Money and Banking in the United States*. Auburn, AL: Ludwig von Mises Institute.

Rumsfeld, D. 2002. U.S. Department of Defense news briefing, February 12.

Ruston, A. 2004. "Fordyce, David (*bap.* 1711, *d.* 1751)." In *Oxford Dictionary of National Biography*. Oxford: Oxford University Press. doi:10.1093/ref:odnb/9877.

Samuelson, P. A. 1973. "Classical and Neo-Classical Monetary Theory." In *Monetary Theory*, edited by R.W. Clower, 170–190. Penguin Education.

Saville, R. 1996. *Bank of Scotland: A History, 1695–1995*. Edinburgh: Edinburgh University Press.

Schama, S. 1987. *The Embarrassment of Riches: An Interpretation of Dutch Culture in the Golden Age*. New York: Knopf.

Scheidel, W. and S. J. Friesen. 2009. "The Size of the Economy and the Distribution of Income in the Roman Empire." *Journal of Roman Studies* 99: 61–91.

Schelling, T. C. 1971. "Dynamic Models of Segregation." *Journal of Mathematical Sociology* 1(2): 143–186.

———. 1978. *Micromotives and Macrobehaviour*. New York: W. W. Norton & Co.

———. 1969. "Models of Segregation." *American Economic Review* 59(2): 488–493.

Schoff, W. H., tr. and ed., 1912. *The Periplus of the Erythraean Sea: Travel and Trade in the Indian Ocean by a Merchant of the First Century*. New York: Longmans, Green, and Co. http://depts.washington.edu/silkroad/texts/periplus/periplus.html.

Schumpeter, J. A. 1939. *Business Cycles: A Theoretical, Historical and Statistical Analysis of the Capitalist Process*. New York: McGraw-Hill.

———. 1943. *Capitalism, Socialism and Democracy*. New York: Harper.

———. 1989. *Essays on Entrepreneurs, Innovations, Business Cycles and the Evolution of Capitalism*. Edited by R. V. Clemence. New Brunswick, NJ: Transaction Publishers.

———. 1934. *The Theory of Economic Development*. Cambridge, MA: Harvard University Press.

Schwartz, H. 1992. "Hegemony, International Debt, and International Economic Instability." In *Current Perspectives and Issues in International Political Economy*, edited by C. Polychroniou. New York: Praeger.

Seattle Times. 1954. "Glass Pits Intrigue Scientists." April 16.

———. 1954. "Laboratory Begins Air Pollution Tests." April 16.

———. 1954. "Mystery Windshield Damage Spreads in Seattle and County." April 15.

———. 1954. "Reports of Damage to Car Glass Taper Off." April 16.

———. 1954. "Windshield Front Quiet in Northwest." April 17.

———. 1954. "Windshield-Peppering Hoodlums Strike Whidbey Naval Air Station." April 14.

———. 1954. "Windshields Pitted as Two Watch." April 15.

Second Thoughts blog. 2007. "Ginko's Going . . . Going?" August 8. http://secondthoughts.typepad.com/second_thoughts/2007/08/ginkos-goinggoi.html.

Sheridan, R. B. 1960. "The British Credit Crisis of 1772 and the American Colonies." *Journal of Economic History* 20(2): 161–186.

Shiller, R. J. 2003. "From Efficient Markets Theory to Behavioral Finance." *Journal of Economic Perspectives*, 17(1): 83-104. DOI: 10.1257/089533003321164967.

Shintaro, I. 1991. *The Japan That Can Say No: Why Japan Will Be First Among Equals*. New York: Simon and Schuster.

Simon, H. A. 1983. "Alternative Visions of Rationality." In *Rationality in Action: Contemporary Approaches*, edited by P. K. Moser. Cambridge: Cambridge University Press.

———. 1996. *The Sciences of the Artificial*. 3rd ed. Cambridge, MA: MIT Press.

Simon, H. A., G. B. Dantzig, R. Hogarth, C. R. Plott, H. Raiffa, T. C. Schelling, K. A. Shepsle, R. Thaler, A. Tversky, and S. Winter. 1987. "Decision Making and Problem Solving." *Interfaces* 17(5): 11–31.

Sloan, P. 2005. "The Virtual Rockefeller." CNN, December 1.

Smith, A. 1776. *An Inquiry into the Nature and Causes of the Wealth of Nations*. Reprinted., New York: Modern Library, 1937.

Social Democracy for the 21st Century: A Post Keynesian Perspective (blog). 2011. 2011. "Debt Deflationary Crisis in the Late Roman Republic." June 16. http://socialdemocracy21stcentury.blogspot.co.uk/2011/06/debt-deflationary-crisis-in-late-roman.html.

———. "Inflation and the Fall of the Roman Empire." June 12. http://socialdemocracy21stcentury.blogspot.co.uk/2011/06/inflation-and-fall-of-roman-empire.html.

———. 2011. "Why Is the Fractional Reserve Account a Mutuum, Not a Bailment?" December 17. http://socialdemocracy21stcentury.blogspot.co.uk/2011/12/why-is-fractional-reserve-account.html.

de Soto, J. H. 2009. *Money, Bank Credit, and Economic Cycles*. Auburn, AL: Ludwig von Mises Institute.

Stiglitz, J. 1988. "Why Financial Structure Matters." *Journal of Economic Perspectives* 2(4): 121–126.

Stiglitz, J. and A. Weiss. 1992. "Asymmetric Information in Credit Markets and Its Implications for Macro-Economics." *Oxford Economic Papers*, New Series 44(4), *Special Issue on Financial Markets, Institutions and Policy*: 694–724.

———. 1981. "Credit Rationing in Markets with Imperfect Information." *American Economic Review* 71(3): 393–410.

Strachan, H. *The First World War: Volume 1: To Arms*. Oxford: Oxford University Press, 2001.

Suetonius, A.D. 121. *The Lives Of the Twelve Caesars*. Translated by J. C. Rolfe. In Loeb Classical Library. Cambridge, MA: Harvard University Press, 1913–1914. Also available at: http://penelope.uchicago.edu/Thayer/E/Roman/Texts/Suetonius/12Caesars/.

Suzuki, Y. 2002. "The Crisis of Financial Intermediation; Understanding Japan's Lingering Economic Stagnation." In *International Financial Systems and Stock Volatility: Issues and Remedies*, edited by N. Sabri, *International Review of Comparative Public Policy* 13: 213–243.

———. 2011. *Japan's Financial Slump*. New York: Palgrave Macmillan.

Svenson, O. 1981. "Are We All Less Risky and More Skillful than Our Fellow Drivers?" *Acta Psycholigica* 47: 143–148.

Sylla, R. 1991. "Financial Disturbances and Depressions: The View from Economic History." Working Paper No. 47.

Swarup, A. 2006. *Investigations into Condensed Matter Analogues of Phase Transitions in the Early Universe and Other Low-Dimensional Phase Transitions.* Ph.D. thesis. Imperial College London.

Swarup, A. and D. Perkins. 2013. *Till Debt Us Do Part.* Lombard Street Research.

Tacitus, *Annals.* In *Loeb Classical Library.* Cambridge, MA: Harvard University Press, 1925–1937. Also available at http://penelope.uchicago.edu/Thayer/E/Roman/Texts/Tacitus/home.html.

Temin, P. 1976. *Did Monetary Forces Cause the Great Depression?* New York: W. W. Norton & Co.

———. 2006. "The Economy of the Early Roman Empire." *Journal of Economic Perspectives* 20(1): 133–151.

———. 2002. "Financial Intermediation in the Early Roman Empire." MIT Department of Economics Working Paper No. 02-39. Available at SSRN: http://ssrn.com/abstract=348103 or http://dx.doi.org/10.2139/ssrn.348103.

———. 2001. "A Market Economy in the Early Roman Empire." MIT Department of Economics Working Paper No. 01-08. Available at SSRN: http://ssrn.com/abstract=260995 or http://dx.doi.org/10.2139/ssrn.260995.

Thaler, R. H. 1993. *Advances in Behavioral Finance.* New York: Russell Sage Foundation.

———. 1997. "Irving Fisher: Modern Behavioral Economist." *American Economic Review* 87(2): 439–41.

Thaler, R. H., A. Tversky, D. Kahneman, and A. Schwartz. 1997. "The Effect of Myopia and Loss Aversion on Risk Taking: An Experimental Test." *Quarterly Journal of Economics* 112(2): 647–661.

Thornton, M. 2004. "The Japanese Bubble Economy." LewRockwell.com, May 23. http://archive.lewrockwell.com/thornton/thornton24.html.

Thornton, M. K., and R. L. Thornton. 1990. "The Financial Crisis of A.D. 33: A Keynesian Depression?" Journal of Economic History 50(3): 655–662.

Thucydides. *The History of the Peloponnesian War.* Translated by R. Crawley, 2004. Project Gutenberg Release #7142. http://eremita.di.uminho.pt/gutenberg/etext04/plpwr10.txt.

Toner, J. and Y. Tu. 1998. "Flocks, Herds, and Schools: A Quantitative Theory of Flocking." *Physical Review E* 58(4): 4828–4858.

Turner, Lord A. 2009. *The Turner Review: A Regulatory Response to the Global Banking Crisis.* London: Financial Services Authority. http://www.fsa.gov.uk/pubs/other/turner_review.pdf.

Tversky, A. and D. Kahneman. 1992. "Advances in Prospect Theory: Cumulative Representation of Uncertainty." *Journal of Risk and Uncertainty* 5: 297–323.

———. 1990. "Anomalies: Preference Reversals." *Journal of Economic Perspectives* 4(2): 201–211.

———. 1981. "The Framing of Decisions and the Psychology of Choice." *Science* 211: 453–458.

———. 1974. "Judgment Under Uncertainty: Heuristics and Biases." *Science* 185: 1124–1131.

————. 1986. "Rational Choice and the Framing of Decisions." *Journal of Business* 59(4): S251–78.

United States Congress Senate Committee on Banking and Currency. 1932–33. Stock Exchange Practices: Hearings Before the Committee on Banking and Currency, United States Senate, Seventy-Second Congress, first-[second] session on S. Res. 84. Washington, D.C.: United States Government Printing Office. http://archive.org/details/stockexchangepra04unit.

United States Department of Commerce. 1975. *Historical Statistics of the US— Colonial Times to 1970*.

Vanderblue, H. 1927. "The Florida Land Boom." *Journal of Land & Public Utility Economics* 3(3): 252–269.

Veblen, T. 1934. *The Theory of the Leisure Class*. New York: Modern Library.

Vernon, J. R. 1994. "Unemployment Rates in Post-Bellum America: 1869–1899." *Journal of Macroeconomics* 16: 701–714.

Vogel, E. 1979. *Japan as Number One: Lessons for America*. Boston: Harvard University Press.

Volcker, P. 2011. "Financial Reform: Unfinished Business." *New York Review of Books*, November 24. http://www.nybooks.com/articles/archives/2011/nov/24/financial- reform-unfinished-business/.

Wilensky, U. 1999. NetLogo. Center for Connected Learning and Computer-Based Modeling, Northwestern Institute on Complex Systems, Northwestern University, Evanston, IL. http://ccl.northwestern.edu/netlogo/.

————. 1997. NetLogo Segregation model. Center for Connected Learning and Computer-Based Modeling, Northwestern Institute on Complex Systems, Northwestern University, Evanston, IL. http://ccl.northwestern.edu/netlogo/models/Segregation.

Wilson, J., R. Sylla, and C. Jones. 1990. "Financial Market Panics and Volatility in the Long Run, 1830-1988." in *Crashes and Panics*, edited by E. White, 85–125. Illinois: Dow-Jones Irwin.

Winkler, M. 1933. *Foreign Bonds, an Autopsy*. Philadelphia: Roland Swain Co.

Wood, C. 1992. *The Bubble Economy: Japan's Extraordinary Speculative Boom of the '80s and the Dramatic Bust of the '90s*. Atlantic Monthly Press.

————. 1994. *The End of Japan Inc*. New York: Simon and Schuster.

Wray, L. R. 2013. *The Credit Money, State Money, and Endogenous Money Approaches: A Survey and Attempted Integration*. Available at http://cas.umkc.edu/econ/economics/faculty/wray/papers/CREDIT&STATE%20MONEY%20JOIE%20revised.doc.

Wudunn, S. 1996. "Big Japan Developer Seized for Blocking Land Auction." *New York Times*, May 28.

Young, G. K. 2001. *Rome's Eastern Trade: International Commerce and Imperial Policy, 31 B.C.–A.D. 305*. London: Routledge.

Index

A Note on the Author

Bob Swarup is an international expert and commentator on financial markets and regulation. He was born in New Delhi in 1977 and educated in India and England. He holds an M.A. from the University of Cambridge and a Ph.D. in cosmology from Imperial College London. He has managed investments at financial institutions, counseled leading hedge funds and private equity firms, worked closely with major think tanks, and advised policymakers. He lives in London with his wife and two children.